Confessions

of an

80 Year-Old Boy

*A Blueprint for
True Happiness and
Successful Living*

STAN HILL

RED OAK PRESS
White Bear Lake, Minnesota

Confessions of an 80 Year-Old Boy — A Blueprint for True Happiness and Successful Living

Printed in United States of America
99 98 97 96 95   10 9 8 7 6 5 4 3 2 1

Art and Design: Mary E. Coughlin
Photo: Lark Gilmer
Editor: Douglas C. Benson
Copy Editor: Doris H. Hill

Library of Congress Catalog Card Number 94-066229

Hill, J. Stanley, 1914-
  Confessions of an 80 Year-Old Boy

  Includes reading recommendations, index and table of contents.

  1. Autobiography   2. Philosophy
  3. Religion   4. Sports
  5. Inspiration   6. Self Help

ISBN 0-9640439-0-4

This book is dedicated to all kids of all ages, especially over 80 years old;

to Doris, whose unwavering love, friendship and steadfast commitment through 56 years of marriage have been a continual source of inspiration, happiness and fulfillment;

and

to our children, George, Jan, Mary, Bev and Rick, whose good lives, friendship and love have brought me riches beyond measure.

"To live each day free from guilt, worry and fear, with opportunities to serve and love others and to exercise both mind and body vigorously — with these goals (and it's taken me over 60 years to come even close) the other things (money, recognition, love from others, and appreciation) come automatically. Christ and others have said it better, but the important thing is: It Works."

JAMES STANLEY HILL in *Who's Who in America*

"All of us have an opportunity to increase our enjoyment of life at the same time bringing benefits to others. The principle of giving to live asserts that if you increase your philanthropic activity, more benefits and rewards will come to you than to those you assist or the causes you champion. You have it in your power to test this formula any time you desire — if you are open to the possibilities and willing to move along the Giving Path."

DOUGLAS P. LAWSON, PhD in *Give to Live*[19]

Contents

Confessions
of an
80 Year-Old Boy

Preface

This is the kind of book that:

- can dramatically improve your quality of life
- I wish I had read when I was younger
- old and young can relate to
- gives you plenty of practical ways to enhance your own life style
- is fun to read.

This book is about happiness, contentment, fulfillment and serenity. I am one of the happiest, most contented, most fulfilled, most serene persons I know. This was not always so. How did I arrive at this fortunate state? That is what this book is all about.

It's a frank and open book with no attempt to glamorize my life or to hide the failures, disappointments, or the less favorable experiences and feelings. As people say, "Let it all hang out." I have used real names except in a few instances where their use might embarrass the people involved (or their descendants).

The word "confession" has two quite different meanings. It can be a disclosure, or it can be an affirmation. I have used it both ways: to disclose my innermost thoughts and feelings, and to affirm my beliefs.

How to Read this Book.

You can read this book from cover to cover, or go first to the subjects that interest you most. Either way, you will find some inspiration in each chapter. Most chapters begin with a flashback (in italics), that shows the stark contrast between my earlier years and my more recent status. It will help you to think, "If he could do it, so can I!"

Each section deals with a subject that has contributed to my happiness; and shares a part of me. Each of you will react differently. Personally, I believe Sections One, Three, Eight and Nine are the most significant. The section on sports is important because it illustrates the boy in me that helps to make life so enjoyable.

Sources of True Happiness and Fulfillment.

But true happiness and fulfillment spring from broader and deeper sources, all of which join in a great chorus to bring us that feeling of a life triumphantly lived. Much of this book is a conscious effort to explore and share those sources.

I had a relatively unhappy childhood and youth. Now each day brings new joys and satisfactions. How was I fortunate enough to have become so fulfilled? So much of it seems to be happenstance — or might it be the guiding of a Merciful Providence? You can also achieve this sense of fulfillment; it is salvation in the truest sense of the word. Here is a sharing of experiences, thoughts, attitudes, and beliefs that created this enviable state. That is the purpose of this book. I wish I could have read it (or written it!) when I was much younger. But I take pleasure in sharing it with you now. If it helps to bring you more joy, contentment and fulfillment — and perhaps some fascination along the way — it will have served its purpose. May you have as much fun reading it as I did writing it!

Stan Hill
White Bear Lake, Minnesota   July 24, 1994

Introduction

*"A long walk is a succession
of small steps."*
Confucius

*A six-year-old farm boy, lonely, totally immersed
in his own thoughts, climbs to the top of a new
80-foot silo, complete except for its roof. His parents
and the farm hands watch in fear and horror, as
he slowly walks upright all the way around the
four-inch outer ledge! Paralyzed into silence and
inaction, they are afraid a word or movement
might cause him to lose his balance and produce
a fatal fall. Having completed his hazardous trip,
he climbs down unhurt.*

Well, here I am, 80 years old today — a long journey, in
many senses, from the lonely six-year-old farm boy! Viewed
from almost any point in that journey, the future would
have seemed incredible, could it have been foreseen.

What guided this incredible journey from a humble, poor
boyhood to total fulfillment as a husband, father, actuary,
army officer, executive officer of a "Fortune 500" company,
member of many boards, personal counselor, entrepreneur,
computer and management consultant, investor, graduate
school teacher, musician, sportsman, author and publisher,
with a listing in Who's Who in America. What is more im-

portant, how did the journey lead to true inner peace and a sense of fulfillment? Was it the result of happenstance, logical choice, or Providence? Or was it a combination of all three? You can help me to decide. I feel certain of this: the journey would have been much more likely to occur if I had known earlier many of the things I share in this book.

Blessings.

Like many of you, I was extremely fortunate in many ways totally outside my control. Let's count these blessings and rejoice in them:

- genes for a sound, although not perfect, body;
- a good mind that does what is expected of it, most of the time;
- parents who loved me, even though they never told me;
- parents who made their share of mistakes, but did their best to make a good human being of me;
- the privilege of living in an economically prosperous country, even though it's often hard to translate that to a personal prosperity;
- never having to go to bed hungry;
- a grandfather and aunts who were fun to be with.

Oh yes, there were some things missing:

- regular elementary schooling (until the fourth grade), college education;
- friends as a young boy;
- facilities for entertainment (no radio, no TV, no movies, no sports, no car, no trike, no bike, no allowance, no ice cream, no parties);
- electricity and indoor plumbing (until I was eight years old);

- playmates, sisters, grandmother (when I was old enough to remember);
- Dental care, adequate medical care.

But I didn't know any better at the time, so I didn't feel sorry for myself.

The Process.

I can state the what's involved in the process of achieving fulfillment briefly and simply. For those who believe in a benevolent, merciful God, it is to seek the will of God and do it with a whole heart. For those who don't, it is to acquire the wisdom needed to achieve happiness and fulfillment, and practice it continually.

On the other hand, carrying out this process takes a lifetime. You can think of it as becoming rather than arriving. Recognizing and pursuing the process develops more quickly for some people than for others. For many people it appears not to develop at all. They feel hopeless because they see their problems as far too difficult to cope with. For many others it appears to develop in the wrong direction. For example, many criminals feel fully justified in their actions because they feel this is the only way they can find fulfillment in a totally unfair world.

This book can help you to develop more quickly in the right direction.

The Real Message.

Oh yes, recognition and material gain were very enjoyable. But let's not let them distract us from the real message of this book: happiness and fulfillment came despite the recognition and material gain and not because of them. I believe these important ends are obtainable regardless of socioeconomic status. The rest of this introduction is a brief attempt to support this belief.

"It is easier . . . ."

Happiness and fulfillment may come more easily to the less affluent. It took me a long time to learn this. I was in my late 60's before I understood the real meaning of Matthew 19:24:

> *"It is easier for a camel to pass through the
> eye of a needle than for a rich man
> to enter the kingdom of heaven."*

For 25 years I was a member of the White Bear Yacht Club, whose membership included some of the wealthiest citizens of the Greater Saint Paul area. During most of that time I was a board member or officer of the club. These activities brought me into close association with people whose inherited wealth was measured in the tens and hundreds of millions. The first-hand insights I gained from these experiences were truly surprising. Although wealth brings relief from the concern of providing life's basic necessities, it adds a whole new set of problems:

- It is often more difficult for the wealthy to acquire a feeling of self-worth ("Could I *really* make it on my own?" "Am I valued as a friend because of who I am or because of what I own?")
- Many of them miss the real joys and satisfactions of work.
- Money often exacerbates sibling rivalries.
- They miss the closeness created when family members help each other, out of financial necessity.
- They are constant targets for people who try to relieve them of a portion of their wealth.
- Some have guilt feelings about their money ("I didn't really earn this").
- Some complicate their lives beyond their emotional ability to deal with these complexities.
- Temptations are greater because there is more time for indulgence and the means are more readily available.

When people say of the wealthy, "I wish I had *their* problems," I know they don't really understand these things.

Poverty is a Relative Term.

Financial poverty is a relative term. Most people living below the poverty line in this country are well to-do compared to people in third world countries.

During the first 25 years of my life, my parents, my brother and I lived on a fraction of the income that is today regarded as the poverty line. And that's after making full allowance for the change in what a dollar will buy. But there was no poverty of the mind or the soul. And we always had enough to eat and a warm place to sleep. This was also true of great numbers of our socio-economic peers.

Starvation and homelessness are another matter. We have no justification for allowing them to exist, at least in developed countries, including the United States. When I speak of financial poverty, I do not include these extreme conditions.

• Poverty of the mind and soul, not financial poverty (as I define it), is the real barrier to happiness and fulfillment.

• It follows, then, that programs that deal only with financial poverty are dealing, therefore, with only a part of the problem.

• Poverty of mind and soul exists at all socioeconomic levels and is equally devastating at all such levels.

• Poverty of mind and soul is not only devastating to the individual; it has serious implications for the future of our country.

• Poverty of mind and soul is commonly inherited. To break this chain is our greatest personal and national challenge.

• Happily it doesn't take much money to break the chain: only the dedication of enlightened people.

And so this book is dedicated to the task of enriching mind and soul. Each of us holds the keys to our own enrichment: the desire and the will to pursue it.

One

Family

It is hard to overstate the importance of family as an influence on our character, body, mind and spirit. How much of this influence is genes and how much is environment? No one knows for sure. But it is important that we sort out what has been a good influence and what has been a bad influence.

The Audio Tapes.

We must also understand that we are quite capable of overcoming these influences, good and bad. Some psychologists have described them as audio tapes, which play more or less continually in our heads. To extend this metaphor, we can re-record these tapes, if we so choose. The stronger the tapes, the harder they are to re-record. Of course, we don't want to rewrite the good parts of the tape. Rather we need to play those parts consciously, as we have heard people do ("my mother always taught me that . . .").

You can easily identify any of the bad tapes: those which lead to criminal behavior, dishonesty, the negative emotions (see Chapter 47), lack of commitment, selfishness, race, religious and ethnic prejudice. The list continues: verbal abuse, physical abuse, violence, and so on. Other bad tapes are more subtle (perhaps even debatable): those which lead to extreme humility, teetotaling, manipulative behavior, psychological game playing, giving of unsought advice, chauvinism, sex role stereotyping, extreme family loyalty, and so on.

Rewriting the Bad Tapes.

Extending the metaphor, you can sometimes still hear a tape that has been erased. When you write over a tape, seldom, if ever, can you hear the old message. It is important, therefore, that we rewrite the bad tapes. Sometimes we can do this on our own. More often we need help: a wise friend, or a professional counselor.

The Good Times.

Most of us are fortunate enough to have (had) one or more family members with whom we have spent many happy hours and have (had) really good times. These experiences form the fabric of our lives. They shape our character and affect our personality. It is good to recall those times and count them among our blessings.

1. Grandparents

"Grandpa, when does your football team play?"
"What?! Why son, I don't have a football team.
What made you ask?"
"Well, Dad says when you kick off we can get a
new car."

This conversation never really happened in our family; but it could have. My maternal grandfather was the only relative who had any money, and he didn't have a lot. He and Grandma spent most of their lives in Merrickville, Ontario, a town of fewer than a thousand people. Located between Ottawa and Toronto, it has only one claim to fame: it is situated on the Rideau River. This river is now a very popular recreational boating area, but when my grandparents lived there, the Rideau carried a modest amount of freight in small barges. Grandpa was the lockmaster. He also had considerable skill in buying and selling horses profitably. My father called him a horse trader. That didn't sit well with my mother.

A Happy Man.

I remember Grandpa as a happy man. His name was Demetrius Crozier. I don't think he liked his first name very much. He always signed as just D. Crozier. He loved to travel and experience new things. And he loved to tell about these experiences—to the point of boring most of the family. But I never tired of hearing his stories, so he was very fond of me. When we lived on a farm in Manitoba, he lived with us. I loved to sit on his knee and count the coins he would take out of his pocket. We had to do this quietly in the kitchen while my parents were in the dining room; otherwise my father would try to borrow the money from him. It was the first money I had seen — and was to see for quite a few years.

A Fateful Ride.

At age 70 (in 1920, perhaps) Grandpa bought a Model T Ford, much against the judgment and will of my parents. My mother forbade me to ride in it. But one day Grandpa spirited me off for a two-mile trip to "the garage" on Main Street. As we drove out of the garage, he failed to see an approaching car. Then, when he did see the other car bearing down on us, he "hit the gas" to avoid a collision. We shot across the street and into a ditch on the other side. The sudden stop threw me against the windshield, unhurt except for a bloody nose.

A bit shaken, but also unhurt, Grandpa rushed me back across the street to the only store in town that had ice— and ice cream. I had never seen either of these wonderful commodities before. The former stopped my bleeding. The latter stopped my crying and sealed my promise never to reveal this fateful incident to anyone. But a telltale bruise on my face caused a confession and an unfortunate sequence of events: Grandpa and I were both grounded, and he had to sell the car.

A Religious Woman.

My memories of Grandma are vague. I was, perhaps, only five when I last saw her. Born Elizabeth Harrison, she was a very religious woman. She spent hours every day reading her Bible. She persuaded me to learn her favorite psalm—the 23rd—and a few other Bible passages. In the evening we would get down on our knees beside the bed and pray: "Now I lay me down to sleep, I pray the Lord my soul to keep . . ."

Paternal Grandparents.

I never knew either of my father's parents. They died many years before I was born, and my father never spoke of them. I believe Grandpa was an importer. He may also have been a sea captain. They must have traveled and lived abroad extensively. My father was born in Halifax, Nova Scotia, one of his sisters in England, and another in India.

Points to Ponder.

- Our grandparents can have a strong influence in our lives. Be conscious of these influences, both positive and negative. Emphasize the positive. Overwrite the negative.

- One of our greatest potentials for immortality is as role models for our grandchildren. If they are not close geographically, strengthen the relationship by regular letter writing.

2. Parents and Brother

"It's no disgrace to be poor, but it's
mighty inconvenient." — My Mother

A young man, in his 20's, is given a seemingly im-
possible task by Cecil Rhodes (of scholarship fame):
negotiate with the tribal chieftains of Africa for land
to build a railroad. This railroad is to run from
Capetown, South Africa to Cairo, Egypt, a total
distance of 7,000 miles!

Adventurer, Soldier of Fortune, Army Major.

I don't know if mile one of track was ever laid. But my
father, John James Hill, came away from this decade of his
life with rich memories of some incredible experiences.
Later on, these memories would provide him with a means
of earning a livelihood.

He joined the British Army during the Boer war (The
Boers were Dutch colonists in South Africa. The mutual
dislike between them and the British colonists resulted in
this war that lasted from 1899 to 1902). He was discharged
as a major, a title he carried proudly as long as he lived.

Construction Foreman.

When my father married Louisa Arletta Crozier in 1908,
she wanted him to settle down in her home town of Merrickville to "a steady job." But such a humdrum life was
not for him. His brother-in-law, D. B. Lindsay, was president of the Temiscuota Railroad. He hired my father as a
construction foreman. My mother said they moved 32 times
while he had that job! She finally insisted that Father make
a change. Again, she pleaded for the stable life of Merrickville. Her pleading was in vain. They compromised on
farming, about which Father knew nothing. The next six
years consisted largely of hard work, crop failure and finan-

cial disaster. We walked away from two farms with little more than the clothes on our backs.

Liquidator.

In 1922 his sister, Annie, persuaded Father to come to St. Paul, Minnesota and look for work. The Northwest Jobbers Credit Bureau collected bad debts for clients who sold merchandise to small retail stores. When the poor retailer couldn't pay his bill, it was Father's job to repossess the merchandise and sell it for what it would bring. It didn't pay much, but it was steady.

It took about a year for him to save a few hundred dollars and make a down payment on a house in White Bear Lake. During that time Mother, my brother Jack and I stayed with her sister in Rochester, New York. The family was re-united in April 1923. Although our family never prospered materially from the move to Minnesota, it was a major turning point in our lives. We were transported from a struggling, intellectually poor farming environment in Manitoba to a milieu that truly became the "land of opportunity" for us. We owe Aunt Annie a great deal . . . . .

Raconteur and Lecturer.

Father loved to talk about his experiences in Africa, and people loved to listen. When Northwest Jobbers Credit Bureau closed, he joined the Redpath Chautauqua. This involved travelling from town to town all over the country during the summer, giving a lecture each afternoon. Chautauqua brought culture (plays, music, magicians, and lecturers) to the smaller communities. The performances were under a tent and people sat on folding chairs.

In colder weather Chautauqua went indoors to meeting halls and theaters and became Lyceum. Father did the Lyceum Circuit. He also lectured to high school students under the aegis of the National School Assembly Program.

I suspect these were the happiest years of his life: he was doing what he loved to do and getting more money than he had ever made in his life.

Too Good to Last.

Alas, the great depression of the 1930's and radio conspired to shut down all three outlets for his lectures. He had a weekly program on KSTP (St. Paul) for a while. The producers insisted that he write his talks and read from the script. Apparently this format was not as appealing as the live talks from a platform. Father's career in radio lasted only a few months.

Unsuccessful Prospector.

Father was convinced that there was gold to be had in the farther reaches of British Columbia and Newfoundland. He had a unique method of financing these forays. He would go to the stockbroker's office (usually Paine, Webber, Jackson and Curtis in St. Paul, where speculators spent their day watching the "ticker tape." They had the two things he needed: a little money and the speculative spirit. He would end up with a few hundred dollars from each of them. In return they received a simple one page agreement to share the profits—that's all—none of these ventures ever made a dime. When his stake ran out, we would wire him bus fare to come home. He continued these forays until his health failed in his early 70's.

A Good Man and a Good Father.

Apart from his wanderlust, Father was a good man. He had high moral principles, which he communicated to my brother and me, mostly by example, occasionally by word. He had an excellent mind and was a voracious reader. When he could find nothing else to read, he would spend hours reading a huge, unabridged dictionary. He could (and did)

converse on almost any subject. He loved to be with people, and liked nothing better than good conversation. He
loved to play cards. Auction bridge (a precursor of contract
bridge) was his favorite game. He also played Norwegian
whist with his cronies.

A Great Sense of Humor.

Father loved to tell stories, especially if they had a humorous twist. He could see the funny side of almost any situation. When I was perhaps 12 or 13, he and I were playing
cards at the kitchen table. Lightning struck the chimney
with a tremendous noise. There was a metal cover over a
hole in the chimney where a kitchen stove had once been
connected. It flew around the room with a great clatter.
Behind it came a great cloud of soot, much of which settled on Father's face. When I said "Look at your face," he
did so in the mirror, and began to laugh heartily. My
mother was petrified with fear. She believed that, when
people were struck by lightning, they turned black. When
she heard him laughing, she was sure it had knocked him
crazy: No man in his right mind would laugh at such a
calamity!

Opposites.

It's hard to imagine a greater difference in personalities
than existed between Mother and Father. She would have
been content (even delighted) to spend the rest of her life
in the serenity and security of the quiet little town of Merrickville. Although she could laugh readily at someone else's
humor, she was mostly a sober, serious person. She could
talk easily with friends; but she was uncomfortable with
strangers. When my parents were with friends, Father carried on most of the conversation.

The Embarrassment of Poverty.

Mother often said, "It's no disgrace to be poor, but it's

mighty inconvenient." But this was only to deny her true feelings. She was often embarrassed and occasionally downright humiliated by our lack of money (see Chapter 39). When we walked away from the second farm, Father borrowed train fare from his sister to get Mother and us two boys to Rochester, New York, where we lived with her sister and brother-inlaw for the year Father was getting settled in Minnesota. We paid no room and board and could make no financial contribution toward the household operations. Although she never talked to us boys about it, I know she felt extremely embarrassed and ashamed. In White Bear Lake her experience with the "Ladies Aid" (as the church women's group was then known) was brief and embarrassing, because she couldn't meet even their modest financial requirements.

Worry and Tears.

Worry over finances was a constant condition for Mother. Many times she would exclaim "I don't know what's going to become of us!" When I came upon her unexpectedly, I would often find her weeping quietly. Yet her father told me she was a happy person when she was young. It must have pained him deeply to see her in such dire straits.

Talents.

As a young woman, Mother had aspired to become a professional pianist; she studied at the Toronto Conservatory of Music. That career ended when her hands "gave out" (as she described it) from the required eight hours a day of strenuous keyboard exercises. She played the piano and/or a small reed organ in almost every church we went to, except the Presbyterian Church in White Bear Lake. There she couldn't quite manage the pipe organ. When we left our last farm, she couldn't afford to move her beautiful "square grand" piano, a wedding present from her parents. We had lived in White Bear Lake several years before she accumulated the $50 needed to buy a used upright. But by that time her hands had become too stiff and sore for her to enjoy playing it. (She never went to a doctor; but I suspect she had arthritis.) The money wasn't wasted, however. It was on that instrument that I learned the joys of playing piano by ear.

Her one source of pride, other than her sons, was her needlework. She crocheted and embroidered beautifully and exhibited her work at fairs in many provinces. What excitement and pleasure there was when the work came back with the ribbons and prize money (the latter carefully saved to buy more materials)! For a wedding present for Doris and me, she took some of her precious dollars and bought a cedar chest. Then she filled it with her beautiful handiwork: quilts, a crocheted bedspread, beautifully embroidered table cloths and pillow cases, doilies—you name it—a real gift of love.

My Only Sibling.

My only sibling is my brother. Christened John Demetrius Lindsay Hill, the family called him Lindsay. He dropped the Demetrius while he was still in school. In his adult life he has been John, or Jack to his friends.

As boys we worked together on the farm in Manitoba. One of our jobs was to hoe four rows of corn each day. That doesn't sound like much; but the rows were a mile long! The corn stalks would quickly become taller than we were. When we wanted a break, we would sit down in the shade of the corn. We would put our hats on the end of the hoe handles and move them so it would look as if we were working. I doubt that we fooled anyone!

Trouble.

One rainy Saturday, we boys decided to do Mother a favor and reorganize the basement. Our brilliant plan was to put everything in alphabetic order. The ham came just before the hammer, the peas beside the prybar, and so on. We were almost done with this magnificent contribution to household order when Mother came home. It's the only time I can ever remember her being furious with us! We spent the rest of the afternoon and evening restoring things to their original order.

More than four years older than I, Jack was more of a role model than a pal. When I was in grade school, it seemed as though I was always wishing I could do what he did. When I would fret about this, my mother would say, "Be patient; your turn will come." Of course, it did; but by then Jack was doing something else I wanted to do also.

In high school his brilliant mind and studious nature made him a straight-A student. When report cards came out, I would always resolve to be like him. When he became valedictorian of his class, that became my most cherished goal. (I missed by .3 of one percent: 94.9 vs 95.2!)

In high school, it seemed to me Jack had more friends than I, dressed better, and had more fun. In short, Jack was a hard act to follow.

College and the CCC.

After Jack finished high school Aunt Lillie and Uncle Justin invited him to live with them in Rochester, New York. This is the same aunt and uncle with whom we lived in 1922. He did so while getting a certificate in mechanical engineering from the Rochester Athaeneum and Mechanics Institute. There he went to school half time and worked the other half for General Railway Signal Company. The Great Depression had begun. Unemployment was over 15%, it wasn't too long before GRS laid him off, and there were no other jobs available. So he joined the CCC (the Civilian Conservation Corps which was a makework program for men who couldn't find a job).

Near the end of his one-year hitch, while fighting a forest fire, he suffered exhaustion and exposure, and came home with a severe pneumonia. We slept on an unheated sleeping porch. I have two powerful impressions of that time. One was Jack's terrible wracking cough which nothing seemed to help. The other was the marvelous mystery of a radio on which you could miraculously get WLS, the famous radio station in Chicago. They broadcast live from the great Aragon and Trianon ballrooms in Chicago. I can still remember those "big band" sounds, and strongly suspect that was what inspired to me start playing the piano.

Real Jobs.

After a slow recovery and a long period of job hunting, there came the great moment when Jack landed his first real job: a quality control inspector at the the Minnesota Mining (now called 3M) rock-crushing plant in Wausau, Wisconsin. Minnesota Mining later transferred him to St. Paul where he worked as a mechanical engineer. One of his more interesting assignments involved the development of the Thermofax, one of the earliest copying machines that produced images on heat-sensitive paper.

**An Outstanding Career as a
Creative Computer Engineer.**

But his true love was electronics. He spent most of his spare time designing, building and rebuilding radio receivers and transmitters. This was an extension of his high school hobby: building and selling primitive radio receivers. During his high school years he would wind wire around an oatmeal box to create the tuning coil. He connected this coil to a piece of galena crystal which reduced the radio frequency signals to audio frequency. An antenna and a simple pair of earphones completed this inexpensive but workable radio. Through this hobby and a great deal of reading he became a highly qualified electronic engineer.

Next came a short period of service with Northwest Airlines, upgrading their radio communications systems. Jack then saw service with the Army Signal Corps in Panama during World War II as a part of the Army Airways Communication System.

He became a "ham" (amateur radio operator) in 1937, and still remains devoted to that activity. After World War II he went with Engineering Research Associates. ERA was one of the very early successful developers of the "stored program computer," a marvelous device that could actually remember instructions you gave it and perform them at a rapid rate!

One of the big challenges in the design of these early computers was to find an effective medium for storing the instructions and other data. Jack pioneered in the development of both drum memories (which stored the data on the periphery of a revolving magnetic drum), and core storage (tiny ferromagnetic doughnuts strung on a grid of fine wires). Jack was published internationally on these subjects.

In 1952 Remington Rand (later Univac, then Unisys) bought ERA. Remington Rand also bought Eckert-Mauchly of Philadelphia (designers of the Univac Model 1, the first commercially available "mainframe"). J. Presper Eckert was placed in charge of all computer development activities. Eckert's management style was in sharp contrast to the more collegial atmosphere that had existed at ERA. The resulting culture clash with the ERA engineers produced great unrest. It was then that William Norris left to start Control Data. Six months earlier Jack had left Univac to start the Electronics Division of Ramsey Engineering, a firm known worldwide for its creative design of sophisticated controls for handling materials, especially in rugged environments. Until that time all of Ramsey's controls had been electromechanical.

Retirement to a Life of Service and Philanthropy.

In his middle 60's, Jack went on a part-time basis. That was about the time entire computers were developed on a tiny silicon chip. He would read of these marvels, think of a brilliant application for Ramsey and develop it.

1977 saw his full retirement from Ramsey Engineering to a busy life of service and philanthropy. Shrewd investments in (and timely divestments of) Control Data and Ramsey Engineering were placed in charitable remainder trusts. These trusts provide the donor and his (her) spouse with an income they can't outlive, a charitable deduction and generous payments to charities of the donor's choice. They also provide relief from tax on the stock appreciation. Most importantly, they provide the donor with the satisfaction of having helped worthy causes.

Another activity that benefits both others and himself is Jack's reading for the blind through the Minnesota Radio Talking Book program. And he works with SCORE (Service Corps of Retired Executives), donating his time to help new small business people with both management and technical problems.

Jack and Catherine live on the shore of Silver Lake in North St. Paul. They are on excellent terms with their three children. He is still my role model.

Points to Ponder.

- My brother was, and is, a positive influence in my life. Because we both lead such busy lives we don't spend a lot of time together, perhaps two or three long lunches in a year. But those times are very precious to both of us.

- Our relationship grows increasingly open. We share values and feelings as well as facts. We are becoming better friends. The process produces growth in both of us.

- We celebrate the joy and happiness of lives made increasingly triumphant by the giving and sharing of our talents and possessions. These are true mountain-top experiences.

- In the process, we rarely have time to think about the inevitable results of aging, loss of friends by death, or other negative aspects of our lives.

- Do we all have opportunities for this kind of sharing and growing closer to our friends and loves ones? Are we taking full advantage of the opportunities for personal growth and joy that they offer?

3. Wife

> *"Happiness is being married*
> *to your best friend"*
> — Author Unknown

It's a beautiful summer Sunday evening in White Bear Lake in September 1934. An 18-year old woman, new to the community, walks to the First Presbyterian Church to attend the young people's meeting. The absence of people puzzles her. A kind woman comes along, explains that the meeting is at the "Manse" (the house where the minister lives), and offers to drive her there. She accepts. The meeting is already in progress. A 20-year old man is quick to notice her beauty and to realize she needs a ride home. After the meeting, he offers. She accepts. He is totally smitten!

The longer we are married, the more I come to appreciate the marvelous truth in the simple quotation that opens this important chapter. One of the most precious gifts in life is friendship. What greater joy is there than in being able to spend time and share life with your best friend? Of course, there's much more to marriage than that. You may have expected me to talk about love and commitment, and the other things that make marriage such a wonderful institution. Many others have written about those things; but I wanted to emphasize friendship.

That First Evening.

We drove for a long time that night. It was entirely different from previous drives with other girls. I wanted to know as much as I could about this wonderful person. (Her recollection: "He asked so many questions!") We sat for a long time in her folks' driveway. The mere thought of physical advances seemed totally inappropriate. I don't even remember if I put my arm around her. I just wanted to be near this person who thrilled me so with her mere presence. I did most of the talking (things haven't changed). Finally it had to end; but not before I asked if I could see her again. The answer (gloriously) was a simple "yes."

A Not-so-smooth Courtship.

I spent many hours thinking of ways we could be together. We walked together, swam together, went canoeing together, read together, went to church and the movies together, rode to work together with her father. In good weather, we would have him let us off a mile or more from work and we would walk the rest of the way. I would walk her to her office, then walk to mine, a few blocks away. At night we would reverse the process: I would walk to her office to meet her so that we could walk together to her father's car and ride to her home. I had another mile to walk home, and another mile to her house again in the morning — I walked a lot that year!

The following January we broke up abruptly over a skiing incident (see Chapter 29). It seems silly now; but the separation hurt me deeply at the time. I really wanted to make her feel as bad as I did. I dated a girl who lived a block away from Doris, and would contrive to walk her by Doris' house as often as I could!

It was a year from the following July before I came to my senses and realized that I was hurting myself. I swallowed my pride and asked her to go dancing with me at the Wildwood Amusement Park. What a heavenly evening! The band played "I'll Never Say Never Again Again," and that became our theme song.

The Pinch of Poverty.

By this time, my brother had come home from the CCC (see previous chapter). My 1928 Essex (the Edsel of the 1920's) was ailing, and my $85 a month wouldn't support four people, the Essex, the mortgage payments and the taxes. So I sold the Essex, we walked away from another home and rented a cheap house in a poor neighborhood on the east side of St. Paul.

Real Love.

I walked the 3 miles to and from work. In the morning I would take the route down which Doris and her dad drove to work. When he saw me, he would let her off and we would walk the rest of the way (usually a mile or so) to work. On "date nights" (a couple of times a week) I would ride all the way home with them and have dinner there. Her CPA employer required Doris to study bookkeeping. So we would spend the evening studying her textbook together. What a marvelous way to learn bookkeeping! Then I would catch the last bus (11:00 p.m.) back to St. Paul, and walk the remaining mile back home.

Saturday night was our "big date" night. I would take the bus or hitchhike to her house. Her generous dad would lend us his car. At the end of the evening the last bus back to St. Paul left entirely too early. But there was a bus to Stillwater that went by her house about 1:30 AM. I would take this bus to Mahtomedi, and catch the 2:00 a.m. owl streetcar back to St. Paul. That's real love!

We're Engaged!

One hot July night in 1937, we were riding along a country road. I pulled the car over to the side of the road and announced "I can't wait any longer." Doris told me later she thought I had to relieve myself! Instead I produced a very modest diamond ring in which I had invested a good share of my meager savings. It was not like the movies of that day where the hero asks the heroine "Will you marry me?" We had known our destiny for months. It was only a matter of when we could afford to set up another household.

By this time my brother was working (for 3M in Wausau) and could share the support of my parents. Father also had found occasional work as a surveyor for a firm of architects (Toltz, King and Duvall). I was making $90 a month at the time. When I told my boss about our plans, he didn't think we should marry until I was making $100. I said I thought it would be nice if he got me a raise to that amount— and he did! That was the largest single raise I had received.

The Wedding Day.

The thermometer stood at 100 degrees at 8:00 p.m. on August 1, 1938 when we were married in the old Presbyterian church in White Bear Lake. This church stood where the First Bank parking lot is today. The wedding party sought relief by standing in their stocking feet on the basement floor. In carrying flowers from the church to his home for the reception, my new father-in-law poked a gladiolus bud in his eye. For hours he couldn't stop the tears from flowing. Everyone thought this stoic man had really become emotional!

A Classic Honeymoon.

My idea of a classic honeymoon was a boat trip to Niagara Falls. Now everyone knows you can't take a boat from St. Paul to Niagara Falls. But a little research showed that an old passenger steamboat sailed from Duluth to Detroit, and another one sailed from Detroit to Buffalo. A very excited young man booked passage on both of them. Between boats we visited Greenfield Village (the Ford museum village in Detroit). We spent a night with Aunt Lillian and Uncle Justin in Rochester before seeing Niagara Falls.

My fascination with trains was almost as great as with boats; so, for the return trip I had booked a train ride for the end of our honeymoon. We boarded the 20th Century Limited in Buffalo at midnight for the overnight ride to Chicago. On this streamlined train, the New York Central Railroad introduced America to a new type of sleeping accommodations: the roomette. Clarence LaFond, a friend from high school band days, was their passenger agent in St. Paul. His information didn't show clearly the capacity of a roomette. In my urgent need to save money I had persuaded him that no railroad would build a roomette to sleep only one person. So he had sold me a ticket for two persons and reserved one roomette.

A Surly Porter — Crowded Quarters.

Each sleeping car had a porter, the 1930's equivalent of a flight attendant. Our porter was out of sorts before we even boarded the train a little after midnight. His greeting was a surly "I waited up over half an hour for you!" When he realized that two of us were going to occupy one roomette, his tone became derisive.

We soon saw why. The narrow single bed hung from a hinge on the wall, like a Murphy bed, and completely covered the wash basin and the commode. The room was so narrow you had to back into the corridor to pull the bed

down. You can imagine the inconvenience and embarrassment of these two shy young people.

The porter's short night's sleep did not enhance his disposition. His look when I placed my 50-cent tip in his palm
was one of most eloquent disdain. It was not the ideal way
to end a honeymoon. However, I did feel that my frugality
was somewhat justified when we arrived home with only
50 cents between us!

56 Marvelous Years.

Of course, we've had our bad moments, even some troubled years. But, on the whole, it is hard for me to imagine
a more idyllic way to spend 56 (and hopefully more) years
of one's life than in the kind of marriage that Doris and
I have had. She deserves more than half of the credit. She
has a husband who must have been very difficult to live
with at times. He could be overbearing, opinionated, insensitive, and just plain inconsiderate. He often made decisions
without consulting her. I am trying to improve.

I won't attempt to list all of her wonderful qualities. Just
put together a composite of all of those qualities you think
a good wife should have, and you'll come close. Perfect?
In her modesty she would be quick to deny it. But the
multitude of good qualities totally eclipse any imperfections.

The Dramatic Moments.

Many dramatic moments in our marriage are well worth
sharing. Some are recounted earlier in this chapter. A few
are recounted elsewhere in this book. See, for example, my
homecoming from overseas army service after World War
II (Chapter 26). Another would be the marvelous surprise
party our children put on for our 40th anniversary. We had
a quiet Sunday dinner with some of our children at the Pic-
cadilly Restaurant. While we were still at the table we
opened a few greeting cards. Then George said "Here's a

card you haven't opened yet." It was an invitation to a reception for us at Lake Drive Church, to begin in about 10 minutes! I said, "Well, I guess we should be there." About 250 of our friends from all the various contexts of our life greeted us at the church. What a wonderful and happy occasion!

Good Luck or Good Management?

Sailors have a saying: "The good sailors have all the luck." In the same sense, I believe this is true of life in general and marriage in particular. We are "lucky" when we acquire an understanding of God's will and an earnest desire to follow that will. It is the only road to genuine happiness and fulfillment—not in some distant future, but right now. Atheists can substitute "wisdom" for "God's will." How does one acquire wisdom? There are various ways, but reading is one of them. That is the prime purpose of this book.

Wisdom During Courtship and the Engagement Period.

- The advantages of being a virgin on your wedding night greatly outweigh the dubious joys of (and benefits of being "experienced" in) pre-marital sex. Most important are the sacredness and mystique that can help to get the new union off to a good start. Also important is the assurance that both parties are free from sexually transmitted disease.

- On the other hand, most marriages would get off to a much better start if the partners included a good book on successful sexual techniques in their pre-marital studies.

- The choice of a marriage partner gets much less attention than it deserves. Most of us wouldn't think of making any other important decision without a great deal of research. Yet the American culture emphasizes romantic love and downplays the serious study of one's prospective long-term mate. Worse, couples discard the idea of examining one another's personalities and attitudes because the one or both feel foolish, or they're afraid that study may destroy the romance.

• How do you do this research? You do it simply by knowing as much about your prospective mate as possible. Don't be blinded by your love. Be very observing. Ask lots of questions during the courtship. If these are tactful, non-threatening, and appropriate, they won't give offense. Most people enjoy talking about themselves and their families. If they don't, watch out!

• Get to know your prospective mate's family well. Not only are you going to see much of them after the marriage, but you can gain many insights into the future by studying the parents. If either parent is abusive (even orally), there is a strong likelihood your mate will be abusive. If either parent is moody, choleric, alcoholic, drug-addicted or "peculiar," etc., there is a good probability that your mate will become moody, choleric, alcoholic, drug-addicted or "peculiar." You must discuss these tendencies openly and frankly, even at the risk of aborting the intended marriage. If your fiance(e) is not willing to discuss these problems now, what hope do you have of resolving them later? If he or she doesn't admit the possibility of developing the parent's bad trait, that is a denial of reality. That denial is a strong signal that you will be unable to persuade your mate to seek treatment if the trait does develop later. If the parent(s) is (are) dead, ask questions: "What was your father like?" "What memories do you have of your mother (good and bad)?"

• Many people marry for the wrong reasons. Some marry just to have sex (it's fun; but by itself it won't provide a lasting relationship). Their mate is exciting and romantic (he or she turns out to be undependable, flighty or whimsical). Some marry in hopes of solving a personality problem (marriage may exacerbate it). Others marry to escape a bad home life (not a sufficient foundation for a good marriage). Still others marry to have children (they can be one of life's greatest satisfactions; but if the marriage doesn't have a stronger basis, they probably won't be).

- The quality of a mate is greatly dependent on where you meet. The likelihood of finding a truly satisfactory mate in a singles bar is remote unless your aim is to spend your life in bars. The likelihood of a successful marriage resulting from a first meeting in church is excellent: most people (but not all) go there for the right reasons. The prospects in a country club are dim: you may get a mate of "good social standing" but not find the real depth that makes a marriage worthwhile. Schools are a mixed bag. The prospects depend largely on the reason the potential mate is there. If the purpose was matrimony, watch out! Some (not all) private schools are custodians of young people whose parents couldn't deal with them. If the parents couldn't cope with the recalcitrant brat, what chances do you have? On the other hand, some of the most successful marriages begin with a college romance. Almost invariably you will find the partners were there for a reasonably serious purpose.

- There must be an open discussion of what each party brings to the table. What are their mutual expectations? Is each party capable of living up to what is expected of her (him)? Most couples discuss differences in *nominal* religion (Roman Catholic vs Lutheran, etc.) and how they are going to resolve them. More important (and much less often considered) are differences in philosophy of life, value systems, and theology (who am I, who—or what—is God, what is my reason for being).

- Never marry a person in hopes that his or her character will improve. People can change; but the odds are against it. If you don't think his (her) good qualities eclipse the bad, or if you think certain bad qualities would impair the relationship, better terminate the relationship quickly.

Wisdom in Marriage.

Doris and I were "lucky" enough to learn and believe much of this wisdom early on. Other things we learned later, even recently. We are still learning. And our bad moments are directly traceable to the lack of wisdom or failure to practice it. But it is never too late to learn most of these things and improve the quality of your marriage. There are many books devoted entirely to this subject. Here is a brief and partial summary:

- A monogamous marriage, free from adultery, can (and should) be both exciting and romantic.

- Excitement and romance don't just happen. A good marriage is like a beautiful garden; you must cultivate it.

- Adultery (read "an affair", if you prefer) inevitably leads to complications and difficulties that far outweigh the temporary excitement and enjoyment.

- It is hard to carry on an affair in secret. Even if you do, it seriously harms all three parties. The adulterous mate carries a burden of guilt, which affects his or her disposition (even a professional actor or actress couldn't conceal his or her guilty feelings). The other mate becomes suspicious, and the all-important element of trust is threatened. There follows, quite often, veiled innuendo or even outright questioning. The guilty mate becomes defensive and petulant, or aloof and moody; and the relationship deteriorates further. At the same time the third party has high expectations of a romantic new life. There are only two possible outcomes, both bad. You consummate the new relationship, but both parties bring a load of guilt to the union that greatly reduces the likelihood of a successful long-term relationship. Or the original marriage survives and the third party feels cheated, used and disillusioned, and ends up with a low self-image.

You may have heard of the minister in this small, poor parish. He made his parish calls on a bicycle, which he lost one day. He was certain that one of the parishioners must have stolen it. Not knowing who the culprit was, and not wishing to confront his congregation directly, he came up with a very clever idea. He preached a sermon on the ten commandments, certain that, when he came to "Thou shalt not steal," the guilty party would confess—or at least return the bicycle. But he never got that far. When he came to "Thou shalt not commit adultery," he remembered where he had left his bicycle!

- The foundation stones of a good marriage are love, commitment, compassion, faith in God, mutual trust, unselfishness, consideration (attention to the mate's feelings and needs), and good communication. If any of these stones is weak or missing, the structure will become unlivable, and will collapse, sooner or later.

- Elements that are not essential, but which will improve the quality of the marriage are humor, good sex, romance, common interests, common values, common beliefs, common objectives, friendship and children.

- True love is an unselfish devotion to the happiness and welfare of your mate. When it exists in full measure in both parties, it is difficult to have arguments about household chores, money and other mundane matters.

- On the other hand, submerging one's individuality leads to unhappiness and can even destroy the relationship. You can say the same for a self-sacrificing attitude worn as a badge of honor ("Look at how much I do for you!"). It is also true of an emotional dependency.

- Do you remember your courtship, when you were on your best behavior? Why not continue this behavior into your married life?

- Good manners, courtesy, consideration, trust, tact, and humor are the keys to good relationships. We practice these in business and in our social relations. How much more desirable it is to practice them in the most important relationship of our life.

- Abuse, even mild verbal abuse, is a symptom of a deviant personality. The abuser must seek professional help, just as urgently as (s)he would for a serious medical problem. The same is true of a psychological game player.

4. Children

"We make a living by what we get.
We make a life by what we give."
— Author Unknown

A 31-year old army major comes home to greet his wife and 3-year old son after being across the Atlantic for 19 months. He looks forward eagerly to getting re-acquainted with them. He is equally avid to meet his 13-month old daughter, whom he has never seen. After a few weeks he realizes how permissively they are being brought up, compared with the strictness he remembers from his own parents. The shock worsens when he realizes their mother is just as conscientious and firm in her beliefs about child rearing as is he in his. He tries to compensate by being even stricter . . .

Happily, Doris and I learned to appreciate the virtues of each others' parenting philosophies and became increasing ly comfortable and relaxed in our respective roles as Mary, Bev and Rick came along.

Happy, Strenuous Days.

Watching and helping our children grow gave us many happy days—and still does. There is not enough room in this book to share more than a fraction of those wonderful experiences. The family vacations, the driving trips to California and Washington, D. C., the train trip to California all create wonderful memories. They were also the most strenuous days of our lives. How Doris ever managed to cope with the demands of feeding, clothing, nurturing, and meeting all of the other endless demands of five children is still a mystery to me—and to them. At the time I didn't give it that much thought. I was too busy trying to balance the responsibilities of an extremely demanding job with those of a husband and father.

How We Perceive Our Children.

We perceive our children as maturing adults. As it is for us, so also for our children, maturing is a process, not a status. Like physical maturing, mental and spiritual maturing (MSM) continues (or can continue), to the moment of death. Like physical maturing, MSM is not a steady process. It occurs in spurts, often as a result of some external influence. We view our children's maturing process with great pleasure and satisfaction. All five of our children are healthy in mind, body and spirit. All five of them are givers. None smokes, nor is any one of them chemically dependent. All are materially successful. Each of them has had her (his) share of problems but has shown the ability to work through those problems. All show the potential to live highly fulfilled, happy lives. All of them treat their parents with loving, friendly, considerate respect.

They differ greatly in temperament, personality, interests, beliefs and philosophies. Each of them is a real joy to be with. Each of them shares one or more interests with us and we enjoy doing things together. How could we be so fortunate?

How We View Ourselves as Parents.

As parents, we made our share of mistakes. As we look back, there are many things we would have done differently. But we carry no guilt feelings, because we did what we thought was right at the time. As a father, there are some things I would have done differently; I would have:

- shown my love more openly, both verbally and physically;

- tried harder to understand their feelings, particularly their frustrations;

- shown my love for Doris and my appreciation of her as a mother more often in their presence;

- been more fun-loving and less serious;

- Encouraged more openness in our communication (for example: "it's OK to be mad at Dad," "you look sad, do you want to tell me about it?" "you look especially happy today, do you want to share?").

There are a number of things I feel we did right. We:

- tried always to remember that an ounce of example is worth a ton of words;

- made ourselves available as much as we could;

- respected them, their privacy and their feelings;

- set the limits as broadly as we could, but insisted that those limits be observed;

- gave reasons for the limits;

- tried to be reasonable and consistent in our discipline;

- gave support and encouragement as much as we could;

- tried to build self respect and respect for others;

- explained the consequences of actions, good and bad;
- never contradicted each other in their presence.
- did our best to support each other's decisions.

An important way to measure our success as parents is to look at the parent in our children. We like what we see.

Today our children are our best friends (but not our only friends). We think of them as the adults they are and treat them as adults. We try (though we don't always succeed) to give advice only when asked. The list of things I think we did right is longer than the list of things I would have done differently. Perhaps we are too easy on ourselves.

Points to Ponder.

- Only now am I beginning to appreciate the tremendous potential for mutual growth and fulfillment that can come from an increasingly open relationship with my children.

- Our culture and upbringing do not normally foster this ideal association. It takes considerable courage on both sides to make the necessary changes. Both parties fear possible embarrassment. We are uncertain. But the risks are well worth it and the fears usually turn out to be groundless.

- It is a slow and challenging process. We have long since quit parenting our children. But the old patterns of parent-child relationships linger on. There is no quick fix.

- As difficult as it is, it is easier for us to reach out to our children than for them to reach out to us. So we must make take the lead . . . .

- I hope my children will always spend time with me because they want to, and not out of a sense of duty. The former is fulfilling. The latter would be hard on us both. This thought gives me the courage to go forward in developing a more nearly ideal relationship.

- The earlier we start the process the better, but it is never too late to start.

- The rewards are so great that we must make the effort and take the risks.

- I still have a long way to go; but at least I'm moving in the right direction.

5. Grandchildren

The phone rang shrilly at 4:00 AM. It was Bev's husband, Dan. I thought I heard, "Aaron weighs 7 and a half pounds; they're both doing well."

Only later that day did we learn that it was Erin, a lovely baby girl! Now at 17, she is a beautiful, talented young woman, about ready to enter her senior year in high school. Being shorter than most of her classmates does not keep her from excelling at softball (state championship at age 15), hockey and basketball. An A student, she has volunteered at United Hospital since she was 13 years old. From the start, her devotion to the hospital seemed to transcend her other interests. When her mother asked why, she replied, "I love to fill out forms!" After some reflection, I think I understand this unusual statement: adults fill out forms, so this activity made her feel like an adult.

All five of our grandchildren are healthy, happy young people: Casey at 13 is a gifted mathematician, as is her cousin, Enoch, at 11. Enoch is also a good pianist with an exceptional musical ear. Not only can he play any tune he hears: he can put the right harmony with it. Eight-year-old John is the little philosopher and conversationalist with an exceptional memory and imagination. Karen, at six, loves to paint, draw and dance. She has had poise and a camera presence from a very early age.

All of them are wonderful house guests. There never seems to be enough time to do all the things we love to do together: play tennis, go sailing, play computer games, enjoy music, dance, read, bake cookies, play cards and other games.

We are told that grandparents shouldn't bore their audience with the bright sayings of their grandchildren; but here are a couple I think are worth sharing:

- John came home from one of his first kindergarten classes and announced, "Mom, the teacher thinks I'm skinny."

    Satoko replied "What a terrible thing for her to say!"

    John's response was, "Don't worry Mom; if she thinks I'm skinny, that's her problem."

- When Casey was about 5, she asked, "Grandma, who drove today?"

    Grandma replied, "Grandpa always drives when we go someplace together."

    Casey: "Who drives when you're alone?"

Where We Differ from Some Grandparents.

Like most grandparents, we find our grandchildren to be a great source of joy and fulfillment. If we differ from some grandparents, it would be in that:

- We have tried to avoid putting pressure on our children to have children.

- Our principal happiness is in seeing the happiness and fulfillment of our children and grandchildren, not in our own.

- We make a conscious effort to be good role models for our grandchildren, and to avoid indulging them.

- Because our children and their spouses provide such full lives for their children, it is a challenge for us to provide further enrichment for our grandchildren's lives.

- Conversely, our own lives are so full that we don't depend on our grandchildren for our own gratification.

- We take every opportunity to praise our children and their spouses for their parenting and are very sparing with unsolicited advice.

- I think of the attainment of age 16 as a "rite of passage" into adulthood. So I now start "one on one" birthday lunches with my grandchildren at that age. I seek the same kind of relationship with them that I am trying to develop with my children.

6. Cousins

A six-year-old Manitoba farm boy is used to playing alone. His joy almost overcomes him on the one occasion when his two girl cousins come to visit for a few days. Showing them the farm, playing games, and just being with them are pleasures such as he has never known before. His sorrow and loneliness when they leave is so great that he runs away.

These two girls, Florence and Lillian, were the daughters of my mother's brother Stanley Crozier. A third daughter, Norma, was born some years later. The family lived in Rochester, New York. Lillian and I were the same age. In the year I lived in Rochester (1922) we developed a strong attraction to each other. I still cherish the dozen or so times we were together that year. In 1929 Lillian and her family visited us in Minnesota. What ecstasy! We were truly "kissin' cousins." Only close parental supervision and the fear of discovery kept us from further indiscretions.

My only other cousin was Jack Rideout, the son of my father's sister Annie. He was about 20 years older than I and seemed more like an uncle. When we first moved to

White Bear Lake (1923) our family had no car. Jack would pick us up and drive us to Green Lake (near Chisago City) to spend the day at his mother's summer cottage. Jack's father had died years before. He and Aunt Annie lived in Cleveland. He married Alice Chalifoux, the first harpist of the Cleveland Symphony. Salzado, the great American harpist, had a harp colony on the Maine coast. When he died, he willed it to Alice. As far as I know she is still operating it.

Jack was a talented freelance industrial designer and made excellent money. In 1934 my father's sister Isabel was hospitalized. Jack appealed to my brother and me to help pay her bill, stressing the fact that my father had never repaid the money he had borrowed from her earlier. My brother had no job and my $85 a month barely kept our family of four alive, so we had to refuse. We never saw or heard from Jack again. He died in his 50's. Later on Aunt Annie and I became good friends again, and she lived with us for several summers before she died.

7. In-laws

"Mixed feelings: when you see your mother-in-law driving off the edge of a cliff in your new Cadillac"
— Author Unknown

Happily, I never felt that way about my mother-in-law. (What's more I've never owned a Cadillac.) The world could have used a lot more people like Helen Dearborn Huelster. A loving, caring person with a great sense of outreach, she was an active leader in her church and in the White Bear Women's Club. She was quick to form an opinion and to express it. There were no assertiveness classes then, but she didn't need one. She made friends easily. She knew who she was and she was comfortable with herself.

The first few times I was in her home I thought the family

must have quite a bit of money. Later I realized what a marvelous environment she had created with relatively little money. She seemed able to make every dollar do the work of three. Never once did I hear her complain about having insufficient money or express a wish that they had more. She read many good books and provided her family with a rich culture.

The Stepmother Image.

Doris' natural mother (Helen Peterson) died of typhoid fever when Doris was two years old. Her father remarried when Doris was six. Doris used to say she was flower girl at her mother's wedding—a statement easily misunderstood.

When I first knew Doris, I resented the amount of housework she had to do and thought, "H-m-m-m, a typical stepmother taking advantage of her stepdaughter." Later I learned the whole story. Doris' brother had been born just two years before we met, and her mother had been seriously ill for months afterwards. There was no money to hire help, so, at 16, Doris had taken over the management of the house. This training and experience no doubt contributed greatly to her ability to manage her own household with the quiet efficiency that she did.

Mother Helen, as Doris referred to her, knew little about the business world and was inclined to be suspicious of those who did, including me. On two different occasions, I was able to clear up serious problems that had developed on titles to two homes they owned. Her gratitude was tinged with the suspicion that I had somehow managed to hoodwink the people involved. She never completely trusted me after that.

Father-in-law.

Wallace Henry Huelster was a good man. A Linotype operator for Johnson Printing, he was quietly proud of his skills. In contrast to his wife, he was a simple, unassertive, almost shy man. He was content to cultivate his garden or repair an appliance at his neatly kept work bench. It would take a potent push from his wife to involve him in a social evening. Yet I found him easy to talk to and derived pleasure in helping him with a project or with the snow shoveling.

You could actually say we were fond of each other. He was generous in letting Doris and me use his car. His great love for Doris was unspoken but so obvious it made me feel as though he had bestowed on me an almost sacred trust in my relationship with her.

Other-in-Laws.

Doris' half-sisters, Helen and Margaret, were bright and energetic. They were 12 and 10 years old when I first met them. I enjoyed playing games with them and watching them grow up. They were like the little sisters I never had.

Their brother, Wally, was only two then. Despite my own questionable reputation as a punster, I take no credit (blame?) for his ability to pun at a very early age. Barely able to talk, he watched a dying fire in the fireplace: "Fire going out — is it going out to lunch?"

All of Doris' siblings are still living, and I always enjoy our occasional visits.

Sharp Contrasts.

The warmth of the Huelster home, both physical and emotional, stood in sharp contrast to my own home. There we spent the winters in the kitchen and slept in unheated bedrooms because the sparse funds wouldn't buy enough fuel to heat the whole house. At Doris' house there was often laughter and games with her siblings, or lively conversation on a broad range of subjects with her mother. My mother and I were alone much of the time. She would spend her evenings working quietly on her needlework, while I studied or read.

The financial stability and relative luxury of the Huelster

household made ours stand out in stark contrast. Our poverty was physically evident, painfully etched in my mother's face, and a source of tension on the occasions when my father was home. Doris cannot remember being in my family home, and I don't remember taking her there. I guess I was too ashamed.

The attraction of the warm, inviting atmosphere in the Huelster home reinforced my intense desire to be with Doris, and caused me practically to live at their house. This would result in an occasional jealous outburst from my mother, which was upsetting to me and, no doubt, to her.

The Huelsters had many large family gatherings. I enjoyed them all, particularly the lively conversations with Doris' cousins, aunts and uncles. The maternal uncles always had strong opinions that didn't always agree, so there was never a dull moment.

Two

Places I've Lived

8. Merrickville

> *"It takes a heap o' livin'*
> *to make a house a home"*
> —Edgar Guest

A two-year-old boy gazes intently through the railing on the second-floor porch of a sturdy brick home. The ground looks a long way down.

You have already learned, in the chapter about my grandparents, that Merrickville is in eastern Ontario. It was a sleepy little town of 600 when I was born there. It was still a sleepy little town, though of 900, when I visited it 60 years later.

I was born in the same room of the same house in which my mother had been born 40 years earlier. That's stability!

The porch scene described above is the only memory of my birthplace that I have retained. The rest you would call hearsay. My grandfather loved to tell stories about Merrickville. And he loved me because I enjoyed them and would ask for more. There were stories about his livery stable, Sam Jakes' store, the interesting times at the locks (where, you will recall, he was the lockmaster). With little or no encouragement, he would tell the one about the runaway horse and many other stories of the horses he loved so well. When I first heard them, they brought excitement to my uneventful life. Now they help me form a picture of the tranquil, comfortable life in a quiet little town my whole family loved. The exception was my father, the adventurer from Halifax. This quiet life bored him stiff.

9. Gainsborough

> *"A hundred men may make an*
> *encampment, but it takes a*
> *woman to make a home."*
> —Chinese Proverb

A large gander accosts a three-year-old boy in the family farmyard. The terrified boy retreats toward the house as fast as he can run. The gander is faster and nips him in the back. The boy reaches the sanctuary of his house, screaming at the top of his lungs. It takes his mother a long time to quiet him. Grandfather tries earnestly to convince him that he can face the gander and put him in his place. He even gives the boy a large whip with which to threaten the gander. But it is all in vain: From then on the gander owns the yard as far as the boy is concerned.

That is one of my three direct recollections of Gainsborough, Saskatchewan, a small farming community about 160 miles southeast of Regina and 10 miles north of the North Dakota border. Another concerns the Canadian Pacific Railway that ran many freight trains by our house, mostly at night. There must have been quite a steep grade nearby. The steam locomotive never seemed to have enough power to make it up this grade the first time—or sometimes the second—or even the third. It would chug-chug-chug loudly up the incline, the chugs becoming slower and slower, until suddenly they became very rapid as the drive wheels spun in futility on the smooth tracks. Then the train would back farther down the slope and take another run at it. Many nights the noise aroused me enough that I would become aware of my mother standing in the window weeping quietly. I didn't know why she was crying, but it made me sad. Years later I understood the reasons. Her loneliness in this strange prairie country deepened her continual yearning to return to the comfortable, secure life she knew in Merrickville. Her inability to cope with many heavy chores that the stronger farm women seemed to handle with relative ease was both frustrating and humiliating. And the frequent quarrels with her husband, who refused to give up this miserable life of hard work, grinding poverty and endless disappointments, all conspired to deepen her abject misery.

Illness Strikes.

My only other memory is no more pleasant than the others. Bronchial pneumonia took me to death's door when I was three years old, and I had to spend many weeks in bed during the sub-zero winter months. The lack of any heat in the bedroom, together with my mother's attempts to provide relief for my wracking cough with steam, produced a thick coat of white frost on the ceiling. My mother tacked a blanket across the ceiling in an attempt to keep the frost from dropping onto the bed. The doctor told her I would never fully recover and that I would be sickly for the rest of my life. What a terrible prognosis to leave with my distraught mother, who was already convinced that this miserable existence would be the death of us all!

It was many years later when I learned that our departure from Gainsborough was an ignominious one. Successive crop failures caught up with us: There was no more credit at the grocery or seed store, and not enough cash to make payments on the mortgage. So we left with our suitcases and our shame. . . and nothing else.

10. Austin

> *"There is no greater grief than to remember days of joy when misery is at hand."*
> —Dante

It is a crisp winter day. The deep, fresh snow, carved into magically exotic shapes by the previous two-day blizzard, sparkles under a brilliant sun radiating from a clear blue sky. This fairyland scene carries a six-year-old farm boy, playing alone as usual, into a fantasy about his magic sled. By climbing a 15-foot snowdrift he is able to reach the roof overhang of a low barn, from where he makes his way to the peak. The swift ride down the barn roof and the exhilarating free fall into a deep snow drift, perhaps six feet below, is in sharp contrast to the rude shock of the sudden stop. The snow is soft enough to prevent any broken bones; but the impact is sufficient to bloody his nose and create a painful bruise across his entire face where it struck the sled. Screaming and dripping blood, he heads for the house and the sanctuary of his mother's arms.

Austin is a small Manitoba farming community located 84 miles west of Winnipeg. Our farm was two miles from town and the one-room school. School was a catch-22 as far as I was concerned. In the summer the school was closed. In the winter the extreme cold and wind, or the deep snow, kept me home. Moreover, my mother dreaded the thought of a replay of the pneumonia that had nearly killed me in Gainsborough. So my schooling was confined to the Fall and Spring months when I could walk the two miles each way. There were also brief periods of schooling when Grandfather visited us. He would hitch Nellie (a retired workhorse) to the cutter (light sleigh) and drive me to school. Father was too busy with the farm chores to perform this less important function.

The One-Room School.

School was a large single room that held about 30 or so kids arranged in rows representing grades one through eight. The one teacher would move from row to row as the day progressed. She would ask the students to read aloud from their "readers," to recite history dates, or to "go to the board" and do their arithmetic. Because of my spotty attendance, I never felt a part of the program. The compassionate teacher must have sensed this, because I never remember being called on to do anything. That was just fine with me, because the very thought of having to get up in front of the class was enough to send chills of terror up my spine.

The centerpiece in the school room was a large stove whose vigorous fire roasted the nearby students while those farther away sat shivering in their coats. Then came the great day when a group of fathers installed a sheet metal jacket around the stove. This shielded the roasting students and created a convection current that carried some of the heat to the freezing ones.

Recess in the winter consisted of opening the windows and stretching the body with a few simple exercises. In the Spring and Fall we would go outdoors to jump rope, play games, and use the one article of playground equipment: a rope swing suspended from the branch of a tree. I didn't know how to jump rope, nor was I invited to join in the games. I wanted to try the swing, but was always elbowed away by the bigger boys. Mostly I just stood around and hoped that no one would say anything to me. They didn't.

A Miserable Environment.

Lunch hour wasn't much better. I would take the cover off the lard pail in which my mother had packed lunch and eat my lunch quickly. Then I would hide myself in the hope that none of the bullies would torment me until school started again. If I didn't have part of my lunch stolen, or have dirt thrown in the lunch pail, and wasn't harassed, it was a good day.

About my only other remembrance of school is of Queenie McKnight, who sat just ahead of me. Poor Queenie was tormented constantly by an itchy head, which she would scratch vigorously with the point of her pencil. The lice would fall onto my desk. Inevitably some of them found their way to my head. When my mother found me scratching, she washed my head with "coal oil" (kerosene) and combed my hair with a fine tooth comb. The whole affair was not very enjoyable. She complained to the teacher, who moved Queenie to the back row.

Happy Times.

There were a few happy times: adventures with Grandpa, visits from aunts and cousins. My aunts would play cards with me, bring me wonderful books, help me read them and teach me to spell. Then they would sit me in the center of a family circle and try to stump me with spelling words. They seemed to delight in my ability to spell, and that made me feel good inside.

Today, as I think about that traumatic experience with the sled I see it as an allegory of my father's farming experience. But I slid down the barn roof only once. We repeated our humiliating departure a second time.

11. Rochester

> "Home is the place where, when you have
> to go there, they have to take you in."
> —Robert Frost

An eight-year-old boy is forbidden by his uncle to play with the neighbor children, or even speak to them, because they are Jews and "dirty wops." A stray kitten assuages his loneliness and becomes his dear friend. The boy follows the kitten out of the third floor dormer window and on up to the peak of the high steep roof. He finds a strange exhilaration in looking down from this pinnacle. He repeats the experience on other days. Eventually his uncle catches him and chastises him severely . . . and there is no more rooftop elation.

Aunt Lillie (my mother's only sister) was a good, caring woman, who had to give up her nursing career because of ill health and her husband's decree. Justin Schopp, her husband, was a medical doctor. Most of his patients deserted him during World War I because of the strong hatred of Germans in Rochester, New York then. By 1922 he was the only person of German ancestry left in this neighborhood. All of the other German families had retreated to friendlier environs, but Justin stuck it out in the old neighborhood. A sharp decline in property values made the neighborhood attractively affordable to Italian immigrants and poorer Jewish families. Uncle Justin hated them all bitterly.

He had converted the large three-story family home into a rooming house by bartering lodging for the services of unemployed carpenters and laborers. He did all the painting himself, even though the paint made him deathly sick.

The only person he loved was his wife. He despised all her family, particularly her brother's wife and my father. He seemed to take particular pleasure in tormenting me until I cried. He persisted in this despite Aunt Lillie's entreaties. Since we had no money to pay for the two-dollar-a-week room we slept in or the food we ate, I think he felt the harassment was justified by his largess.

When I think about Justin's life, there are many unanswered questions. Did his chronic colitis contribute to his bitterness, or was it an effect? Did his failure as a medical doctor make him a misanthrope, or was it the other way around? Why did he stay in this neighborhood he hated? I have the impression that his parents were strict to the point of severity. How did this affect his personality? At one time he played piano in the Rochester Symphony orchestra. Why had he not touched the piano for years? Why would he not let anyone else touch it? Why did he keep it?

School.

P.S. #29 was my first experience in a large, fully graded school. The large building and the bustle of seemingly endless numbers of children terrified me. The first day, my mother had a conference with the principal. They had difficulty deciding what grade to put me in. I was old enough to be in the third grade, but my mother could produce no evidence that I had completed second grade work. So they put me in the second grade. It was an uneventful experience. I don't remember being asked to recite or anyone speaking to me, and I was relieved that no one did.

During this year my father lived with his sister, Annie, in St. Paul while he sought work and accumulated a few dollars to move us. We moved from Rochester in April 1923, so I missed the last several weeks of school and received no credit for my time spent. But I must have learned a few things. . .

12. White Bear Lake

*"He is the happiest, be he king or peasant,
who finds peace in his home."*
—Johann Wolfgang von Goethe

*A nine-year-old boy, accompanied by his 13-year-old
brother, walks over a mile on a hot summer day to
enjoy the cool waters of a beautiful lake. When they
feel thoroughly refreshed, they trudge home again.*

The town of White Bear Lake, Minnesota is located 12
miles northeast of St. Paul on the largest lake in the greater
St. Paul area. In 1923 it was a quiet bedroom community
of about 2,500 people. The Northern Pacific railroad bisects
the town geographically. Then, it also bisected the town
socio-economically, and we lived "on the wrong side of the
tracks." Nevertheless, it was the best home my mother had
ever known since her marriage.

My father's job didn't pay much, and I don't think he
liked the work or the lack of adventure; but it was steady.
It wasn't hard to keep up with the Joneses, because the
Joneses didn't make much money either. My father made
friends quickly with many families in the area, and they
soon formed a card club that provided many happy
evenings.

School.

Shortly before we left Austin a classmate of mine had been
killed while playing on the train tracks. To go to the third
grade in White Bear I would have had to cross 13 railroad
tracks. The fourth grade was in a school on our side of the
tracks, only half a mile away. Those railroad tracks so terrified my mother that she persuaded the superintendent

of schools to try me in the fourth grade, even though she couldn't show that I had completed second grade work.

For the first time in my life I could attend school regularly. I loved it; most of the teachers were caring people who seemed to understand this extremely shy farm boy. Back then the White Bear elementary schools were organized in "half grades": 4A, 4B and so on. Happily, I justified my mother's strong faith in me: The teachers "force fed" me so that I did a full year's work each semester and continued to skip grades. The process was accelerated in high school, where I skipped the entire sophomore year and graduated from high school two months before my 15th birthday.

Paying the Price.

Although I was pulling down A's and A + 's in my studies, I would have gotten F's in both sports and my social life, had they been graded. It wasn't lack of time that caused me to flunk these latter two areas; I just didn't have the skills. I will recount my miserable experiences at sports in a later section.

Flunking Social Life.

Because of my extreme timidity and because I was only 13 when I started my junior year, I just couldn't be jump-started in the social arena. The very thought of attending class parties and dances terrified me. I totally avoided them until late in my junior year. Our class adviser had noticed my absences, and he tried to get me involved by recruiting me to help organize a party. Even that didn't work; it was a very stormy night and only a few kids turned out. I felt it was my fault that the party was a flop. There was one consolation, however; the adviser and I, and the other two classmates who had organized this dismal failure, cleaned up the remaining gallon of ice cream!

I felt attracted to several girls in the class, but was too timid to let them know. One girl made some gentle overtures to me. Once, she put perfume on a small felt pennant and presented it to me with a shy smile. Her gesture touched me deeply, but I didn't know how to respond. She mistook my lack of response for rejection, and the romance died before it had really begun.

Missing the Mark.

Because my brother had graduated as class valedictorian in 1927, I dearly wanted to do the same. A misunderstanding with my senior English teacher caused me to miss this mark that was so important to me. She had persuaded me to be business manager of the senior class play. I thought (and still think) she had said, in consideration of the many hours I would need to spend on the play, she would excuse me from writing the final theme.

The biggest job of the business manager was to solicit about 48 ads for the program. They sold for $5 each (about $50 in today's money). I had spent many, many hours canvassing the local business and professional establishments. The evening before the program had to go to press I had only 47 ads. After dinner I walked the mile to the downtown area and looked desperately for a business that was still open, and whose proprietor I hadn't already solicited. I found only one, a small barber shop I had never even been in. Haircuts were 50 cents then. I told him my story and asked for his ad. He was most reluctant. In a final burst of desperation I said, "Mr. LaBelle, I've never been in your shop before; but if you will buy this ad, I promise to get at least 10 haircuts from you." He smiled and pulled a five dollar bill from the cash register.

The Crushing Blow.

The first school day after the play, the teacher asked me to stay after class. She thanked me for my good work on the play. Then she said, "Your final theme was due over a week ago. You didn't turn it in. It's too late now. I will have to give you a D for the semester." I was shocked, deeply outraged, and disappointed beyond all description. That one bad mark knocked my numerical average down to 94.9% My friend, Harry Green, ended up with 95.2%. I had lost the coveted valedictorian position!

This disastrous experience taught me a valuable lesson: Always get important agreements reduced to writing. Another important principle that I learned many years later is the right of appeal. If I had known this then, I would have insisted that the teacher go with me to the principal. It would have been her word against mine, but he might have given me the benefit of the doubt.

No College.

By 1929 radio had brought culture into most homes, and my father's income as a Chautauqua lecturer had largely evaporated. He made a little money lecturing in schools, but it was not very steady. His luck was no better at lecturing on the radio. I have no idea how seriously he took my mother's entreaties to "get a real job," or what the job market was for a 55-year-old man with a very spotty employment record. But he was unemployed. He had defaulted on the contract for deed for our house. When he could no longer talk the former owner into waiting for his money "until things got better," an FHA loan came to the rescue.

Two years earlier my brother had moved to Rochester, New York to live with Aunt Lillie and Uncle Justin and attend college. We needed every penny I could earn to help with the mortgage payments and buy a little food. So even a generous scholarship would not have enabled me to go to college.

People have asked how it was decided that my brother would go to college and I would work. I don't think any of us thought of it as a deliberate decision. It was just "the way things worked out." I believe my brother had thoughts of helping me through college when he got established; but, by the time that happened, I was already committed to an actuarial career.

The Self-taught Driver.

The lack of jobs in White Bear Lake forced me to find work in St. Paul. Riding the bus to work and back six days a week would have cost $3.00, exactly one third of my $9.00 gross pay. I saved the money by hitchhiking the 13 miles to and from my job, morning and night, winter and summer. On a typical day I would walk about a mile and a half in the morning and perhaps the same at night. On the rare occasions when I couldn't get a ride, I considered it a minor financial disaster to have to pay 25 cents to take the bus. One morning, as we approached downtown St. Paul, the driver who had picked me up that day said, "I'm late for work; can you drive my car to the service station?" The service station was about a mile away through the downtown traffic. I had dearly wanted to drive a car, but never had the opportunity, since neither my folks nor most of their friends owned one. So I simply said, "Yes."

I had never driven before, but I had watched many drivers and felt I would be able to make it just one mile. I don't remember ever being so excited and nervous as when I slid across the front seat and under the steering wheel of that beautiful convertible. My left leg shook violently as I tried to let the clutch out slowly. The car bucked and jerked in unison with my leg. But the car did pick up speed and, miraculously, I made that mile without mishap, and drove into the service station. With a mixture of exhilaration, relief and triumph, I turned the keys over to the attendant and walked away, realizing how fortunate I was to have completed this foolish mission without serious consequences.

My Very Own Car.

By 1932 my brother was sending home most of the money

he made in the Civilian Conservation Corps. I was making over 50% more than I had at my first job, and I was able to save a little money. But that spring I blew virtually everything I had saved ($350.00) on a 1928 Essex Coupe with a rumble seat, an option in which the trunk was replaced by a seat that opened backwards. The salesman told me it was very sporty and would make me "the man about town." I learned too late that the Essex was the Edsel of its day, and the rumble seat went over like a lead balloon. Some of my friends derided me for this foolish purchase. One night I felt particularly embarrassed when my girl friend and I came out of a movie house on a frosty night. Some wag had drawn in the frost: "My Essex, does yours?"

The Essex was more of a liability than an asset. Oh, it brought me some new "friends" who had no car of their own, and it expanded my social life a bit. But the many nights I spent cruising and trying to keep that darn car in running order hampered my home study program. I was never very proficient at repairing it and had to pay for expensive repairs, which it seemed to need frequently. It ate up the money I should have been saving, and even some that could have improved our home life. And it caused strained relations with my father, who told me repeatedly, "you have no business owning a car," and fussed continually about the money it consumed. The frequent nights "on the town" worried my mother.

The Forced Sale.

By 1934 my brother, Jack, had found work with 3M in Wausau, but the job barely paid enough for him to support himself. Meanwhile, the Essex seemed to need almost continual repair. The financial and parental pressures became so great that I felt forced to sell the car. I couldn't find anyone who wanted to buy that unpopular junker and had to take what I could get from a used car dealer. I believe it was $15.00.

Walking Away from Another Home.

In 1935 3M transferred Jack to St. Paul, and he moved back home. In 1937 he and I called a family council and persuaded my father and mother that we could live more cheaply by renting a home in a low rent area. We chose a house on St. Paul's East Side, on Bush Avenue, a block and a half west of Johnson Parkway. The rent was about the same as the mortgage payment had been, but we saved the taxes and the insurance payments. Jack would be just a few blocks from his work. I would no longer have to hitchhike; I could walk the 3 miles each way to and from Minnesota Mutual's office.

In the extremely depressed market we couldn't sell the house for the mortgage balance. So it was Gainsborough and Austin all over again, with one exception: since our meager furniture wasn't mortgaged, we moved it along with our clothes.

Points to Ponder.

- How did the early years of loneliness and poverty affect my life? For good? For bad? I think most of the effects were positive.

- Despite the physical hardships, there was little psychological trauma.

- Although we lived in poverty in White Bear Lake, it was so much better than what had gone before that it felt good.

- The absence of early formal schooling appears not to have been a lasting handicap. I had more than made up for it by the time I graduated from high school.

- With one exception (my Algebra teacher, Mary Williams), I don't remember my teachers as being out of the ordinary. But I seem to have retained much more knowledge from my high school education than have my peers. How much of this is due to genes? To having

a role model, valedictorian brother? To the high expectations and faith of my parents? To the complete absence
of social life that allowed me to focus on my studies? Or
is it due to a marvelous school superintendent (C. H.
Christenson) who seemed to take a personal interest in
my progress? To a very high motivation to learn? To a
great curiosity about things? To a continuing vigorous
use of my mind and knowledge in many aspects of my
life? I believe they all have played a part.

13. St. Paul

*"The worst feeling in the world is the
homesickness that comes over a man occasionally
when he is at home."*
—Ed Howe

I'm afraid my mother was the real loser in the move to
St. Paul. She missed all of her wonderful friends, the familiar
surroundings, her church, and the card parties terribly. She
felt very keenly the shame of "losing our house," the best
home she had enjoyed in 29 years of married life. The rest
of us had a life outside the new home; she didn't. I don't
think she ever got to like that new neighborhood, which
was already showing signs of decay (it is now a wretched
slum). But I never heard her complain.

Even though it was a long walk to work, I enjoyed the
new sights and sounds and, most of all, the blessed relief
from the uncertainty of hitchhiking. My stay in the rented
house was relatively short, since Doris and I were married
just a little over a year after my family moved to St. Paul.

The Apartment.

In preparing for our marriage Doris and I had read that

a family should not spend more than a quarter of its income on housing. That worked out to be $35.00 a month (about $350 in today's dollars), which didn't buy much of an apartment even then. After much looking, we had to stretch that up to $39.50. This covered the rent on a furnished one-room, third floor walk-up apartment on Summit Avenue (St. Paul) just west of Rice Street. This, too, was a decaying neighborhood. The apartment looked small, even by 1938 standards. A nine-by-twelve rug left only modest margins of bare floor around the edges of the all-purpose room.

The unit had a "Pullman kitchenette," which was like a short, narrow hallway containing a stove, a sink, a small counter and a few cupboards. Despite the apartment's miniscule size, it was superior to several others we had looked at. Instead of a "Murphy bed" (which hinges down out of the wall) the stationary bed was in a little alcove that was separated from the room by a curtain. To get to the tiny bathroom, you pushed by the curtain and squeezed around the end of the bed.

A few years ago an episode of The Cosby Show included a scene in which the newly married daughter and son-in-law have moved into a small, grungy apartment in a low-class district. The young woman's parents, Dr. and Mrs. Huxtable, come to visit. The focus of the scene is the expression on Mrs. Huxtable's face as she views the squalid setting that her beloved daughter has chosen to call home. Her facial expressions speak volumes as she tries politely to conceal her disgust. I had a strong sense of deja-vu as I watched that show. It was virtually a repeat of my mother-in-law's first visit to our apartment.

No Room for Us.

The one room was about the size of an average bedroom in today's houses. It contained a davenport, an upholstered chair, a drop-leaf table and two dining chairs. There was just enough room for the beautiful cabinet radio my brother, Jack, had given us. The apartment was so small that there was barely room to stack the boxes containing our wedding presents and our modest belongings on the minimal floor space that wasn't occupied by furniture. We tried to leave narrow aisles for us to navigate, but it was a tight fit. Then came the challenging process of bringing some order out of this chaos. The situation reminded me of that puzzle with 15 squares and one blank in which you must get the 15 numbers into sequence. You must move a dozen or more squares just to get one number where you want it. But, in a few days the boxes disappeared and we had a cozy little home that we found very pleasant.

A Meager but Happy Life.

There were many good things about this living arrangement. We could walk the mile each way to work together, and the housekeeping chores were simple. We could also eat out and take in a show at least once a month. Our friends would come for bridge occasionally. Once we even squeezed in two tables of bridge, but it was very cozy. I spent weekday evenings studying. Doris cooked, sewed or did other household duties. She worked most Saturdays and I studied. Sundays we would take the bus to visit her folks in White Bear, or the streetcar to visit mine on the East Side. What with year-end closings and tax returns, the winter months were busy times in the CPA offices. So, in addition to a full day on Saturday, Doris had to work many Sundays. Then I would study or go to see my folks.

We budgeted very carefully and went without rather than overspend. Each of us kept cash ledgers, and balanced them carefully against the few dollars in our possession. With this frugal existence we could come close to living on my $100 a month and save practically all of her $40. We couldn't even dream of accumulating enough money to buy a house, but we knew the money would come in handy for something. Mostly, we felt that, if we had a child, we could continue our lifestyle on my income.

A Strenuous but Memorable Trip.

By 1940 we felt we could take some of our savings and blow it on a trip. The Greyhound Bus Company offered a "circle tour" ticket that allowed us to go Los Angeles by way of Spokane, Portland and down the Pacific coast. We could then come home the more direct southern route through Las Vegas and Denver. We could get on any bus we chose and get off wherever we wished as long as we stayed on this circle route. Always wanting to get the most for our money, I persuaded Doris that we were young and strong enough to go sightseeing every day and sleep on the bus at night. We spent six days going to LA, 3 days in LA, and six days returning. On that entire 15-day trip we slept in a bed three nights at the house of her cousin, Edythe, in San Francisco and one night in a hotel in Spokane!

After an intensely uncomfortable first two nights, we became quite adjusted to our seats for beds, and the rest of the trip was tolerable. We saw a great deal of this country and found the trip exciting and enjoyable. The ride through the Cascade Mountains on the narrow, winding roads with their steep grades and tight curves gave us much the same chilling thrills as a roller coaster. I haven't found any other couple who have taken a similar trip.

The Blizzard of 1940.

Much has been written about this famous blizzard in early November, which caused the deaths of so many hunters who were fatally trapped by the sudden change in the weather. In a very few hours, bright sunshine and mild temperatures were replaced by raging winds, heavy snow, and sub-freezing temperatures. Doris and I were both allowed to leave work early. We arranged, as usual, to walk the mile uphill to our apartment together. It was a cold, arduous trip.

The morning had been sunny and mild. Radio storm warnings were rare then, and there were none that morning. Our light coats and footwear offered scant protection from the vicious onslaughts of the violent weather. The tremendous wind drove the blinding snow so hard that it stung our faces and our eyes. The worst blasts drove us to seek shelter in doorways or building recesses. If none of these inadequate shelters were near at hand, we would grab the nearest sign post or light pole to avoid being blown down.

How do You Spell Relief?

Powerful waves of relief and thankfulness poured over us as we finally reached the warmth and safety of our apartment. The trip had totally exhausted us and chilled us through and through. We were so numbed that we had difficulty unlocking our door. We were victims of moderate hypothermia, which numbs the mind as well as the body, but we didn't even know the word then.

The extreme fatigue combined with the hypothermia were probably the perfect formula for pneumonia, but our healthy bodies and a merciful Providence apparently protected us from this dreaded outcome. As I think about it now, it was a risky, foolish trip. But we didn't realize how severe the weather was until we were well on the way, by which point we were eager to get home and the buses had quit running.

Once we arrived, I compounded the initial foolishness by donning warm clothes and overshoes, and going back out to help motorists up the steepest part of the Ninth Street hill. Doris was quite upset by my failure to heed her vigorous (and wise) protests. I'm much more, but not totally, receptive to her wise counsel today.

Our First House.

At Minnesota Mutual Life, I used to browse in the ample

library that was part of the large office of Henry Allstrom, Vice President and Actuary. I had run across a book by Irving Fisher, a noted economist of that period. He had a theory about inflation that was not widely accepted at the time. Fisher argued that, when the United States finally came out of the Great Depression, we would see inflation at unprecedented rates. He further advised individuals to protect against the consequent loss of their purchasing power by putting a major portion of their money into something other than "promises to pay." This was his expression for savings accounts, credit unions and savings bonds, which were the popular forms of assets for the people of modest means then.

When I was inducted into the Army in February 1941, we gave up our apartment and Doris "moved back home." I was "permanently assigned" to the Reception Center at Fort Snelling (just south and west of St. Paul). My first application for Officer Candidate School had been turned down because I didn't have a college education. So it looked as if I might remain at Fort Snelling "for the duration."

The trip to White Bear Lake was too long and expensive to make every night. Doris and I realized how fortunate we were to see each other on weekends, but we longed for the opportunity to live together again. My bosses at the Reception Center seemed very appreciative of my mental quickness and my willingness to do any assigned task. They promoted me just as rapidly as the rules would allow: Private to Private First Class, then Corporal, Sergeant, and then Staff Sergeant. This rank paid about the same as I had been making at Minnesota Mutual. Neither Doris nor I had any living expenses, so we were saving virtually all of our combined total gross pay.

These circumstances caused me to think creatively about ways we might live together. A house in the Highland Park area (a good neighborhood in the southwest area of St. Paul) seemed like the ideal answer. Property values were increasing in that area, and I could walk the four miles to Fort Snelling. The early rising, the eight-mile walk and the late dinners seemed like a small price to pay for the priceless privilege of being reunited with my Beloved.

Joint Venture.

Doris and I spent many pleasant weekends house hunting. The cheapest house we could find had an asking price of $5,500. We didn't have enough money to buy a house on our own; so I approached my bachelor brother, Jack. I explained Irving Fisher's theories to him and proposed a bold plan: we would split the down payment and the principal portion of the mortgage payments equally. I would pay the balance of the mortgage payments, the real estate taxes and insurance instead of rent; when we sold the house, he would get half the proceeds. He agreed!

How great was my excitement when I signed an Earnest Money contract for $5,000 and presented it to the seller! He refused the offer; but he quickly agreed to my suggestion that we split the difference, and we signed the modified contract.

Our Dream House.

This four-bedroom semi-bungalow still stands unchanged at 1764 Palace Avenue. The living room was larger than our entire apartment, so it seemed huge to us, although the whole floor plan, downstairs and up, consumed just over a thousand square feet. With two bedrooms down and two up, you had to come downstairs to go to the tiny bathroom. But we owned the place and we loved it. Most importantly, it brought us together again. . . .

Buyer's Guilt.

When I visited Minnesota Mutual and told some of the senior officers what I had done, their unanimous reaction was a combination of horror and disbelief. How could I, an (otherwise) smart young man, do such a foolish thing! I can remember specifically the President's remark: "You'd be a lot smarter coming out of the Army with cash in the bank than being saddled with a house you probably won't want."

I went away feeling I should consult the nearest psychiatrist. When winter came, the pangs of guilt only increased. Waves of remorse poured over me every time I heard the oil burner come on. All I could think of was how large that fuel bill would be.

These terrible feelings were compounded when Doris became pregnant with George. We had discussed the likelihood that I might be in the Army a long time, that we might be separated, and we had decided that we should "let nature take its course." Nature didn't wait long! In the 1940's pregnant women quit work the moment they began to show, so we were quickly reduced to one income.

Moonlighting.

To assuage my guilty feelings, I decided to augment our modest income by moonlighting. Perhaps I overdid it. Before long I had, not two, but four jobs. My daily routine started like this: up at 5:00 AM, walk to Fort Snelling, do the bookkeeping for the Post Tailor, breakfast in the mess hall, and morning at my regular army job. After a quick lunch, I would teach math to a group of enlisted men who paid me so that they could pass their Officer Candidate exams. When I finished my regular army job, I would eat a quick dinner in the mess hall, do the bookkeeping at the Officer's Club, and walk home. Then I would prepare my math lesson for the next day, and fall into bed a little after midnight.

Doris would still be asleep when I left. I would see her briefly before she went to bed; but we did have our weekends. I seemed to thrive on this strenuous regimen, partly because I felt I would be able to ease up a little after my next promotion. Mostly I enjoyed all of my activities, except the three months of basic training. Even that was interesting because I learned so many new things.

A Full House.

Like us, our good friends Jack and Mary Lou Schneeweis gave up their apartment when Jack was drafted. Then, when he was assigned to work at Fort Snelling, they needed a place to live, so they moved in with us. We still had a couple of empty bedrooms so we rented one of them to Grant Kuehn, a very fine young enlisted man with whom I had developed a friendship at Fort Snelling. We all enjoyed the arrangement, I especially because the room and board they paid helped to relieve our strained finances.

In the culture of the 1940's, it was not customary for a couple to announce the wife's pregnancy publicly. People even avoided the use of the word as much as possible. We quietly told our parents that Doris was "in a family way," and that was it.

When she began to have serious attacks of morning sickness, our roomer friends were quite concerned. Jack had the stomach flu at the time, and said to Doris, "Maybe you've got what I have!" This gave Doris and me a private laugh, but we still didn't explain the real cause.

The happy arrangement lasted for only weeks: Grant and Jack were "shipped out" and Mary Lou moved back in with her parents.

The Pace Increases.

My daily routine became even more strenuous when Doris developed toxemia and became extremely ill. I had to cook her meals and do the household chores. She became so dehydrated that you could pinch her skin and a sharp ridge would remain. It was soon obvious that she needed more care than I could give her. In a conference with her mother we decided that she should move "back home" again until her health improved. So we had come full circle!

A Welcome Relief.

When the Army accepted my third application for Officer Candidate School I went to Fort Washington, Maryland. My classmates were complaining about the tough regimen: from 6:00 AM to 10:00 PM. But it felt so marvelously luxurious to get eight hours of sleep every night that I felt as if I was on vacation!

When my brother, Jack, was drafted into the Army, my parents moved in with Doris, who had returned to our house in Highland Park. This move saved the rent payments on the house on the East Side and provided company for Doris. The arrangement had a third important advantage that only I appreciated: It justified the purchase of the house and erased the last vestiges of buyer's guilt! Jack was discharged before I was and moved in with Doris and my folks. He lived there until he was married two years later.

A Strenuous but Pleasant Life.

As I will explain more fully in Section V, our eldest two children, George and Jan, were born while I was in military service. Mary, Bev and Rick weren't born until I was out of the Army and had completed my actuarial exams in 1947.

In December 1945, after World War II, I was the first man to return to Minnesota Mutual from military service and was given a challenging job. Because of the extreme shortage of skilled personnel at the office, the heavy responsibilities I carried, and the urgent need to complete my professional studies (more about these things later), life was strenuous. There would be a couple of four-week to six-week periods each year when I would work virtually two shifts. Apart from that I managed to keep my work time down to about 50 intensely packed hours a week. But, beyond work, I felt I had to study over 30 hours a week to complete my actuarial exams in the shortest possible time. I would usually be home just in time for a six-o'clock supper with the family and a brief time afterward with our kids, George and Jan.

Doris would get them to bed promptly at seven, and I would begin my five hours of evening study. For a while I had great difficulty staying awake until midnight. Then I found a solution: if I couldn't stay awake after 11:00 PM, I would set the alarm for an hour earlier in the morning and complete my five hours then. This system not only provided the requisite hours of study, but it also gave me increased motivation to stay awake!

Saturdays I spent a full eight hours at the office—not working, but studying. We reserved Saturday evenings and Sundays for family, a little yard work, social activities and a little recreation. This regimen was heavily tilted toward work and study, but we contented ourselves with the idea that it was temporary, and an investment in the future. It also avoided giving our children the feeling that "Daddy's too busy to play with you." I was always available to them during the time when I was home and they were awake.

A Workaholic?

Doris cooperated beautifully and without complaint, although she occasionally expressed concern that I would become a workaholic. I tried to dispel that concern by pointing out that true workaholics don't work to meet their commitments, but rather to escape from a bad family situation or some other unpleasant environment. She still thinks I'm a workaholic, and I'm still unable to convince her otherwise.

I really don't think I overwork, nor do I believe that hard work for long hours causes either fatigue or burnout. Fatigue comes from working at something you don't enjoy. Burnout comes from a combination of fatigue, frustration, disappointment and disillusionment about your work. Working hard at something you feel you're good at, in pleasant surroundings, and with a feeling of accomplishment is one of God's great gifts. This is especially true if you find the work creative, or if you can do it with associates with whom there is friendship, camaraderie and mutual respect.

Doris was also concerned that I would get into a pattern of 60-70 hour work weeks, as she had seen some of my associates do. I assured her that I would never let this happen to the detriment of a well-balanced family life. And once I completed my studies, it never did.

The Bottom Line

In 1953 we sold the Highland Park house for almost 2½ times what we paid for it. When my brother was drafted, he didn't feel able to continue the joint purchase arrangement. I had already been commissioned, Doris was keeping the books for the White Bear Yacht Club, and we had been able to save considerable amounts of money. So we felt wealthy enough to buy his share of the house. Besides providing good housing for many people, the house had yielded us a compound rate of over 9% on our investment (government bonds were yielding less than 2½% at the time). On top of that, since we had prepaid the mortgage in full, the proceeds enabled us to create a very substantial equity in the "expensive" lakefront home.

14. Mahtomedi

"Home is where the heart is."
— Pliny the Elder

A 14-year-old high school senior hears his parents and their friends discussing "that terrible community" called Mahtomedi. According to them, it is a den of iniquity: Gangsters from Chicago hide out there; they have a night club there with "all sorts of goings-on"; they call it a "speak-easy" because they sell bootleg whiskey there! After they hear this, his parents forbid him ever to go near this evil community.

On a stormy winter night in January 1952 our friends Jack and Mary Lou Schneeweis were playing bridge at our house in St. Paul. Mary Lou said, "Gee, you folks should move to Mahtomedi so we don't have to drive 35 miles round trip in weather like this to play bridge." She went on to tell us how great it was to live in Mahtomedi: "It's a wonderful place to raise kids, with good churches, good schools, convenient stores, etc." I responded, "We wouldn't want to live that far from work unless we could live on the lake." (Mahtomedi is on the east shore of White Bear Lake, about 15 miles from downtown St. Paul. Pronounced Maw-toe-mee'-die, the name was derived from an Indian word for White Bear Lake.) Mary Lou exclaimed, "I know just the place for you!"

She went on to describe this picturesque four-bedroom home on almost an acre of wooded lawn sloping down to 140 feet of lakefront. She recalled her fond memories of playing as a child in this grand old house, which had been built in 1896. The owners had tried to sell it two years earlier when they moved to California. When it didn't sell, they leased it. She offered to get the owners' permission for us to look at it. I accepted.

The Home of My Dreams.

The tenants had rented the house for a song and didn't want to move. So they pulled every trick in the book to avoid showing it to us. After a couple of months of vain attempts to make a date, we caught them outside one day and insisted on seeing the inside. They discouraged us in every possible way from buying. We learned all the bad points of the house; they even pulled up the living room rug so we could see how terrible the floor was.

The list of drawbacks seemed endless. The 19th century

kitchen had a patched linoleum floor, with patches on the patches! Its open sink had a sidearm drain board; steep, narrow stairs led to the laundry tub in a dirty, dingy basement, whose outside door had rotted away because the drain didn't work. The entrance from the street required you to walk around the kitchen table and through the dining room to get to any other part of the house. The unsightly icebox, built through an exterior wall, added to the unattractive scene. It was a great invention at the turn of the century; the iceman could replenish the ice without entering the kitchen. But it was an eyesore in this day of modern refrigerators. There was no coat closet. The facility for coats, hats, boats and mittens for seven people was totally inadequate. It was a series of hooks on the wall of the small powder room that adjoined the kitchen.

The upstairs wasn't much better: The one bathroom that served the four bedrooms had an ancient, fourlegged tub. The open washbasin was of the same vintage. And the toilet, with its dark wood flush-box located near the ceiling and operated by a pull chain, was a genuine conversation piece! The carpets were shot or even non-existent, exposing worn, softwood floors. Closets were small and inconvenient. The house was heated by an ancient steam boiler that vented its energy through a series of unsightly radiators of various sizes and shapes. A real estate expert told me the boiler seemed sound, but was "apt to let go any day." The entire house needed re-decorating badly. The exterior was also sorely in need of paint. The lawn was a hayfield that the tenants hadn't raked or mowed for two years. The 19th century carriage shed, which served as a garage, was totally dilapidated, had a suspicious slant, and showed more bare wood than paint.

Before we had gained access to the inside we had thoroughly inspected the yard and the lakefront. George, age nine, was too excited to contain himself. His words are inscribed indelibly in my mind: "We like the lake, we like the yard, we like the trees, we like the outside of the house; there's nothing left but the inside of the house; let's buy it!" My enthusiasm was at about the same level. Jan, age 7, cried because I had told her the house was "on the lake" and this one was "far away" (100 feet)! The three younger ones just wandered around.

Doris had serious misgivings about the risk of drowning posed by living on a lake with five kids ranging down to a toddler. (Her concerns were heightened when a neighbor girl fell off the dock and drowned 2 weeks after we moved in!) She also expressed many other valid concerns: giving up her Palace Avenue friends, enrolling three children in a new school over a mile away, having no stores within walking distance. She felt that living so far from the city with only one car and a bus line that operated infrequently during the day and on weekends would severely restrict her activities.

I made many promises: I would have the kitchen completely rebuilt just as soon as we could find a good contractor. I would put decent closets in the bedrooms. I would convert the pantry into a laundry room, and install drawers and a coat closet in it. I would re-carpet upstairs and down and help her redecorate the whole house. I promised to take the bus to work so that she would have the use of our only car. I couldn't promise anything about the eyesore next door; but I expressed a strong faith that someone would improve such valuable lakefront property before too long. The combination of George's and my tremendous enthusiasm finally overcame her good judgment and she reluctantly agreed to move.

The owners were in California, so we negotiated by mail. I don't remember the asking price. I do remember my "final offer" of $21,000 with another $2,000 for the furniture. The latter was mostly old and not what we wanted. But it would help fill the space (over twice what we had) and the owners were eager to dispose of it.

Keeping my Promises.

To our great delight, even before we moved, a wealthy couple had rebuilt the adjacent eyesore into a picturebook house and had beautifully landscaped the yard.

We didn't want to miss even one precious summer at the lake, so we moved before rebuilding the kitchen. I kid Doris about drawing 801 plans before she had the kitchen the way she wanted it. During the rebuilding she cooked on a hot plate in the dining room, where the contents of the kitchen were stacked around the walls. To save money, I laid the floor tile, did the counter tops, and built a hard-wood radiator cover, and we worked many hours sanding and varnishing the great expanse of cabinets. But we all survived and the beautiful, modern kitchen turned out to be well worth all of our sacrifices.

Endless Work.

When I wasn't at work, it seemed as if I spent every waking hour building closets, laying carpets, sanding, painting, varnishing, papering, and replacing bathroom fixtures. At the same time, I was trying to beat that huge lawn into shape.

There was no place for the kids to play in the winter, so I partitioned half of the basement, tiled the floor and the ceiling, put in fluorescent lights and painted all the walls in bright colors. To our horror, we discovered that this huge house was served by only one 30-amp circuit plus the current for the stove. We couldn't use the coffee pot and the toaster at the same time. When we had company, and had extra lights turned on, if we plugged in the coffee pot the whole house would go dark!

Buyer's Guilt Revisited.

When the plumber came to do the new utility room, he was very upset by all the illegal plumbing he found in the basement. He said he would have to replace it or the inspector would never approve the new work. That extra expense, plus the cost of installing a 200-amp service and rewiring a good share of the house, ate up most of our cash reserves. What's more, the oil bill for a sub-zero January would have heated our little house on Palace Avenue for the whole winter. Finally, we discovered that, through a quirk in the Minnesota property tax law, the real estate taxes were going to be much higher than we anticipated.

The Palace Avenue house didn't sell for almost a year after we moved, so we had the expense and trouble of maintaining two houses. Doris was convinced that we were going bankrupt. All this unanticipated expense compounded my initial buyer's guilt. I drew plan after plan to prove to Doris and myself that we could sub-divide and sell off part of that beautiful lot to deal with a financial emergency should it occur. I showed the plans to Doris, hoping to encourage her. Happily I never breathed a word of this to anyone else, for it would have upset the whole neighborhood. To assuage his buyer's guilt the man who bought the house from us in 1987 did share his plans to subdivide with neighbors, and they were extremely upset. I now feel it was extremely fortunate that neither he nor I ever went through with any of those plans. It would have destroyed that beautiful lot.

Risk Has its Rewards.

George, Jan and Mary liked their new schools and made new friends. We counted 45 children in our family and the eight families nearest us. Most of them would assemble in our yard for nightly games. We decided that raising kids was much more important than raising grass, and encouraged this activity. I restored a high swing that the former owners had installed between two trees. I painted the old teeter-totter and built a large sandbox on the old slab that had once held an under-sized garage. The loft of the old carriage shed made a marvelous playroom on rainy days, and came equipped with an old bed that made a great trampoline.

Under Doris' patient instruction and encouragement our children all became good swimmers and loved the lake, as did their friends. They all became excellent sailors and had relatively little concern about what to do with their time. We liked the fact that so much of their free time was spent in wholesome activities near home.

The neighbor children soon invited George, Jan and Mary to Sunday School at the small Methodist chapel just a block from us. Doris and I continued to take Bev and Rick with us to church in St. Paul. One Sunday morning Bev stood up in her crib and announced firmly, "If I can't go to church with George and Jan and Mary, I'm going to stay in my bed!" That was the signal for us to transfer our membership, which we did promptly. We became the 99th and 100th members of this small congregation, and served this church happily for the next 30 years, Doris as the volunteer secretary and office manager and I as the treasurer. Under the leadership of Harold Trost, an inspired pastor, the church grew quickly. I chaired the building committee for our new church building, where we watched with gratification as the membership grew to about 450.

Fulfillment of the American Dream.

Doris and I made many friends among the neighbors, at church, and in the Parent-Teacher Association, where I soon was elected treasurer and later president. The PTA was a large and active association then, involving a majority of the parents. Our many activities brought us into close contact with teachers, principals and the superintendent; many of these people became good friends. This close involvement paid large dividends, I believe, in our children's attitude toward school. We encouraged them to work up to the full level of their ability, expressed interest in their progress, and helped them over rough spots in their homework. We advised them (when requested) on their choice of classes, and encouraged them to participate in band, choir and other activities. Apart from that, I never recall saying a word to them about attitude, deportment, or attendance; but the teachers considered them model students.

The Empty Nest.

In 1969 all five of our children moved out. George and Mary were married, Jan opted for apartment living, Bev started her ski instructor career in Vail, and Rick went to the Air Force Academy. Doris says the most difficult adjustment was learning to cook for only two instead of seven. She and I were filling our lives with community service work, and I had just started a new business. Except for Mary (she and Dave moved to Puerto Rico) the children "came home" quite frequently. We had long since decided that we should live our own lives and let our children live theirs. So neither of us ever really experienced the negative feelings, and even depression, often associated with the "empty nest syndrome." In Section Nine I will expand on the personal benefits of community service, but I must emphasize here its importance in easing us through what could have been a very difficult adjustment.

People used to ask me, "What are you going to do with that big house when all of your kids leave home?" My standard answer was, "The folks who sold it to us were in their late 80's; we have plenty of time to decide."

The Investment of a Lifetime.

In 1987 we sold the house for over 16 times what we had paid for it. That works out to be an 8.25% return compounded annually: much more than we could have realized in bonds or CD's. What is more important, we had 34 years of idyllic living. I cannot imagine a more ideal environment in which to have had our family grow up. Both George and Rick have bought homes on the shore of White Bear Lake. I believe that makes a strong statement about our choice of locales.

Points to Ponder.

How did we achieve a home situation that far exceeded our fondest dreams in every way? Was it:

- Good luck?
- Hard work?
- A willingness to take a reasonable risk?
- Careful planning?
- Taking advantage of opportunities?
- Wisdom and knowledge?
- God's will (or the workings of a merciful Providence)?
- The result of seeking to do God's will?
- Frugality?
- Genes?
- The result of a good upbringing?
- A combination of all of these factors?
- Something else?

15. White Bear Lake Revisited

> *"Home interprets heaven. Home*
> *is heaven for beginners."*
> —Charles H. Parkhurst

A nine-year-old boy sits alone on the shore of White Bear Lake, gazing dreamily at the lake and his surroundings. He marvels at those beautiful houses along the lakefront. He lapses into a daydream and enjoys the heavenly thoughts of living in one. But he knows they are only for the wealthy and that he will never have enough money to buy one.

In 1985 my grade school classmate, Ted Glasrud, built some beautiful condominiums on the northwest shore of

White Bear Lake. Doris and I found the plans intriguing; but before we could decide if we were ready to move, the best units had all been sold. Our friends, Jock and Twinks Irvine had bought the unit we liked best, intending to rent it out until they were ready to move. They thought that would be seven to ten years. So we rented their unit and moved in June of 1987.

Many of our friends asked, "How could you bear to give up that beautiful lakefront home?" My answer always was, "Only for something better." Everything was beautifully done. All the rooms are large and bright. The 2,800 square feet of living area gives us more room than we had in the home we sold. During the first summer we felt as if we were on vacation at some lovely resort. The large window walls give us a much better view of the lake than we had before. Before the lake level fell, the water came right up to up to the edge of the lovely garden and tennis court on which we look down. The Jacuzzi and the walk-in shower provide us with luxuries we hadn't previously known except when we were on trips.

An Exciting Time.

Our old furniture would have looked out of place in the new condo, so we sold everything except a few special pieces. What exciting fun it was to attend our own estate sale! Even cleaning the huge accumulation of junk that had accumulated in our basement and garage provided its own humor. I rented a 10-cubic-yard dumpster, the kind usually used for construction debris. The young man who delivered it said, "Going to do some remodeling?" I replied, "No, just some housecleaning." He looked at me as if I had come from another planet! Three days later I had heaped it so high I was afraid it wouldn't clear the overhead wires.

For the first time in 40 years we furnished a house with all new furniture. What fun we had picking and choosing. We had an experienced interior decorating consultant who was a real joy to work with. The third bedroom makes a great office, which we have furnished with "his and her" large teak desks, electronic typewriter, computer, laser printer, copier and computerized FAX machine. Doris and I both do so much volunteer work that we use all this equipment well.

Coming Home.

When we moved to the new condo in June of 1987, it was exactly 50 years after my family had walked away from the old home in White Bear. To our pleasant surprise, Doris and I found many friends from that period. They looked a bit older now, but they still recognized us! Many of them were active in the White Bear Historical Society, of which we were already life members. They welcomed us warmly and put us to work. Doris was elected secretary of the Society, and I was elected treasurer a year later. We found several of our old friends in a nearby church. But the church lacked the quality in its ministries (preaching and music) and the energy that we enjoy at St. Andrews Lutheran Church in Mahtomedi (the super-church that I will describe later).

A Triple Celebration.

In February 1990 we bought our unit from the Irvines. The closing was on the 16th. The four of us went to lunch and celebrated three great events: Doris' birthday, Jock's birthday, and a mutually pleasant, satisfactory and advantageous transaction.

New Friends.

We already knew 10 of the 18 families in the condo complex when we moved in. At the condo association's 1990 meeting I was elected to the board, and in 1991 I was elected president. So now I know all the residents, since I welcome all the new ones and help them get established in their new homes. We have become good friends with one of the wonderful couples, Jack and Bev Pfaff. Jack is one of my two favorite tennis singles opponents. He is almost 15 years my junior. But I don't often think of that, and he is nice enough to ignore it. We not only get an enjoyable workout; we carry on a continual banter about our intense rivalry. I call us "bitter friends."

How could we be so fortunate? We enjoy a beautiful home that leaves nothing to be desired, easy maintenance that leaves Doris and me time and energy for our many service activities, and many friends. Many of our friends have winter homes in Florida or Arizona. Because of our year-round commitments, however, this long absence would be inappropriate for us. What's more, we enjoy the Minnesota winters. My many winter sports provide both enjoyment and the needed exercise. Doris seems happy and content just to enjoy the beautiful winter landscape, although she claims to miss her only "winter sport": shovelling snow!

The freedom from household maintenance, yard chores, and concern over an empty house allows us to do considerable travelling, which we enjoy most when travelling with our family. We go sailing with Mary and Dave in Panama, and enjoy bridge, snorkel trips, whale watching and tennis with Jan and Loren in Maui. Skiing with Bev, Erin, Casey and Dan in Vail and Keystone is great sport for me. We have explored Australia with Mary and Dave. We have also enjoyed skiing in Vail with Mary, Karen and Dave, and showing Mary the elegance of a new luxury cruise ship while transiting the Panama Canal.

Some of these experiences have been unforgettable. Biking down the slopes of Maui's dormant Haleakala volcano with Jan's husband, Loren in 1991 was breathtaking with excitement and beauty. After watching the famous sunrise from the 10,000-foot summit, we coasted over 38 miles to the seacoast. Most of the way down we gripped the brakes hard and still cruised at over 20 miles an hour. We started down through a freezing, misty cloud, bundled in sweat-shirts, gloves, and rain suits. As we broke out of the clouds into the brilliant sunshine, the temperature rose quickly and we began to shed our layers. The spectacular view was like nothing I've seen before or since. We looked down on cascading mountains, punctuated by tightly curled ribbons of the steep, winding mountain road on which we were descending. The rich green valley was a jigsaw of bright color and the deep shade of the cloud patterns. That whole enchanting scene was bordered dramatically by a mountain range to the north and to the west, with the fringe of brilliant white surf and the bright blue of the Pacific extending in all directions that were not occluded by mountains.

Two parts of our trip in Australia are equally memorable. Standing on a prominence at the extreme southwest corner of the continent, we gazed southward and felt that nothing but ocean separated us from Antarctica. Then we turned to the West to look across the Indian Ocean and wonder what mysteries lay beyond. It was an enchanting moment. On the other side of this continent, three time zones away from our southwest experience, we spent two beautiful, exciting days cruising up the east coast. Aboard our friend Andrew Campbell's beautiful 65-foot racing yacht, we sailed from Brisbane to Mooloolaba.

My trip to Japan with Rick's wife, Satoko, was a rare privilege that produced an experience available to few Americans. (Satoko was born and brought up in Osaka.) We lived, ate and slept with three Japanese families, those of her sister in Osaka, her brother in Tokyo, and the Takaha-shis in Kobe. I was prepared to be treated with courtesy, respect and generosity (and I was); but I was totally overcome by the unexpected outpouring of warmth and love that I felt in every home. We played, we laughed, we embraced, I was really "one of the family." They went incredibly far out of their way to entertain us and to show us all the beautiful and marvelous sights. And, of course, we exchanged gifts.

Comfort and Security.

Wherever we may travel, we're always delighted to return to our home on White Bear Lake. We feel extremely happy and comfortable here. We feel secure in the thought that we have no reason to move again as long as we enjoy enough health and energy to take care of ourselves. And the wonderful home care services that have developed give promise of extending this idyllic existence well beyond that time. Truly, "The kingdom of heaven is at hand."

Three

People I've Known

*"The happiest business in all the world
is that of making friends,
And no investment on the street
pays larger dividends.
For life is more than stocks and bonds,
and love than rate percent,
And he who gives in friendship's name
shall reap what he has spent."*
— Author Unknown

People are the most important influences in our lives. If we allow ourselves to be surrounded by people with pessimistic and cynical outlooks, we will tend to become pessimistic and cynical. If we are with people who have a positive outlook, our own view of life becomes more positive. If we are often in contact with people of high moral standards, our own morals improve. And so it goes for value systems, disposition—you name it.

This principle is most important when we are younger. It is vital, therefore, that we surround our children with good people. The strongest of these people will become their role models. The others will round out their lives. I can remember my mother encouraging me to spend more time with certain boys. I knew even then that she thought well of them.

The process works even when we are older. I spend most

of my time with younger people. This occurs mostly because of our common interests and activities: business, community service, and sports. These young folks stimulate me, energize me, and make me feel young. When I am with them, I am rarely conscious of the age difference. What is the effect on them? Many of them say, "You're my role model for my own advancing years." The less active ones say, "You inspire me to (be more active), (get more exercise), (do more for my community)." Occasionally one will say, "You depress me because I can't (don't) do as much." To this I usually reply "You can if you really want to," or "What would happen if you tried?"

Givers and Takers.

Too many people my age spend their time complaining, criticizing, talking about "the good old days," and wallowing in idleness and even hedonism. We have so little in common that I don't spend much time with them. They have little or no motivation or desire to change. The attempts I have made to encourage them into a more active, productive life style have met with little success. They have many complaints, both real and imagined. They demand much of others. They are the takers.

Of course, there are notable exceptions. These people are truly alive, vital and continuing to make significant contributions to the welfare of their families, friends and the community (or even the world). How fortunate they (and we) are! They are a joy to be with, work with, and play with. They find pleasure and happiness in their worthwhile activities. They demand little of others. They have few complaints, either real or imagined. They are the givers.

16. Friends and Friendliness

*"The only way to have a friend
is to be one"*
— Ralph Waldo Emerson

*A seven-year-old farm boy feels a deep loneliness.
There is no one near his age within miles. The adults
are all busy with their own affairs. He dulls his
sadness with trance-like day dreams. He is friendless.*

Friends come in a great variety of sizes and types: close friends, family, coworkers, members of the same church, club or lodge, hunting and fishing partners - you can add to this list. They add important dimensions to our lives, and we to theirs. Good friends are givers, not takers. They take pleasure in sharing and caring. They stand in sharp contrast to the would-be friend whose chief concern is in meeting his (her) own selfish desires. They accept us as we are, don't try to remake us, and don't expect us to be perfect.

My Best Friend.

My best friend is my wife (see the quotation that begins Chapter 3). She meets fully the description of a good friend. She spends a major portion of her waking hours doing things for other people and expects little or nothing in return. Each of us has many other interests, but we look forward to the time we spend together. She is a joy to be with. For too many years I took these qualities for granted. I try now to express my appreciation more and to reciprocate. She makes no demands of me and rarely even expresses a desire. I try hard to be sensitive to her needs and to meet them. I'm afraid there are times when I don't succeed.

Children as Friends.

My children and I are good friends. They meet the definition of a good friend, and I try to do the same. Of course, there is a special relationship between parents and children. But I like to emphasize the love and friendship aspects rather than the duty and respect. I think they provide the basis for a much happier and more fulfilling relationship. I hope they feel the same way.

Close Friends.

Truly close friendships require sharing of inner feelings, trust and emotional risk-taking that not everyone is capable of. Such friendships seem to be more common among women than men. Men are much less apt to share their true feelings with each other. Their communication tends to be on a more casual level. Besides my family, I have only one close friend. Hod Irvine lives in Boston. We see each other less than once a month. But we communicate much more often by telephone and electronic mail. Our times together are a genuine joy. They are growing experiences for both of us.

Psychology professor Jess Lair[6] presents an interesting quality of friendship, mutual need. This quality exists in many friendships, but I don't think it is either a necessary or sufficient basis for friendship. If this mutual need is an emotional dependency, it may destroy the relationship rather than enhance it.

Relatives as Friends.

Someone once said, "Our relatives are forced on us, but thank God we can choose our friends." What a highly unfortunate attitude! Granted, there is an occasional relative who can be difficult. Yet, most of our relatives can be our good friends if we show them the same courtesy, consideration, respect and warmth that is needed to be anyone's friend. Since most of us feel some obligation to spend some time with these people, why not make these times into opportunities for additional friendships?

Other Friends.

Most of my friends are the people with whom I spend time during the day, in business, sports, board and committee meetings, and in other community service activities. I find myself attracted to these people because they are vital human beings. Most of them respond quickly to any display of friendliness, and the bonds grow readily. Occasionally they lead to a sharing of concerns, feelings and interests that transcends the original purpose of our being together. How much more fun it is to have these kinds of daily relationships.

Age is not a factor in the quality of these friendships. My friends range in age from 7 to 90. Nor does the difference in ages affect the degree of friendship — at least as far as I'm concerned. I hope it's the same for them.

Friendliness.

It is hard to have friends without being friendly. What does it mean to be friendly? My dictionary says it is to be warm, welcoming. I would add that it is also to express a genuine, caring interest in another person. Most people respond readily to such expression. The nature of the response depends largely on the other person. If (s)he has been brought up to be reserved or undemonstrative, you may feel rejected at first. Children (and a few adults) may be timid or shy or even afraid. But that apprehension usually goes away after your second or third overture. If it doesn't, don't take it personally or feel disliked. That person is probably incapable of responding. Your only emotion should be sympathy.

Friendliness doesn't have to lead to friendship. It can be a happy adjunct to courtesy, which is the lubricant for the gears of human contact. Whatever you call it, it can add a delightful dimension to your daily life. It can help you through the tough days. You will be much less tired at the end of the day. It can even leave you feeling buoyant.

Psychologist Abraham Maslow, in *The Farther Reaches of Human Nature*[9], describes peak (or mountain top) experiences. I find that experiences like these occasionally result from this exercise in friendliness. For example, the person who waits on you at a restaurant usually wears a name tag. I think this is a wonderful idea. Try calling that person by name. Ask, "How is the day going for you?" You will be pleasantly surprised at the response. It will make your day as well hers or his. If that person serves you more than two or three times, you will have a friend. If you like music, tell the piano player in the hotel lobby, lounge restaurant or club how much you enjoy the music. Comment on particular numbers. You will have an immediate friend. Most people treat such professionals like part of the furniture. Make friends with the person who brings your paper, your mail, the telephone repairman. Above all treat them like people and not like robots. Doing so will enrich your life as well as theirs.

17. People Who Have Changed My Life

> *"People seldom improve their lives*
> *when they have no other model*
> *but themselves to copy after."*
> —Oliver Goldsmith

The complete list of people who have changed my life would be a long one. Of course, there were my parents and other family members. You have already read about them. A few, however, have had such a dramatic and significant effect that I must tell you about them. They are in chronological order.

Ellsworth Alan Roberts.

"Bob" Roberts was Vice President and General Counsel of the Minnesota Mutual Life Insurance Company in 1930. He was also President of the Engineers' Club. My father spoke at a lunch meeting of this club early in 1930. During lunch Bob asked my father about his family. Apparently my father said something about my being good at math and unable to afford college. Bob suggested that I look into the possibility of becoming an actuary. He stated that companies were more interested in an applicant's character and potential ability to pass the actuarial exams than they were in a college degree. The rest of that story is in Chapter 20.

After I went to work for Minnesota Mutual I went to Mr. Roberts' office to thank him. At age 16 I was terrified of facing this busy dignitary. But his graciousness and courtesy were combined with a handsome smile and upbeat attitude that gave me a feeling of worthiness. I needed that badly. I don't remember what he said or what I said. But I went away vowing that I would try to be like him, even though I never expected to really be a vice president.

A few years later Bob spoke to the Home Office Life Club. This was a group of aspiring young supervisors. His message was: Be generous in giving your time and resources to others; you will be rewarded beyond your fondest dreams. It was the first time I had heard that message. But it really impressed me, mostly because my role model had said it.

Bob went on to become president of Fidelity Mutual Life in Philadelphia. As a 2nd Lieutenant just out of officer candidate school, I visited him in his beautiful penthouse office in Philadelphia. He was as gracious as ever, took me to lunch at his private club, and again sent me away feeling good.

His funeral was in the huge Plymouth Congregational Church in Minneapolis. The eulogy made me realize what a truly great and beloved man it had been my privilege to know. Again I went away vowing to try to be like him. So Bob was a positive force in my life even after his death. . . .

Anne Grant Rideout.

Aunt Annie was my father's sister. Her influence on my life was both indirect and direct. It was she who persuaded my father to move to the St. Paul area. No one can say what would have happened to me if he had continued to farm in western Canada. It is hard to imagine that life would have been as good. It certainly couldn't have been better.

By example, Aunt Annie taught me how to live. She lived until she was 93. She never lost her desire to learn. Her interest in new places, people and things was inexhaustible. She continued to work at her profession (genealogy) right up until the end. She saw humor in almost everything. She expected the best and went for it. She treated people with courtesy and respect and expected the same from them — and got it. She was a classy lady. She enriched the lives of people with whom she came in contact. I was strongly reminded of her when I saw the movie "Driving Miss Daisy."

Harold Joseph Cummings.

Harold was assistant sales manager for the Minnesota Mutual Life Insurance Company when I went to work there in 1930. He was the most energetic man I ever knew. You could feel the energy when he walked into the room. He made friends with everyone he met. When he talked with you, you felt like the most important person in his life.

When Harold believed in some cause or some project (and these beliefs were numerous) his enthusiasm knew no bounds. If he enlisted you in a cause, you couldn't say no. No one who met him ever forgot him. He had friends and admirers in every part of the country. He had a tremendous sense of humor and was fun to be with; but he never had fun at others' expense. He treated people with courtesy and respect and expected the same of them.

Harold was a great community leader. As Chairman of the Board and President of one of St. Paul's major companies, he was in constant demand to lead this or that major civic project. He frequently did. He lent not merely his name, but worked tirelessly for these projects; and they never seemed to fail. One example illustrates his great creativity and imagination: When he was president of the St. Paul Athletic Club, he felt that the club needed a rooftop restaurant. The board of directors was dubious that it could be made to pay. Harold said, "If you will approve this project, I will see that the restaurant is filled every night for the next three months." Knowing Harold, the board went along. He rented Dancing Waters (computer controlled fountains with colored lights) and had it installed on the top of the building across the street. He persuaded the major downtown corporations to absorb the cost. The Summit, as the new restaurant was known, sold out all nights for the next two summers.

At the time I never thought of Harold as a role model because his qualities seemed inimitable. I now realize that, perhaps subconsciously, I acquired some of those qualities to a modest degree.

Doris Huelster Hill.

Many of you have heard successful men say, "I owe it all to the little woman." This statement has always raised some bothersome questions in my mind: Why did she have to be little? Do they really mean it? How does she feel about it? It's hyperbole; didn't he or others have anything to do with his success? I don't owe it all to Doris, but she has certainly been a wonderful influence in many ways.

Without even saying anything she caused me to settle down to the serious study needed for passing my actuarial exams. My devotion to her made it unthinkable to goof off as I had been doing before I met her. She showed respect for my time and efforts by putting her own interests second. This gave me the strong motivation I needed to use my time effectively.

Her love and devotion have been priceless in their enrichment of my life, and in giving me the strong emotional foundation needed to face the many problems that we all encounter, such as setbacks in business, difficult relations with business associates, problems in sorting out my priorities and similar problems. Her respect for me gave me a badly needed increase in my self respect. These qualities make it impossible for me to treat her with anything other than the utmost love and respect. Likewise her total faithfulness has kept me totally faithful to her. Her giving nature inspires me to be more giving. Since she demands nothing, I am strongly impelled to find more things to do for, and with, her. People ask me, "How do you manage to get so many things done?" or "How do you have so much energy?" As I write these paragraphs, I realize another important answer. Many men I know consume much of their energy trying to solve their marital problems. Our marriage has been a great source of energy rather than a drain on it. I see so many of Doris' wonderful qualities in our children. This, in turn, makes fatherhood all the more marvelous and fulfilling.

I could go on and on; but perhaps you get the point: meeting Doris was the best thing that ever happened to me.

Harold Trost.

Harold was a very successful minister in a large church in Lombard, Illinois when he developed serious health problems. The doctor told him, "You must either retire or take a small country church." Our church wasn't exactly "country," but it was small, with just over 100 members. He was the friendliest, most engaging man I ever knew. Every day he would lunch at the local lunch counter with whoever was sitting next to a vacant stool. He would come away with a new friend. If the new friend wasn't already active in some church, he would usually come away with one or two new church members!

Harold taught me how to become a much more friendly person. We loved to trade stories, talk theology, philosophy, the state of the community or the world, anything. It didn't matter what the subject was, it was always a delightful experience just to be with him. He taught me to let my business relationships be much more friendly, upbeat and lighthearted. When he talked with you, you always felt that he respected you and cared about you. Once, when I was having trouble with some of the theological tenets I had been taught, he told me it was OK to question them and to develop my own personal theology. That has made me much more comfortable with God, with myself and with other people.

Turning the Tables.

Under Harold's leadership our church membership quadrupled. When he reached retirement age, he was still going strong, but the policies of his denomination required him to retire. For the first time in the 20 years I had known him I saw him become deeply troubled. He felt (rightly) that he had much more to contribute to the world and that his superiors were very wrong in denying him the opportunity. His many arguments with them were futile and he became depressed and full of self-doubt. It was now my turn. I became his counselor! I persuaded him to accept his retirement in good grace by looking on it as a God-given opportunity to serve in a new and different capacity and environment. He could have a new and exciting beginning. After all, he had done most of what he could do for his present church and the people of the community. Why not retake control of his own future? I offered him a vision of new opportunities to use his still wonderful talents in new settings and make many more new friends. He chose to work as an interim pastor; and he became an outstanding one. He continued to love and serve people almost to the day he died.

Who Helped Whom?

I had recently gone through a similar crisis in my own career. Fortunately I had been able to apply the process of viewing major life changes as new beginnings to my own life. To some extent Harold had taught me how. I have had many occasions to apply it since. It works every time. I now tell people, "I have too many beginnings and not enough endings!" During my years at Minnesota Mutual I had counselled many people concerning their careers. But it was always at a very objective level. Harold had taught me to deal with the whole person. I developed respect for my own ability as a personal counselor. The opportunities to use this skill seem endless. When the other person extends sincere thanks, I always reply, "Oh, I thank you: you have done more for me than I have done for you!" They often go away looking puzzled, but I really believe they do give me at least as much as I give them.

I owe Harold Trost a great deal. . . .

18. People I Would Rather Not Have Known

Happily this list is not a very long one. Will Rogers said, "I never met a man I didn't like." I can't go quite that far, although I enjoy most people, and can usually find some likable qualities. However, I doubt if many of us go through life without running across a few people who are exceptions. I have encountered a few of these. They are the people whose values are so warped that their effect on others is largely negative. Dishonesty, deceit, greed, envy, dirty tricks, animosity, spite and just plain hatred seem to play an important part in their lives. They reject totally any attempts to appeal to their "better nature" and all efforts to change them. In short, they are wicked people. It serves no good purpose to name them; a couple of short descriptions will serve to typify them.

The Tabulating Supervisor.

This man's position as tabulating supervisor (TS) gave him marvelous opportunities to be of service and help to people. Instead he spent much of his time and energy protecting his little empire and frustrating people who he felt threatened it.

During World War II I worked very closely with some creative people who did wonders with IBM tabulating equipment. When I came back to my civilian career I realized what marvelous potential this equipment had for relieving drudgery and offsetting the rapidly rising costs of our business. But we had no such gear; instead, I found our equipment outmoded and underutilized. The TS reported to another department head, so I could not tell him what to do. He resisted all my efforts to persuade him to modernize. Working through my superior and his, I got permission to set up my own little tabulating workshop in a room next to the regular tabulating department. In that room I installed some state-of-the-art equipment. Unfortunately, I was still dependent on some of the older equipment, the use of which I was to share.

In this close and unpleasant relationship I really had my eyes opened to an incredible world of deceit and pettiness. Other departments would wait days for important reports that were done and sitting on the TS' desk. His explanation to me was, "I don't want to spoil them by giving them too good service, so I just tell them they're not done!"

When I would ask for permission to use an idle machine, the answer often was, "No, I'm going to need it shortly." I would then watch the machine sit idle for much longer than I had needed it. If I started to use a machine, even with his permission, he would often come along and peremptorily take my work out of the machine with a curt "Gotta use this right now." I would watch him do some trivial job and leave the machine without even telling me it was free. Occasionally I would track the cards he had used and find they had no significant purpose!

His own people were embarrassed and frustrated with his antics. He often treated them not much better than he treated my assistants and me. Morale was low and the turnover rate was high. As I look back on it, I suspect the TS managed to hold his job only because he had grown up with it, and the company culture was very laid back; they never laid anyone off and rarely fired anyone.

I could live with the personal frustrations because I was accomplishing great new things in my little room. But I couldn't live with the extreme anguish he caused for my hardworking assistants. They would spend hours wiring a very complex control board, only to have the TS grab it off their desk and pull the wires out with a barked "Gotta have this board!" They would then walk into his area and find idle boards! When they were not there, he would move their work to a remote storage area and deny any knowledge of its whereabouts.

After several such instances I threatened to blow the whistle on him. I said, "You have deliberately sabotaged my people's work." His reply was, "I haven't done that lately!" Through this confrontation he realized that I was ready to turn him in and that I would have witnesses. I had finally found the only way to motivate him. That was fear. What a sad working relationship!

He died a few years afterward. I don't recall the final diagnosis; but I suspect his negative emotions contributed to his early death.

Incredibly Bitter Hate.

This man was the founder of a small company in which he had persuaded a relative and some of the relative's friends to invest. It became quickly evident that something was amiss, and the investors appealed to me for help. It didn't take much investigation to discover that the founder was not merely a poor manager. He had grossly misrepresented the value of the company and was diverting what little money the company had to his own ends. What followed is a long story, but the part that is pertinent to this subject can be stated briefly. The investors fired the founder and threatened to sue him for misrepresentation and misuse of their funds. They asked me to manage the company on an interim basis and help with their suit. The founder refused to negotiate a settlement; but events worked out so that he was forced to repay some of the money. His interest in the company was reduced to what I felt was more nearly fair, so the investors were content to drop their suit.

Not surprisingly, I didn't make many brownie points with the founder. He fed his hate with false beliefs. He told his family and friends that I had cheated him out of his rightful share in a lucrative business. To support this statement he told his daughter he couldn't afford a wedding reception. At that time the stock he still owned in this company was worth well over $100,000 and was actively traded. He bristles with hate on the few occasions when I happen to see him. He refuses to speak to me, even to answer a "hello." My only emotion toward this man is pity. This hate has visibly darkened his countenance. Think what it has done to his soul! Think what it will do to his body if he continues to harbor it (see Chapter 46: "The Negative Emotions").

Four

Business

*"It is only through labor and painful effort,
by grim energy and resolute courage,
that we move on to better things."*
—Theodore Roosevelt

*An eight-year-old boy is eager to earn some spending
money. He and his mother and brother are living with
an uncle while his father looks for work in another
city. The uncle, who raises beautiful peonies, suggests
that the boy cut a bunch and sell them on the busy
street in front of their house. He tries for two hours
to sell his first bunch. No one is interested . . . .*

*A 13-year-old boy rises at six o'clock on a summer
morning, eats a quick breakfast, and walks to a
vegetable farm about two miles away. After 10 hours
of weeding long rows of beets, carrots and cabbages,
and a short break for lunch, he trudges home again
— bone tired, but a whole dollar richer.*

It was a long road from weeding vegetables to becoming
Chairman of the Executive Committee of the largest printed
circuit manufacturing company in the western world. But
the path was stimulating, absorbing, and, for the most part,
pleasant. The next seven chapters will share a few of the

more interesting milestones I encountered.

The road had several detours, and the signposts were often confusing or even non-existent. Some of the significant events seem to be the result of happenstance, or just dumb luck—what Charles Dickens would have called "a concatenation of circumstances." But to a large extent I believe that a merciful Providence silently guides those of us who seek to do His will. Or, if you prefer, having the proper mind set, striving to do the best possible job at any task, and being alert to opportunities can create a lot of "luck."

19. Early Employment

My first regular job was that of office boy for the Belding-Heminway Silk Company. They were wholesalers of silk products; stockings and thread were the principal items. At age 14 I was mildly shocked by their stocking slogan, "Blow, blow, let the wind blow, for there's nothing to fear with Beldings to show!" I swept the floor, dusted the shelves and ran errands for the order filler, the shipping clerk, and the manager. The order filling process fascinated me and I would beg the order filler to let me help him; but he would never let me. The shipping clerk let me help him occasionally, and I took delight in doing so.

The Great Northern Railway.

Charlie Burlingham lived a block from us. He was a very nice man who gave me rides to and from work. He thought it indecent that an industrious young man was making only $9.00 a week. So, on his own he arranged for me to have an interview with Frank Sprain, the Auditor of Overcharge Claims at The Great Northern Railway, where Charlie repaired Ediphones (wax cylinder dictating machines). This was the first time I had ever been in the private office of the department head of a large corporation. At age 15 I was scared to death. But Mr. Sprain was a gentle, kindly man who made me feel as comfortable as he could.

After a brief interview he introduced me to Jake Keller, the chief clerk. Today we would call him a manager and he would have four or five supervisors working for him. He sat at a massive desk in the middle of the long side of this large room and supervised the work of about 30 men and one woman. A gruff man, he would shout out the sur-name of any employee he wished to talk to, and the employee would hurry to his desk. I held him in great awe. He told me I would work as a file clerk and introduced me to the other two file clerks. They spent much time telling off-color stories and stumping me with double entendre questions, such as, "Did you ever eat at the Y?" My naive "Oh yes" would send them into gales of laughter. The chief clerk would yell out an oath and tell us to quiet down. My embarrassment delighted them, but they seemed to like me. I felt like a little brother. I certainly learned much about the ways of the world.

The Practical Joke.

When a claim examiner wanted a file, he would yell out "Hey, Kid!" That was my signal to report to his desk. The normal request was for a file. One day an examiner pulled out a box with just a few brass paper fasteners in it. He said, "I'm almost out of junction points. Go see (a name) on the fourth floor and ask him to lend me some." I dutifully made the trip and returned to report that gentleman was almost out also and couldn't oblige him. "Then go see (another name) on the sixth floor." After about the third futile trip the chief clerk yelled at me, "Hey Kid, don'tcha realize they're pullin' your leg? Now get the hell back to work!" The whole office roared with laughter, while I fought back tears of embarrassment.

Concealment?

The department processed two kinds of claims. The "regular claims" were those filed by shippers who felt that the freight clerk had used too high a rate to bill their shipment. These claims were handled promptly. The "relief claims" were filed by freight agents who exercised their authority to settle smaller claims in which they could easily determine the adjustment. They then applied for reimbursement, or "relief." These claims were processed as time permitted. After the examiners approved them, they stacked them in huge piles on top of the file cabinets. The railroads had fallen on hard times and would hold up payment of these claims for months, until the comptroller would decide they had enough revenue to "book" them. I didn't understand this process until years later. Today I'm sure an independent auditor would insist that they be booked promptly as a liability. I still don't understand why they weren't so treated then.

The file clerk job paid $1.95 a day for a six-day week. When the mail clerk was sick, I would fill in for him. That job paid $2.05 and was much more enjoyable. I looked forward eagerly to a promotion to mail clerk, but the job never opened up while I was there.

The Band.

Great Northern had an excellent band. The director, George Ghimenti, worked as a claims examiner. He was a friendly man, and I enjoyed talking with him. When he heard I played the trumpet, he recruited me to play in the band. The band had colorful green uniforms trimmed in red and gold, and it made three or four public relations trips a year. Before the next scheduled trip after I joined, however, revenues had dropped so sharply that trips were suspended indefinitely. But band members were allowed to keep the best perk: a "card pass." Sometimes called an "annual pass," this precious piece of cardboard could be used on almost any Great Northern train. You merely presented your pass to the conductor, told him where you wanted to go and he issued your seat check. It was that simple. There was no restriction on the number of trips: you could travel as often as time permitted. Other employees worked 20 years before they received this cherished benefit; but band members received card passes immediately.

It was wonderful! At age 16, I was the envy of older employees who didn't yet have 20 years of service. They had to apply for "trip passes" and were limited to two each year. I took several trips to Duluth and a couple to Winnipeg. I was not quite 16 when I received permission from my parents to go to Seattle all by myself! It was an exciting, enjoyable six-day trip. I slept in a coach seat all but one night, because I couldn't afford the extra charge for a berth. I stayed awake most of the one night I did have a berth because I didn't want to miss the experience of going through the famous Cascade Tunnel, the longest on the North American continent. For the whole eight miles I stood on the open veranda as the train wound its way through the tunnel. The scenery wasn't spectacular, but there was something fascinating about the experience that I didn't want to miss.

A Frugal Trip.

My total budget for the trip was only $15. I spent half of this for the berth the night we went through the Cascade Tunnel, since that was the only way I would be allowed on the observation platform. The other half had to provide food for the six days. It wasn't much food!

The train arrived in Seattle in the morning; I would be boarding it again that evening for the return trip. Meanwhile I spent the day walking the streets of Seattle. The dock area particularly fascinated me, with all its mysterious freighters from ports around the world.

Being Followed.

I had been walking for a couple of hours when I realized the same man had been walking behind me for quite some time. I was too naive to know what his intentions were, but I sensed that they were not honorable. I quickened my pace. He quickened his. I hurried to the busiest street I could find and managed to hop on a streetcar just as it was starting up. I watched for a stop that had a streetcar waiting to go in the other direction. My timing was perfect. I was able to run around the one car and hop on the other before it began to move.

By sliding down in an inside seat I felt I would be hard to see from the outside. After riding for a couple of miles, I felt it was safe to leave the streetcar and continue my walk. What a relief it was to be free of my "friend"! Some of my precious food money had gone for car fare; but I felt it was worth it. I had no more adventures that day.

I Get in Trouble.

The trains from St. Paul to Duluth were jointly operated by the Great Northern Railway and the Northern Pacific Railway. My card pass was valid for these trains, but it was not valid on the Northern Pacific commuter trains that ran between St. Paul and White Bear Lake. However, I discovered that my pass looked just like the Northern Pacific passes except for the name of the railroad on the top line. I contrived a way to put it in my billfold so that this line was concealed. That worked very well. John Brown was the conductor on the Northern Pacific train that I rode to work and back. He was "blind in one eye and couldn't see out of the other." His eyesight was so bad that I rode free for several months.

I knew many people on the train. One of them was an older man from our church who had worked 18 years for the Great Northern. One morning I saw him stop the conductor and say something to him as he pointed back toward me. When he came to me, the conductor grabbed my billfold out of my hand, jerked the pass out of it, and told me firmly, "This pass is no good on this train, you'll have to pay your fare."

Tempering Justice with Mercy.

A few days later, the Vice President and Controller paid Mr. Sprain a visit. He buzzed for the chief clerk. After some conversation, the latter shouted for me to come in. Mr. Sprain said, "Stanley, you have committed a very serious offense for which you could be fired. Mr. Keller (the gruff old chief clerk) says you are a very good worker. Don't EVER do anything like that again!" With tears in my eyes and a shaky voice I thanked him and assured him I wouldn't. I was so weak I could hardly walk out of the office!

20. Minnesota Mutual
Life Insurance

Encouraged by the suggestion of Minnesota Mutual Vice President "Bob" Roberts that he look into a career as an actuary, a 15-year-old boy visits the company offices and knocks timidly at the open door of James McIntosh, Associate Actuary. McIntosh is in his late 50's. His thick Scottish brogue betrays his origin and belies his 30 years in Minnesota. His general manner is brusque and stern. A conversation follows:

McIntosh: "What do you want?"

Boy (nervously): "I want to be an actuary."

McIntosh (almost contemptuously): "The wor-rk is harrd, and I don't think ye can do it; but if ye want to tr-ry we'll take yer-r name."

The boy has difficulty speaking clearly because of his nervousness. He manages to recite his name and telephone number. With a mumbled "Thank you" he beats a hasty retreat. That is the sum total of his employment interview.

A few months after his 16th birthday he is called to come in and fill out an employment "application." It is a blue-lined notebook page overprinted to provide a place for date, name, address, telephone number, age and person to call in case of emergency.

At \$52 (\$459 in today's dollars) a month, no social security, no pension, no insurance, no unemployment benefits, no pay for overtime (and there was tons of it!), the company was not really risking much. But I was deliriously happy. I had started my career. It was Thanksgiving 1930, and I felt I had a lot to be thankful for.

Then and Now.

Some of the contrasts between the office of the 30's and today's office world are interesting. By today's standards. yesterday's office seems primitive, since it had:

- No computers. All office records were hand written. Calculations were made on mechanical calculators either cranked by hand or driven by a noisy motor the size of a large grapefruit. Adding machines were too big to sit on a desk. They were mounted on a rolling stand that was pushed from desk to desk and shared by half a dozen "cl-a-ar-rks" (as McIntosh called us).

- No word processors. Letters were either drafted in long-hand, or dictated into a wax-cylinder recording machine and sent to the "steno pool" for transcription on clattering typewriters. The senior officers had their own secretaries, who took dictation in Gregg shorthand.

- No lighting standards. Incandescent, low wattage bulbs covered with frosted "globes" were sparsely distributed over high ceilings. If you were lucky, you sat under one or near a window. Some of the more affluent senior clerks (who made a munificent $60 a month) brought their own desk lamps and got permission to plug them in. No air conditioning. Summer brought heat and humidity. Deodorants were not yet in common use, though some of the more fastidious women masked the odor with cheap perfume. We men just stunk. If we sweat too profusely, we would have to roll our shirt sleeves down or wear black cotton "sleeves" to keep the moisture from soiling our papers. There were no ceiling fans, and portable fans were not permitted unless prescribed by a doctor. We welcomed breezy days; but if the wind was too strong, the windows had to be closed to keep the papers from blowing around. Paper weights were a necessity. Winter brought drafts and incredibly dry air that caused nasal passages to ache. "Ventilation" meant opening the windows a crack; but this usually resulted in arguments about drafts. Most of the men, and a few women, smoked. By mid-morning the air was heavy with blue smoke. Some of the more progressive department managers would insist that we open the windows wide during our 10-minute morning and afternoon recesses. That helped to clear the smoke, but then we'd have to wear coats for the next hour or so until we warmed up again. Spring and Fall were the delightful seasons when the air was (relatively) fresh and we were comfortable all day.

- No vending machines. You could get candy bars at the cigar counter in the lobby, but only before or after working hours. You could also buy soft drinks there, but you weren't allowed to bring them back to your desk. That didn't really matter, though, because there was no way to keep them cold. And few of us could afford them, anyway.

- No coffee machines. Most of us couldn't have afforded the luxury anyway. A few bolder, more affluent employees would sometimes sneak across to the Ryan Hotel for a cup, even though it was against the rules.

- No copying machines. Letters were typed as "the original with 2 carbons," or whatever number was needed, up to 6. If more than that were needed, the letter was typed twice. Memos needing many copies were typed with "ditto" carbon, a very messy process in which the carbon side was up. The reverse image (on the back of the original) was then laid on a damp gelatin plate, and as many as 30 to 50 copies could be made from it. If copies of an existing document were needed, they could be made on the "Photostat," a huge camera that produced paper negatives (white letters on a black background).

- No music. Piped music came about two decades later. Portable radios were not yet available, but it didn't really matter because we couldn't have afforded them and wouldn't have been allowed to use them.

- No cafeteria or dining room. The lunch room had tables and chairs where we ate our brown bag lunches. Years later the company hired a lunch room attendant who made coffee and sold milk. On payday the more affluent would go across the street to the Ryan Hotel for lunch.

- No ball-point pens. We used straight pens dipped in inkwells. When ball-points first came on the market, the general counsel forbade their use. Someone had told him that the ink would fade or disappear. I guess he had never tried to wash it out of a shirt pocket!

- No partitions or divider panels. Normally, desks were placed end-to-end in long rows across an entire large room. If limited space wouldn't allow this, two rows would be placed back to back, so that we sat facing each other across the width of two desks.

- No carpeting. With the exception of senior executive's

offices, the floors were tile or terracotta.

- No acoustic tile. With hard ceilings, floors, and walls, the clattering typewriters and calculators produced a barely tolerable noise level, which was highly distracting.

- No flexible hours. Time cards were kept in large racks on the wall by the door. You "punched in" by placing your card in the slot of the time clock. If you were on time, the time was recorded in blue ink. If you were even a minute late, it was red ink. If you had more than two red marks in a half-month, the next card had a red top. For the next half month it stood out among all the white cards with your name highly visible, and was a cause for shame.

- No overtime pay. After a few years an enlightened management gave us 50 cents for "supper money." I would spend half of this for a couple of White Castle hamburgers and a malted milk, and the other half for bus fare home. Wage-and-hour laws came later. If the work began to pile up, our supervisor would declare an overtime session, and we would all work an extra three hours. Two or three weeks of steady overtime was a regular routine at year-end. Every couple of years the publication of a new dividend scale or rate book would require six to eight weeks of solid overtime.

- No subsidized public transportation. At 25 cents a ride, bus fare would have consumed a quarter of my gross pay. So I hitchhiked most of the time. Charlie Burlingham and Al Schweitzer, a couple of not-so-near neighbors were particularly generous and friendly. Two or three of us became "regulars" with Al. We each gave him 25 cents a week to "help with the gas." Carpooling was simply an economic necessity. I promised myself I would repay these and other gentlemen's generosity by doing the same thing when I had a car. I am often sorry today that the high rate of hitchhiker crimes precludes doing this for others.

- No sick leave or personal leave. We received one week of vacation a year (this gradually increased to two weeks for ten-year employees), and were "docked" for all other absences. An exception was that we were given a half-day off to attend funerals in the immediate family.

An Early Scare.

I had been working in the Actuarial Department only a few months. I found the work to be very easy, but my penmanship had never been too good. One day I was given a rush job that involved writing several long columns of figures. In my haste to complete the work on time, I got the numbers misaligned in one column. Mr. McIntosh, who had given me the job, took the result to his boss. The latter flew into a rage at the sight of this "sloppy work." "Mac" came back to my desk, visibly upset. He completed my tongue lashing with the words, "Ye cawn't do wor-rk like thaht and stay in the Actuarial Department." That night I was still very shaken. I tried to read the want ads to see what I might do if I were fired. But there were so many tears in my eyes I couldn't see the print.

Routine but Enjoyable Work.

We spent most of our days using noisy calculators to grind out column after column of numbers on large work sheets. (The expression "grind out" came from the characteristically loud grinding noise the calculators made as their gears meshed rhythmically to do the thousands of multiplications.) We would start a sheet by copying hundreds of numbers out of large books of actuarial tables.

Occasionally the formulas we used involved taking square roots. Since our primitive calculators couldn't do that process, we had to look up the logarithm of the number, divide it by two, then look up the "antilog" and copy it to our work sheet. I found this process very cumbersome and felt that there must be a better way. So I invented a way to find square roots with the calculator. It saved considerable time and was a lot more fun.

At the end of every month I received a stack of large sheets filled with thousands of numbers printed by our IBM tabulators. (Known as electric accounting machines, they could add and print the totals of figures from large volumes of punched cards. From these sheets I would take a 7 or 8-digit number, enter it into a ledger and add it to another number and finally write the total in the ledger. This process was repeated several hundred times. I was supposed to use my desk calculator for the additions, but I found it was quicker for me to add them mentally. I taught myself how to write the totals from left to right as I added them in my head. I made sort of a game of it, which relieved the monotony. Since no one else seemed able to do this, I felt a little pride in having mastered the process.

I have described just a couple of the tedious jobs to provide the flavor of the routine work we did in the 1930's. Gradually, the cumbersome calculators were replaced by smaller, faster and quieter models. My boss, Walter Chapin, was a creative innovator who introduced some labor-saving processes. But there was to be no major breakthrough in productivity until the arrival of the computer 20 years later. Despite the labor-intensive nature of the insurance business, however, the cost of insurance was reasonable because we made less than 35 cents an hour. Manual laborers were already doing much better than that.

I Goof Off.

The routine drudgery of an actuarial clerk's work soon overcame the original novelty and excitement of having a job. I was promoted to a "change clerk." We change clerks calculated the cost of changing a policy to a different plan of insurance, the cost of reinstating a lapsed policy, and other transactions. This work was a little more stimulating, but it, too, lost its challenge after a year or so. I became bored, and I fooled around when I should have been working.

I had been hired with the understanding that I would pass the actuarial exams by studying at night. The objective was to become a Fellow of the Society of Actuaries. If I passed one exam a year, with allowance for a couple of failures, I would achieve my fellowship status in 8 to 10 years. I had bought a car, however, and I spent my evenings cruising around when I should have been studying. When I failed to pass any exams for two years in a row, Walter Chapin called me to his desk. As gently as he could he told me, "Neither your current work nor your progress on the exams has been satisfactory. You can no longer work in the Actuarial Department. But there is an opening for a clerk-typist in the Group Insurance Department if you would care to try it."

A New Start.

This crushing blow brought me to my senses. I resolved never to goof off again. The year was 1934. That was also the year I met Doris and began to take my life seriously. I took the new job, even though I had never used a typewriter. I sold my car, which relieved much financial pressure, as well as pressure from my father! I taught myself to type. I resumed my actuarial studies.

The "Group Department" was a new, small unit consisting of a woman supervisor and a woman clerk typist. I became the third member. Both of the women were very friendly and helpful in training me. I found the work interesting, but mostly I was thankful to have a job. I worked diligently and learned the group insurance business rapidly. Both of the women had "steadies," so there was no romance. But we became close friends and had many earnest conversations. I learned a great deal about life from them.

My First Promotion.

Two years later the supervisor got married. Married women were not allowed to work in those days because they would deprive a man of a much-needed job. The other woman didn't want the responsibility, so I became the new supervisor. With the promotion came a raise of $10.00 a month, the largest raise I had ever had. I reported directly to James McIntosh, as did Walter Chapin, my former boss. Even though Walter had much more responsibility, I derived much satisfaction from being on the same reporting level. I was on a roll!

The Big Raise.

When Doris and I were married in 1938, I was making only $75 a month. My bosses didn't think a married man should make less than $100 a month, so they raised my salary to that number. I felt rich!

This happy status lasted for about two years. By then the ominous clouds of World War II had darkened our emotional skies. Almost all of our evening conversations, with or without the company of friends, turned to very somber thoughts and questions. They were the same questions young people ask today in threatening times: Would America get drawn into the war? Would married men be drafted? Would fathers be drafted? Who would be called first? How and where would our wives live? Would our marriages survive the separation? What would we do for money? How long would the war last? Was it true that Franklin Roosevelt actually wanted us to get involved? (We hated him for the very thought!) How many of us would come back alive? How many would be maimed? What would happen to our jobs? Our careers? Who would do our work? "So on, ad infinitum."[12]

A Wonderful Surprise.

My active military service lasted from February 1941 until

December 1945, almost five years. I had managed to pass one actuarial exam while I was stationed in New York. I had prepared fully for another two, but I had been unable to take them because I was stationed in Italy. Because of my very early entry into the military, my separation came relatively early. My pay and allowances as a major were almost twice what I had been making when I left Minnesota Mutual. Our family of four was living quite comfortably. How were we going to adjust to a drastic reduction in income? What kind of job would I get?

I was not at all prepared for what happened next. For the first time in my life Henry Allstrom, a full vice president of Minnesota Mutual, took me to lunch. We went to the Minnesota Club. I had never set foot in this most prestigious of St. Paul's clubs. Allstrom told me that there was a desperate shortage of skilled people in the company's Actuarial Department. The military had taken all the skilled manpower. (Women didn't aspire to actuarial careers then.) They had hired Walter Rupert as Associate Actuary, but despite working 70 hours a week he could only attend to the absolute essentials. The company sorely needed a new rate book, the research, production and publication of which would require many months of highly skilled effort. Many other important tasks also had been left undone, such as recruiting, selecting and training half a dozen new actuarial students.

I Am Overcome!

Allstrom went on to say he was very impressed with my leadership abilities: I had been promoted 13 times during my army career. My diligence in pursuing my actuarial exams while in the Army and the management ability I had shown in the Group Department also impressed him. I was the first man to return from service. He didn't know if any others would be returning to the Actuarial Department. If I would accept the challenge, they would start me at $300 a month (double my rate when I left). There would also be a raise every six months, and possibly a promotion to Assistant Actuary in a year.

Was this actually happening to me, the guy who had flunked out of the Actuarial Department 11 years earlier? Or was I dreaming? I was so overcome with surprise and excitement that I couldn't speak. Allstrom mistook my silence for concern about the salary. He apologized that it couldn't be more, but promised to put in another raise at three months! I accepted the job immediately, asking only that I be given a week or so to get re-acquainted with my family. Then I hurried home to tell Doris the wonderful news.

Strenuous Times.

The next few months were extremely strenuous. I plunged into new and exciting challenges, and I felt pulled in five major directions. It was very important that I spend time with my family. My actuarial exams must be completed as soon as possible. There were constant reminders of the huge backlog of critical projects that were virtually screaming to be done. Yet I knew I had to take time to recruit, select, hire and train some qualified assistants. Failure to do that would make me a prisoner of this chronic overload. Finally, people were already pushing me to "do my duty" at church, school, United Way and other service organizations. Above all, I must keep my health and my sanity.

Prodigious Efforts.

Initially, it wasn't unusual to put in 70 hours a week at the office. Many days I would spend a full work day in my managerial role, go across the street to the White Castle for a quick bite of "dinner," then put in almost another full shift on research. This research required technical actuarial training that none of my willing assistants had. On supposedly "normal" days I would hurry home for dinner, spend time with George and Jan until they went to bed, and then try to study for five hours before I fell asleep.

Many evenings I just couldn't stay awake for five hours (i. e. until midnight). So I would set the alarm early enough to finish my five hours in the morning.

Long Hours

Doris was concerned about my 60-70 hour work weeks. She was afraid I would ruin my health as well as our family life. I tried to reassure her that this was a temporary pattern, and that as soon as this office backlog was caught up and I had adequate help, I would reduce my work week to a more normal 45 hours. I would make a 50 hour limit a hard and fast rule. My immediate goal was to pass the four remaining actuarial exams in two years. Then we would have a normal life. She wasn't very reassured. This made me all the more determined to stay on track and fulfill my promises to her.

A Wonderful Boss.

Walter Rupert was a wonderful boss. He was friendly, considerate and understanding of my inability to overcome the tremendous backlog as quickly as both of us would like. He taught me an incredible amount about the practical aspects of actuarial work, business, managing my work load, getting on with other people. He expected much of me; I delivered, and he showed his appreciation. When he moved to my community in the late 1950's, he insisted on driving me to work and bringing me home, and would never even let me buy the gas. We had many wonderful conversations on the way to and from work. This superb relationship was fortunate. He remained my boss for the next 21 years as we went up the corporate ladder together. When he retired, he was Chairman of the Board, President and CEO; and I was his right-hand man.

Survival.

My work at Minnesota Mutual continued to be quite demanding. Fortunately, while in the army I had learned, of necessity, how to banish worry and cope with stress. I had become a consummate optimist. When needed, I could put in 17 hours of vigorous mental activity without fatigue or strain—and I still can. I believe most people have the potential to do this. But it takes rigorous conditioning to relieve ourselves completely of all negative emotions (see Chapter 42). We must also fill our minds and hearts with a strong sense of purpose and self-worth. You will read more about this later.

Another valuable aid to survival was my method of prioritizing the work. At least weekly I would make a list of all my unfinished projects, and indicate how long it would take me to complete each one. Walter Rupert and I would then go over this list and decide the order in which the tasks should be done. This process had several benefits. Walter knew what I was up against, and he knew I was working on the right things. Most importantly, I derived a strong sense of partnership and a feeling that we were doing the best we could to overcome the backlog.

The Society of Actuaries.

Becoming a Fellow of the Society of Actuaries is as significant to a career actuary as receiving a Ph.D. is to any other profession. Unlike a doctorate, however, fellowship in this society has no academic prerequisite. What is required is a prodigious amount of study to pass a long series of extremely difficult exams covering a wide variety of academic subjects: higher algebra, calculus, statistics, probability, numerical analysis and financial math. A straight-A college math student has about an 80% chance of passing one of these exams. The probability of success drops off sharply to about 5% for a B student.

After these subjects comes actuarial science, a tough

course that combines probability and financial math with instruction on mortality tables, disability tables, and a variety of other tables. Altogether, the exams in these areas compose the first third of the series. The remaining exams cover all the other disciplines that are involved in the complex operations of a life insurance company. They include selection and rating of risks (from the medical, occupational and lifestyle aspects), accounting, contract law, life insurance law, regulation and taxation, investments, pensions, policy contract drafting, valuation of contract liabilities, and the myriad ways to compensate an agent.

Even for the survivors of the early exams, the pass rate on the later exams drops below 50%, and below 40% for some exams. I spent over 3,600 hours of intensive study preparing for them. No wonder there were only about 500 Fellows in the United States then. Some wag has defined an actuary as a person with a rare form of insanity: so rare that it becomes highly valuable!

A Great Day for Rejoicing.

One day in June of 1947 I opened the (eagerly awaited) envelope from the Society of Actuaries that contained the "pass list." There was my name in the relatively short list of successes. I WAS A NEW FELLOW! I called Doris immediately to share the great news. My feet barely touched the ground as I ran for the streetcar. The 15-minute ride seemed to take forever. I was eager to begin the celebration with Doris. It was her victory as much as mine. She was the one who had motivated me to resume my studies in 1934. She had borne most of the weight of caring for home and family while I was concentrating on work and study.

Now we could begin to live like normal human beings. I could keep my many promises to Doris about the home projects I would do "after my exams." I could perform the duties that were expected of me at the PTA, our church and other community organizations. We could play bridge and spend time with our friends. We could take our children to amusement parks, the zoo and on other outings. We could see our parents and siblings more frequently, and take in an occasional movie.

The Challenge of Balancing Obligations.

Walter Rupert made it plain that it would take 50 hours a week at the office to do what he expected of me. He also made it plain that, as I progressed up the corporate ladder, I must do my share of travel and entertaining. In turn I made it plain that I did not intend to slight my family or community obligations. He wasn't too happy with my response, but I felt it important that he not expect more than I was prepared to deliver.

People used to ask me, "Which comes first, your family or your work?" I would answer, "They're both important. When there is a crisis in our family, it comes first. When there is a crisis at the office, my work comes first. But normally, I will balance my time between them." As a result, I never felt guilty about the time I spent in either context.

I brought home a brief case regularly, but I never opened it until the children were in bed. Until then, they came first. None of them ever heard, "Go away, Daddy's too busy to play." They occasionally remark appreciatively about that; it gives me a good feeling.

Building a Strong Actuarial Department.

The technical aspects of my work gave me no difficulty, nor did the managerial or supervisory aspects. I treated the supervisors who worked for me in the same friendly, helpful and understanding way that Walter Rupert treated me. They appreciated that treatment and responded well.

Finding new people to staff a growing department did present a challenge. To meet it, I had to develop some creative methods of recruiting top flight actuarial students. There were only about half a dozen colleges and universities around the country that had programs for actuarial students. I made only one recruiting trip to these schools, and was very disappointed at what I found. The bottom two-thirds of the students in the programs were not of the quality I was looking for. The top third could command starting salaries far above what I was willing or able to pay. So I decided that there must be more than enough students with the exceptional potential I wanted right in the Minnesota colleges and schools.

Allies in Academia.

The University of Minnesota had no placement program then, nor did the private colleges in Minnesota. I developed friendships with the heads of all their mathematics departments and told them of the wonderful opportunities I had for their outstanding students. They were astonished that a busy executive would take the time to counsel individually with these young people. The word got around these schools that Minnesota Mutual was the place to work.

In a few years I had more gifted students than I needed and was able to refer them to my friends in other companies. But I continued to give each of them an interview sufficient to counsel and advise them of their potential in an actuarial career. If I hired them, I gave them plenty of support and encouragement in their careers. I urged them to set goals for themselves and reviewed their progress with them regularly, always emphasizing their interests and their growth. Oh yes, it took much precious time to do this, but the investment paid big dividends.

Appreciative Young Friends.

Posting job opportunities had not yet become a common corporate practice. But I continually watched for promotion opportunities anywhere in the company for my key people. I would advise them of the opportunity, suggest that they interview and let me know how it went. When they came back I would discuss with them the longer term prospects of that position compared to what they had. Some moved, some stayed. But all of them remained with the company and became my staunch, loyal and appreciative friends.

A well-meaning friend in another department suggested that I was too altruistic for my own good and that I was building other departments at the expense of my own. I thanked him but suggested that he look at the fact that my department was continuing to grow rapidly in both numbers and quality. He went away a bit puzzled. Moreover, the company's senior officers appreciated that we now had an effective management training program that benefited the whole company.

This apparent paradox convinced me, more than ever, that altruism beats narrow self-interest every time. It was just one of the many examples that "casting your bread on the waters" is a practical, highly effective way to live your life.

Corporate and Personal Growth.

Under the dynamic leadership of Harold Cummings, Minnesota Mutual grew rapidly. The Actuarial Department and I grew with it: I was promoted to supervisor, manager, assistant actuary, associate actuary, assistant vice president, associate vice president, vice president, and finally to senior vice president. The promotions were always welcome, but the real satisfactions came from other things. The greatest of these was helping actuarial students achieve their potential. Finding better ways to do things and continually striving for quality in everything we did, also brought a strong sense of fulfillment.

Meeting Walter Rupert's high expectation of me was also very gratifying. Working creatively with Harold Cummings in our efforts to develop exciting new sales presentations brought many mountaintop experiences.

Difficulties at Work.

My rapid rise in the company created jealousies and friction with some of my peers in other departments. These hard feelings were exacerbated when I pushed them to perform according to my expectations. For example, our law department drafted new policy contracts to the specifications I provided. I thought their wording was entirely too cumbersome and difficult to read. I began drafting the contracts and insisted that they confine their changes only to those necessary to comply with the law. I would challenge them vigorously when they went beyond this limit.

Our tabulating (IBM) department was particularly backward and inefficient. When I couldn't persuade the department head to raise his standards, I fought for (and received) the right to set up my own IBM unit.

When people in other departments were slow in meeting their commitments on projects in which my department was also involved, I was not bashful about pushing them. When this was not effective, I would complain to their department head. Most of these department heads were 10 to 20 years older than I. They didn't take kindly to being pushed by this young upstart, even when they couldn't deny the rightness of the complaint.

"I'd Rather be Right . . ."

There was a hit play on Broadway in the 1940's entitled *I'd Rather be Right Than President.* I am afraid these words were close to being the motto by which I lived my office life then. I didn't enjoy upsetting these people, but I felt I would lose my integrity if I ceased to push for the best.

In that same era William White, an author and sociologist, wrote a controversial book about the corporate culture. One of his themes was that companies rewarded their "team players" and discouraged the truly creative executive. Another was that corporations treated their executives so well that they became prisoners. He went on to say that the result was mediocrity. I resonated strongly with these ideas because I saw them at work in my own company. I vowed that I would never sacrifice my integrity or my independence for the mundane rewards of the team player. These strong feelings made me even harder to live with for my peers.

The Corporate Shrink.

In the late 1950's Minnesota Mutual retained a consulting industrial psychologist. We called him the "corporate shrink." His primary mission was to help us screen applicants for key positions, but he was allowed to spend some time trying to improve relations between the company executives. I called it "oiling the corporate gears." Many of my peers thought this was a foolish waste of money, but I was a strong champion of the program. The psychologist, Ted Lindbom and I developed a high degree of mutual respect, and he helped me in many ways. He also helped me greatly in understanding the difficulties Doris was going through as the wife of a rapidly rising executive.

But Ted and I didn't always agree. One morning he came into my office visibly disturbed, probably about some tactless approach I had taken with one of my peers (there were many). He began, "Stan, if you want to be president of this company, you . . ." I interrupted him, "Ted, what makes you think I want to be president?" He was so flabbergasted that he blurted out, "Well, you ought to want to be!"

I think Ted really thought I was presidential material, but knew I would do better if he could help me take some rough edges off my personality. He was probably disappointed that I wasn't even willing to try. But I felt so strongly that to mellow out would be a compromise of my principles.

The Cost/Price Squeeze.

Billing and collecting premiums, calculating and paying dividends, and many other routines were very labor-intensive. Many of our life insurance contracts had been sold years earlier in the days of 40-cent-an-hour office clerks. The premiums on those policies were grossly inadequate to pay the expenses we were incurring in the 1950's. This inadequacy was placing a serious strain on the company's finances. Improving manual work methods made only a slight dent in the problem. I had reduced the labor in my department by the creative use of the newer IBM tabulating machines, but the great bulk of the company's heavily labor-intensive work was done in another department. I began to search eagerly for a more effective solution to the problem.

Pioneering Research.

In the early 1950's I began to read about an exciting new invention that had not yet become a commercial reality: the "stored program computer." The Society of Actuaries formed a "Committee on New Computing Machines and Recording Devices," of which I became a member. We visited the laboratories of IBM, Honeywell, the Bureau of Standards, Bell Labs, Univac, and other organizations that were building prototypes of these fabulous machines. My brother, Jack, was working on a similar invention at Engineering Research Associates. ERA was bought by Univac and Jack became project engineer on a machine that was sold as the Univac II, a very popular computer then.

SEX?

At the same time, I helped organize a group of likeminded explorers from several major Twin Cities companies. One member jokingly suggested that we call ourselves the Society of Electronic Xerographers (SEX). But we quickly agreed on the Twin Cities Electronic Data Processing Associates

(TEDPAC). Each month we invited the officer in charge of computer research in a major company to come and speak to us. They were happy to talk to two dozen prospective customers; there were no computer salesmen yet. We became known as the best-informed computer prospects outside the New York City area. We were true pioneers.

The Big Battle.

Unfortunately, most of the labor-intensive, repetitive work that these machines could take over was done in the Controller's department, not mine. He belonged to a professional association called the Life Office Management Association (LOMA). Salary scales were rising rapidly during this period, and computers offered a way to hold down people costs. I tried to persuade him to join me in a project that would utilize one of these exciting devices to relieve the intense pressure of soaring expenses at Minnesota Mutual. Unfortunately, he refused firmly, despite my earnest pleas. Instead he showed me a short article in the LOMA journal. It was LOMA's official opinion that computers had no future in the life insurance business!

I took my case to Walter Rupert. He arranged a meeting of the senior management committee at which the Controller and I argued our positions. I extolled the virtues of these marvelous machines, their expense-saving potential, and the positive effect this progressive step would have on the company image. My opponent gave them all copies of the LOMA article. He went on to argue that this project was high risk at best, wouldn't save any money, would be very disruptive, and would lower morale. He then threw his Sunday punch: did the company really want to risk the loss of its precious records by putting them on magnetic tape? They would become invisible. If this newfangled machine broke down, we would have to restore all the records by sprinkling iron filings on the tape! The resulting delays and prohibitive costs would ruin the company. I countered with a verbal summary of the Society of Actuaries' very positive report on the potential of computers in the life insurance business. I'm sure I did a miserable job of concealing my contempt for my opponent's unenlightened position.

The senior officers were torn. From their questions, it was obvious that they felt themselves to be in a difficult position. They were struggling with a tough issue about which they had no personal knowledge. It was equally obvious that they would not be unanimous. When they had heard all our arguments, they went into executive session.

The Seeds of Bitter Strife.

Walter brought me the news: I had a green light to form a computer department, buy a computer and proceed with the necessary programming and installation. The operation of the tabulating (IBM) department would also become my responsibility. He expressed strong enthusiasm for the project but grave concerns about the road blocks I would run into.

He was so right. Because more than one department was involved, the entire project would be under the control of a committee chaired by the vice president and corporate secretary. He was also the office manager. A nice enough man, he was very conservative and somewhat older than the rest of us. He knew nothing about computers and wasn't about to learn. And he had not forgotten what he felt was the verbal abuse that I had heaped on the controller during the original battle.

At every meeting the controller tried to throw road blocks into the project. He played skillfully on the chairman's conservatism. He wanted to continue the old operations in parallel for two years! I felt two months was adequate. The office manager proposed a compromise of six months. I had little choice but to accept. And so it went on issue after issue.

The First Computer.

The Metropolitan Life Insurance Company of New York

was the largest life insurance company in the world. They bought the first commercially available computer: the Univac I. It was a huge water-cooled affair. Since it wouldn't fit through a doorway or on an elevator, they had to knock a large hole in the side of the building and hoist it into place with a large construction crane. A "sidewalk engineer" remarked, "If that machine is so damn smart, why can't it figure out how to get itself into the building!"

Costing over a million dollars, its "high-speed" memory was ingenious, but slow and cumbersome. A quartz crystal converted the electronic impulses into sound waves at one end of a long tank of mercury. At the other end, another crystal reconverted these vibrations into electronic impulses. Once a piece of information was fed into the tank, you couldn't access it until it came out the other end. This brief delay provided a memory of sorts, since the computer circuits weren't burdened with this information for a few seconds. The Univac II also used this "acoustic delay line" as a high speed memory; but it substituted piano strings for the mercury tank. The term "high speed" is highly relative, since such millisecond delays in accessing the data in memory could not be tolerated in a modern computer.

Our First Computer.

There was a bewildering array of methods for storing data in those early days. Included were mechanical relays, vacuum tube "flip-flop circuits," acoustic delay lines, Williams (a form of cathode ray) tubes, magnetic drums, metal tapes, acetate tapes, and mylar tapes. Ferromagnetic "cores," chips, and discs had not yet been invented.

We chose a Burroughs Electrodata Model 205. The "high-speed" memory was a magnetic drum. There were four large Mylar tape drives for "permanent" storage. Then there was a curious device for "intermediate storage." It looked like a deep coffin. The inside was divided into 50 vertical bins, each just wide enough to accommodate a 3/4 inch ribbon of mylar tape. The tape fell in a ribbon pattern into the bins. Over the top of these bins ran a pair of read-write devices propelled by a worm drive. This whole contraption allowed the programmer to access a relatively large volume of data much faster than searching a reel of tape end-to-end.

By way of comparison, an inexpensive PC today can do many thousand times as much work, and the information is available from its high-speed memory in billionths of a second.

The Salesman Goes Into Shock.

We had studied every option available to us before choosing this machine. There were no computer salesmen in the Twin Cities. I called the Burroughs headquarters, and they sent a young salesman up from Chicago. He was prepared to give a two-hour presentation on the merits of this wonderful machine. Instead, after about 15 minutes of coffee and small talk, I asked him if he had his order pad handy. He turned white as a sheet. I was afraid he was going to faint and fall off the chair. This was his first sale!

Although we weren't quite through with our research, I was 90% sure we were going to go ahead. The $250,000 price seemed very reasonable. I asked him if we could sign an option to buy at this price and if so, what would the terms be. He didn't know, but he would call headquarters. As he hung up he said, "You can have an option if you will write the contract." He had not asked what the price of the option was. I dictated a one page option agreement with a $100 option price, ran it through our law department while he waited, and signed it on behalf of the company. He was on his way before noon.

A year later we decided to go ahead. The price had gone up over $80,000. That $100 seemed like a very good investment!

Pioneer Programmers.

I had asked Bill Lutz, an advanced actuarial student, to head the systems and programming project, and assigned Bill Gilbert, another actuarial student, to help him. I had some difficulty persuading Lutz that this project would advance his career, rather than set it back. A few weeks later we visited my actuary friend, Chuck Pestal, at Northwestern National Life. He had embarked on a similar project a few months earlier. When we ran out of specific questions, I asked him, "Chuck, if you were to do it again, what would you do differently?" He grinned at me and said, "Ask for my old job back!"

These early computers were delivered with absolutely no packaged software, except for a primitive operating system, which was on a reel of magnetic tape. To start the system, you placed a short strip of paper tape containing the "bootstrap" instructions in a tape reader. Then you keyed in the first instruction and pressed the start button.

We started writing our own software even before the computer arrived. There was no Assembly Language program. We had to write all of the machine instructions in a regular decimal code. (That system doesn't exist today; instead hexadecimal numbers are commonly used for coding machine language.) The instructions were not very powerful: about 30 of them would do what one instruction would do in today's powerful languages. We had to decide where every digit of data would be stored in memory. We charted these decisions on a "memory map" so we would know where to find each digit.

By the time we had a few segments of our system programmed, Burroughs had installed a demonstration machine in its Minneapolis office. As a part of the sales contract, they provided us a number of hours of time on this machine to test our programs. When it was our turn on the machine, we would anxiously run our new program segment. When the computer encountered an error, we would run the program step by step and try to figure out what was wrong. If we were successful, we would run frantically to a paper tape punch to correct the error in time to make another test.

It was an exasperating, exhausting, inefficient process. In an attempt to improve matters, we would spend countless hours "desk checking" the program before we tested it on the computer. We were enormously relieved when our own machine was delivered and installed.

A World-Wide Attraction.

We were the second life insurance company in the world to use the "consolidated functions" approach in the application of a computer. Today this would be called the single data base. Insurance company officers from as far away as South Africa came to see our operation. The controller had argued strongly that, for security reasons, the computer room should have no windows. I argued equally strongly that security would be better if we put 30 feet of ribbon windows in the wall facing the corridor. That way visitors could get a good view of the operation without having to enter the room, which was always locked. Happily I prevailed. I don't know what we would have done with those hundreds of visitors we had otherwise.

My articles reporting on our project were published internationally. For lack of time, I had to limit the number of speaking engagements I accepted in various parts of the country. It was an exciting time.

My Love Affair.

The arrival of Fortran was the creative actuary's dream. This computer language was developed originally as a mathematical tool. I found dozens of applications for it in actuarial research. Writing these programs became a hobby with me, and I spent many evenings in this activity. I would kid Doris by telling our friends, "If Doris ever files suit for divorce, the co-respondent won't be another woman: it will be a computer." Her reply was, "Yes, and I think I could deal better with a woman!"

Some of these research applications were so huge that they would run all night on the computer. I would start the programs when the regular operators left in the evening, and pick up the output first thing in the morning. One morning I came to work to find that a well meaning operator had stopped my program because he didn't think it was doing anything! I learned to leave a note on the machine.

The Lobbyist.

In 1959 U. S. Treasury officials introduced a bill in Congress that would tax life insurance companies on a radically different basis. Bill Lutz, my associate actuary, pointed out that it effectively taxed the interest on the millions of dollars of municipal bonds we held. Since we didn't think this provision was legal, we attempted to get it changed. As tax officer for the company, working for that change became my principal duty for the next several months.

First I visited our two trade associations. One of them gave me a cool reception. Its principal supporters didn't have many municipal bonds, and they were afraid to jeopardize the gains they had made on other issues. The other association wouldn't take an official position (for the same reason), but its officers gave me access to their files and some moral support. Those files and some research in the office of the Minnesota Insurance Commissioner helped me to identify other companies with large municipal bond portfolios so I could seek their support.

The bill was the product of some brilliant minds in the Treasury Department. They explained the offending provision in a clever way that made it look legal. There was no hope of educating congressmen or the legislative assistants on the intricacies of the bill. So I prepared a simple illustration showing the taxes that two companies would pay. These companies were identical, except that one had a million dollars of idle cash and the other had invested the million in "tax exempt" bonds. The latter company paid over $30,000 in additional taxes.

Exciting Times.

We went to Washington to persuade key congressmen and senators that this provision was illegal and unjust. I had interviews with Wilbur Mills, Chairman of the House Ways and Means Committee, and Harry Byrd, Chairman of the Senate Finance Committee, and other key figures on Capitol Hill. These interviews were arranged by our Minnesota congressmen. It was exciting to meet and talk with these famous people. When I had enough time between appointments, I visited the hearing rooms and sat in on a number of fascinating hearings, which were not yet being televised.

Our little group of lobbyists met for dinner each evening and planned our strategy for the next day. The treasury men were vigorous in opposing us and came up with new material and arguments every day. This material was based on arcane technical provisions in the bill. Most of our group were attorneys. They were happy to leave the financial analysis to me. I would often work until after midnight and present my findings to them at breakfast. They were truly apologetic about my having to work so hard. But I found the challenge very stimulating and was truly glad to meet it. Moreover, it was much more enjoyable than spending the evening in a hotel bar.

Strenuous Times.

When I flew home each Friday evening, I bought a ticket to return Sunday afternoon. Saturday mornings I briefed Walter Rupert and President Harold Cummings on our progress, or the lack of it. Saturday afternoon was a precious time with my family. I was chairman of the building committee for our new church. We met almost every Saturday evening. After church and dinner on Sunday we would head for the airport again. I didn't give up my Washington hotel room for 17 weeks.

"A License to a Lawsuit."

The outcome of this vigorous struggle was a subtle compromise that gave neither side a clear victory. One brilliant attorney in our group called it "a license to a lawsuit." Among the various companies affected by the law there were hundreds of millions of dollars in taxes at issue. So we decided to sue the U. S. Government, knowing full well they would take us all the way to the U. S. Supreme court.

I spent a good share of the next 6 years engineering this lawsuit. The first job was to raise the money needed to fund these long legal proceedings. We estimated it would cost about $750,000 in attorney's fees. (That would be about $3,000,000 in 1994 dollars.) I really enjoyed visiting the presidents of the companies who helped us. It would usually take about half a day to brief these gentlemen on the project and secure their commitment. I used a precise formula that distributed the cost among all the participating companies in proportion to the value of the municipal bonds they owned. I never had a refusal. They were all very supportive and appreciative of the time I was taking to run this project. One of them was Lloyd Bentsen, who later became the distinguished senator and vice-presidential candidate we all know from the 1988 debates. He is now Secretary of the Treasury under President Clinton. I had a tremendous respect for him 25 years before. He is a marvelous gentleman.

A Witty and Gracious Remark.

Another outstanding gentleman was Stanford Z. Rothchild, President of the Sun Life Insurance Company in Baltimore. Fifty years earlier his father and uncle had immigrated from Germany. One opened a small dry goods store; the other started a fruit stand that later became a grocery store. When they had saved $15,000 between them, they bought a controlling interest in Sun Life. It was a struggling little company selling industrial insurance: The agents would walk their territories (called "debits") each week collecting the five cent weekly premiums from the factory workers.

It was Stanford who had built the company into the large, successful company it was in the 1960's (and still is). I learned from his son that he was a brilliant student. He had graduated magna cum laude from the University of Michigan Graduate School of Actuarial Science and passed all of his actuarial exams with top scores by the time he was 21. He had to wait until he was 25 to receive his fellowship degree because that was the minimum age!

He was a great leader and businessman, a modest man and a gracious gentleman. But he had always wondered whether he would have been able to achieve success if he had been poor like his father and uncle. When I congratulated him on his outstanding academic achievements, he thanked me and asked, "What was your school?" I replied, "Hard knocks; I've been working full time since I was 14." "That's the best," he exclaimed, "I couldn't get in!"

Attorneys.

During our lobbying phase we had retained the Washington, D. C. law firm of Scribner, Hall and Casey to advise us. The senior partners were all well connected politically. Fred Scribner had become Undersecretary of the Treasury, Leonard Hall was Republican National Chairman, and Bill Casey held various jobs in the Administration, ending up as head of the CIA.

We were assigned to a bright junior partner named Thomas Thompson. Tommy specialized in life insurance company taxation, and spent all of his time at it. I used to kid him: "Tommy, this complicated new law is your life annuity!" He was a great help to me in selecting trial attorneys for the various phases of our trial: federal district court, circuit court of appeals, and the U. S. Supreme court. I spent many days visiting these attorneys and giving them a "cram course" in the intricacies of this arcane law. It was one of the few situations I know where the teacher paid the students high fees for the privilege of educating them! But it was much cheaper than having them spend countless hours researching it on their own. I did respect these men, however, for their special skills as outstanding trial attorneys.

Atlas Life vs United States of America.

The selection of the ideal company to be our test case was another important task. Tommy Thompson laid out the criteria for the ideal representative, but it was my job to pick the actual company.

I had become well acquainted with the fine man who ran one of trade associations in Chicago. We had acquired a great deal of mutual respect and trust, but it still took courage on his part to allow me access to the association's confidential files, from which I could readily extract the data I needed for my quest. I swore never to reveal any of this data, and no one ever laid eyes on it but me. It took days to review the files of over a thousand companies and extract the data for a few hundred of the most likely candidates. After dinner, I would ride "the El" to the Illinois Institute of Technology in South Chicago. There I rented time on their powerful computer to analyze my data.

Tommy and I finally picked the Atlas Life Insurance Company of Tulsa, Oklahoma. Luckily they were a client of Tommy's and he introduced me with a telephone call. Even though we would pay all the expenses, it took me two full days with the chairman of the board, the president and the general counsel before I could persuade them to start the lawsuit. Atlas Life vs United States of America is now one of the leading cases read by students of life insurance company tax law.

A Bitter Lesson.

The whole project was an exciting, enriching, growing and educational experience. The hardest lesson, however, was the final one: I learned that you can have the finest legal case in the world and lose it if the court is biased against your cause. We lost in the district court because the judge never understood the issue. We won in the 8th Circuit of Appeals with a unanimous decision, but the Supreme Court was another matter.

Chief Justice Earl Warren's Court (the Warren Court) was known for its liberalism. Its majority seemed to view all tax exempt bonds as loopholes for the rich. The fact is, this exemption is based on the fundamental principle of states' rights. One of these rights is for state and local governments to issue bonds whose interest is free from federal income tax. This exemption had been upheld without exception until the Atlas Life case. As a consequence, state and local governments have been able to finance roads, bridges, schools and all other elements of our public infrastructure much more economically.

Of course, this results in higher federal income taxes, but this progressive tax seems more socially acceptable than the relatively regressive real estate taxes that are so commonly used to fund state and local governments. The only other incursion on tax exemption occurred recently when Congress imposed a partial tax on income from social security. Under this law a person who invests idle cash in "tax-exempt" bonds pays a higher federal income tax. It will be interesting to see whether anyone tests this law in court.

A Better Lesson.

As you may have surmised, the Supreme Court ruled against us. It was my sad duty to report this regrettable news to all our supporters and constituents. Of the 75 companies involved, I never heard a word of criticism or recrimination from any of them. Nor did I receive any from my own bosses. Instead, I received words of gratitude, understanding and praise from many of them. The lesson was simple but forceful: If you are honest and open with people and give them your best effort, you will never regret your actions, regardless of the outcome.

Professional Activity.

The Society of Actuaries always needed members who were willing and able to spend time on committees. The largest of these was the education and examination committee. Along with recommending educational policies to the board of directors, these volunteer committee members spent endless hours preparing examination questions and grading exams. I served on this committee for many years, as well as on the computer committee and the committee on papers. The latter committee selected the manuscripts to be published in our professional journal and provided much editorial comment to the authors.

The membership elected me to the Society's board of directors and then to one of the four vice president positions. The principal duty of vice presidents was to plan meetings, choose the principal speakers, and select timely topics to be discussed in the numerous workshops and forums. We then had to lay out the program in detail and recruit scores of participants. Fitting these activities around an already demanding work schedule was a challenge.

The Society president is expected to travel almost half time and the Society did not even pick up his expenses. To me this seemed like an imposition on the employer. There was always a good supply of candidates eager for the honor, so I never allowed my name to be put in nomination.

A Major Reorganization.

In 1966 Harold Cummings retired and Walter Rupert became Chairman of the Board, President and Chief Executive Officer. I was made a senior vice president and placed in charge of a number of departments whose employees constituted about 60% of the entire home-office staff.

In running the actuarial department I had always insisted that my officers and managers set realistic personal goals for their careers. Then I would advise them on the course of professional training and development they would need to undertake if they were to reach these goals. Finally, I would review their progress with them each year as part of the annual review of their work.

In the reorganization, I acquired many new officers and managers, and spent many days just getting better acquainted with them. I was shocked to find that few of them had any real focus on personal goals, nor were they pursuing any program of professional development. Many of them didn't even view themselves as having a profession.

The LOMA Fellowship.

The Life Office Management Association (LOMA) had been founded many years ago to enable managers in life insurance companies who had no other professional specialty to view themselves as professional managers. The Association had established the Life Management Institute to help these managers obtain both the technical expertise and the supervisory skills they needed to excel in their jobs.

Leading by example had always seemed the best way to me, so I decided to attain my own Fellowship in the Life Management Institute (FLMI). The 10 half-day examinations were given during a single week each year, and students were expected to take one or two exams a year. It seemed to me that the sooner I got my "flimmy" the better example I would be. Much of the material was already familiar to me because of my actuarial training and my long experience working with these departments. And I was already "test wise." So in the Fall of 1967 I decided to take all 10 of the exams when they were given the following spring. I called Al Harris in the human resources department:

"Hi Al, I've decided to get my flimmy, would you please send up a set of the text books."

Al asked, "For which part?"

"All of them," I replied.

"All of them!" he exclaimed incredulously.

"Yes," I said, "the sooner I have my flimmy the better."

In a little while Al appeared personally at my office door with 70 or 80 books on a hand truck. "Where do you want them?" he asked, half amused and half bewildered.

"Just stack them in the corner," I replied, "And thank you very much."

An Interesting Challenge.

Inquiry revealed that one person had managed to pass all 10 exams in a period of two years. I thought it would be fun to see if it could be done in a year, with seven winter months to prepare. If I covered three books a week, I could make it. I could spend only a few hours a week on this project, so I would have to get through a book in an hour or two. I must also have a method for reviewing the material quickly, since there would be very little time for that just before the exams.

The method turned out to be simple and effective. I skimmed the books looking for any unfamiliar word or thought. When I found one I dictated this information briefly onto a tape cassette. Some books took only a few minutes. Others took hours; but the average rate was satisfactory.

Exam Week.

Doris and I had spent the previous two-and-a-half weeks

on a delightful trip to Hawaii. On this first trip, we wanted to see as much as we could. We stayed in two different places on each of the four major islands. We filled the days with guided limousine tours and the nights (after dinner and a local talent show) playing bridge with our friends Herb and LaVerne Cherry. There was no time to even think about the upcoming exams. We were having too much fun.

We arrived home late Sunday evening. The exams began the next morning. During breakfast Monday morning I listened to the tapes for the first exam. At lunch I listened to those for the second exam. And so it went for the week. Most of the questions covered material that seemed familiar, but like many multiple choice exams, some of the questions seemed to have more than one right answer. I finished the tenth exam Friday afternoon, content that I had done a satisfactory job.

Little did I realize that I had set a national record in LOMA for having passed all of the exams in one year.

Taking Stock of My Life.

By 1960 I had seen several of my office predecessors retire to a life of relative unhappiness. Many of them looked forward to a life of travel and leisure, only to find it relatively empty. Some fought the idea of compulsory retirement; they weren't ready to be "put out to pasture." Others just quietly retired and died. Their spirit would die almost immediately, and the body would follow in a couple of years. Only a few seemed genuinely happy and fulfilled.

What secrets had these exceptional few learned? There were many books on preparing your finances for retirement. None dealt with preparing the larger aspects of your life. I began to look carefully at the retired individuals I knew, both happy and unhappy. The difference soon became apparent. The happy ones remained vigorously active and usefully productive. They were the givers. The unhappy ones were living in idleness and leisure. They were the takers. The contrast was clear, even dramatic.

An Exceptional Man.

The most notable among the exceptional retirees was Harold Cummings. He was in great demand as chairman of major fund drives, in which he took a very active role. He was in equal demand as a speaker, and he was a dynamic one. He wrote books. He counseled younger people. He gave of himself freely to those who asked, as much as his waking hours permitted. Before he retired he had been doing most of these things to the extent the duties of his office permitted. He continued to be active, happy and vigorous into his early 90's.

Two Fundamental Principles.

There were other, if less dramatic, examples. They all seemed to point clearly to two fundamental principles. First, everyone should retire to something, not from something. Second, retired people thrive best on activities with which they are at least somewhat familiar.

From these principles it follows that we need to do certain things well before retirement from our main career. First decide with what productive, useful activities we are going to fill a major portion of our lives after we leave our first career. Then start doing these things, to the extent time permits, at least 10 years beforehand. Finally, look forward to the day when we can begin to spend most of our time at these important things. You will read more about these matters in a later section.

Everyone's list of worthwhile activities will look different. That doesn't matter. What matters is that they are things you enjoy doing because you do them well. My original list looked something like this:

- Manage my own investment portfolio
- Enrich the lives of our grandchildren

- Serve on boards of community service organizations and be their treasurer
- Do personal counseling
- Be available to my children when they need me
- Of course, there was to be time for sports, reading and some travel.

How It Turned Out.

The actual list turned out much the same, but with some differences. In the process of learning investment management I realized that the most significant factor in the success of a company was the quality of the people who ran it. In studying these people, I discovered I had the qualities needed to run a business. So I decided that running a business of my own would be challenging and worthwhile if it provided a service that would help people solve their problems.

After managing my own investments for several years, it became apparent that I had neither the time nor the skills to achieve the results that the professionals could. Besides, my other activities were much more personally satisfying.

I find the hours spent with my grandchildren to be both pleasurable and highly satisfying, and I feel that I do contribute to the enrichment of their lives. The only problem is that, with both their busy schedules and my own, there never seems to be enough time.

I have served on many more boards and committees than I thought I would. And I have certainly spent a lot more time as treasurer of various organizations. My years as treasurer of various organizations now total well into the second hundred and are still mounting!

The amount of personal counselling is much greater than I expected, as is the variety: The subjects include financial planning, estate planning, careers, starting a business, getting a job, selecting computers, doctors, attorneys and accountants, the emotional, substantive and procedural problems of divorce, marital and family relations. I am always careful to refer cases that are beyond my skill level. Most of these experiences are highly gratifying. The only exceptions are three people with severe emotional problems. In each of these three cases I made certain that the individual was getting professional help, but neither the professionals nor I seemed able to produce significant improvement.

Happily, our children seem self-sufficient in almost every respect. There are occasional requests for advice and moral support. These never go unanswered and, of course, they get top priority.

The sports (tennis, biking, sailing, down hill and cross-country skiing) and travel activities are getting their share of time; but I read only about 10 to 15 books a year. I would like to do more reading, but I content myself that I will "graduate" to more reading when I'm unable to do other things.

I have been much more active in other businesses than I expected to be; and, for lack of time, I turn down numerous invitations for still others.

The satisfactions and pleasures of writing and publishing were totally unforseen.

As you read on you will see that I left Minnesota Mutual ten years earlier than I had expected to.

Too Far Ahead of My Time.

Traditionally, the life insurance buyer chooses a plan that he thinks he can afford: term, whole life, 20 payment life, and so on. As (her) his financial status changes, a different plan may be more suitable. It is awkward and expensive to change the old plan to a more appropriate one. More often the policyholder just lives with the old plan.

In the mid-1960's, after considerable experimentation,

I came up with a concept that was a fundamental departure from the traditional pattern of plans. Under this concept, only one plan of insurance would be needed. It would separate the two elements of a life insurance policy: insurance and investment. Each year the policyholder could raise or lower his premium to adjust the rate of investment accumulation to a more appropriate level. I proposed to call it the "flexible life plan."

No one liked the idea. Harold Cummings felt that the agents would be upset by the necessary changes in their commission structure. Walter Rupert felt that the tax implications would be troublesome and that our premium income would decline because people would pay only the minimum premium.

I was deeply disappointed, and felt that the idea was too good to forget. So I presented it as a paper to the Society of Actuaries. The paper was immediately accepted and published in their professional journal. A decade later the identical concept was introduced by another company. They called it the "universal life plan." It became a runaway best seller and was copied by many other companies.

Another Exciting New Concept.

In 1967 I became fascinated with a new idea in computers with which Control Data Company had been experimenting: the touch-sensitive, interactive terminal. You could program this remarkable device to display a menu on the screen of a cathode ray tube (a "monitor" in the language of today). When the user touched the screen in the area of his choice, the screen would display another menu that was appropriately responsive to his decision.

I had a vision of using this marvelous invention in our business. Life insurance is most appropriately sold as an integral part of a comprehensive personal financial plan. The most successful insurance agents do this. There is a serious problem, however. When prepared in the traditional manner, a good financial plan requires a great expenditure of time by skilled people. Consequently, many people who need such planning cannot afford it. Oh yes, there are many "estate planners" offering their services; but the good plans still cost too much money. Most of this skilled time is required in two areas. First, the planner must elicit a large quantity of information from the client. Then s(he) must analyze this data in ways that require much table lookup and computation.

Most of these two functions could be done by a computer and a monitor with which the client can interact easily. I spent weeks learning about this new device and determining its applicability to the financial planning problem. The new devices weren't completely perfected, and they couldn't be driven cost effectively by the newly released mini-computers. Both of these obstacles would be overcome in a few years; and it would take that long to develop and test the very sophisticated programs needed.

So once again I presented this radical idea to our management, and again no one liked it.

The Double Whammy.

What I am about to share with you, only a few people have known until now. It was February 1969. Walter Rupert had retired and Frank Briese had succeeded him as Chairman, President and CEO. All of my departments were running smoothly. I was spending a significant portion of my time in teaching, community service, and exploring further opportunities to harness the power of the newer computers. The ways in which they could be used to revolutionize the life insurance business seemed endless — and very exciting.

One morning Frank asked me to come to his office. As gently as he could, but very plainly, he laid the double blow on me. He didn't think I was earning my pay in my present activities, and he didn't see how the company could use my talents. The board thought they should have a younger person than I to succeed him, and he had no intention of nominating me. I was welcome to stay on, but there would be no more salary increases. He really thought I might find better opportunities elsewhere. If I chose to go, they would be very generous with severance and retirement pay.

Our pension plan provided for retirement as early as age 55. But the 10 years less service credit and the "actuarial reduction" because of the longer annuity period would reduce the income drastically. Instead of the normal pension of 40% of final salary, I would be entitled to only about a third of that amount. Frank offered to put me on leave with full pay for four months, so I would be eligible for early retirement. He also offered to supplement the meager pension with a "deferred compensation" income that would bring my total retirement income back to 40% of final salary. In addition they would pay me full salary for a year following the four months, and half salary for a year beyond that. Frank suggested that I "think it over" for a day or so and let him know what I had decided. I left his office in a stunned daze.

Saved from a Horrible Fate.

I was living the nightmare that all men in their fifties dread! My first reactions were all normal, and all bad. This can't really be happening to me. It isn't fair after I had given them the best 39 years of my life. William White[13] was right: They don't want creativity, they want mediocrity and "team players."

That night I tried to think rationally about my options, but my emotions wouldn't let me. Shame, anger, resentment, disappointment and an incredibly strong sense of loss continued to overcome all attempts at logical thought.

The next morning was no better. I decided I needed help. I sought out Mike DeMann, who was then our "corporate shrink." I had a great deal of respect for his knowledge and understanding of people. He tried his best to be helpful; but I don't really remember much that he said. That evening I decided the answers must lie within me. If I was half the man I wanted to be, I must take control of my life. Before I could make a sound decision, I must rid myself of all these negative emotions. I must view this crisis as an opportunity to build the kind of future life I had been thinking of.

That was the key! Minnesota Mutual was really offering me a wonderful financial springboard from which I could leap into the new career I had dreamed of: my own computer company!

The next morning I visited Frank Briese briefly and told him I had decided to accept his offer. I think he was a little puzzled and somewhat overcome at my cheerfulness. I suspect my mien may have looked even a little conspiratorial!

Most importantly, I had been saved from the fate of all too many middle-aged men and women: overwhelming feelings of loss, and even bitterness, that the best part of their lives is behind them. Every night before climbing into bed, I would stand on our sleeping porch, looking out across the lake, which is just as beautiful at night as it is in the daytime. I would silently review all of my blessings. I continued this therapy for about eight months.

Points to Ponder.

- Hard work never causes burnout as long as we continue to be highly motivated. Frustration and disillusionment can cause burnout, and worse, if we don't deal with these negative emotions promptly.

- If we want to gain other people's support we must deal with their feelings and their agendas. At Minnesota Mutual, I applied this principle with great success in working with my managers. I failed to apply it in working with my peers. Why? If I had applied it with them, how would the results have differed? For the company? For them? For me?

- Clearly, the most important factor in the success or failure in any phase of our lives is how we view the situation. Do we recognize the vital importance of this principle? Do we realize the additional power it gives us over our own destiny? Do we act accordingly?

- Do we look consciously for thoughts, ideas and mind-sets that will motivate us to "do the right thing" and give us the strength and courage to follow through with difficult tasks? If we did this more often, how much could we improve our lives?

21. Digiplan

> *"The substance of the eminent*
> *Socialist gentleman's speech is that*
> *making a profit is a sin, but it is my belief*
> *that the real sin is taking a loss."*
> —Winston Churchill

The same day I gave Frank Briese my answer, I called the office of the Secretary of State and ordered a pamphlet on how to incorporate a company. Control Data called their touch-sensitive screen the Digiscribe. I wanted to call my company Diginalysis; but my daughter, Jan, thought that sounded too much like a heart medicine. So I decided to call it Digiplan.

My "Home Office."

I shopped the Twin City area for suitable office space. Then it dawned on me. This wouldn't be the kind of business where customers or clients came to see me. Why not office in our home and save the rent money, commuting time, and the frustration of rush hour traffic? In 1969 the only people who officed in their home were those who couldn't afford an office. So I kept quiet about this decision. Little did I know that I was on the leading edge of a trend that has become quite popular!

Developing an Idea.

Control Data had leased equipment to Biomedical Computer Systems, Inc. (BCSI), a new company in St. Paul. BCSI was attempting to develop programs, using the touch sensitive screen, to take medical histories. This idea would substantially reduce the time a doctor needed to elicit and record all the information for a complete medical history.

I leased time from BCSI for my own developmental work. Learning to write the programs that would drive the screen through the scores of displays needed was a fascinating challenge. Developing the script that collected the data in a cost-effective, interesting, but thorough way tested my creativity and honed my writing skills. I worked feverishly developing the interactive estate planner. Eight months later I was ready to demonstrate the process to potential buyers.

A Fascinating Idea.

The leaders of the financial community came in large numbers to see this exciting new concept. They showed an interest far beyond my expectations. The introductory screens explained that this was only a demonstration, and that it would be some time before they would have a serviceable product. But they sat in front of the screen(s) for 30 to 40 minutes working their way through the entire set of displays. Many of them insisted that I promise to call them when the product was ready.

An Idea Before its Time.

Control Data could not seem to get the bugs out of the Digiscribe. Nor could they get the computer prices down to a level where either BCSI or I could make our product cost effective. Reluctantly, I decided to shelve the project for an indefinite period. But the inquiries still came in. A consulting firm in Atlanta was sufficiently enthusiastic about the idea to present it to American Express. They told me the proposal made it as far as the board room where it became the victim of political infighting. Shades of my earlier struggles to introduce computers at Minnesota Mutual!

Creeping Consulting.

Before starting Digiplan, I had picked the brains of a number of people whose business acumen particularly impressed me. I am especially indebted to two of those people. One was Larry Rybka who was Minnesota Mutual's general agent in Akron, Ohio. Larry's agency was consistently number one in the company, year after year. I made a trip to Akron just to learn from him. Larry said, "Service the hell out of your first client and you will never have to worry about having enough business." The other was Newton Ablahat, Vice President for Planning and Development at Investors' Diversified Services in Minneapolis. Newt said, "Your business will be very successful, but probably not in the way you are now thinking. Be alert for opportunities that present themselves."

They were both right. While I was still working on the Digiscribe project my business friends started to call saying, "I hear you're in the computer business. I have a problem with my computer system. Can you help me?" I did. Soon the callers began to say, "(someone I had already helped) says you were a great help in getting his computer system going. Could you come and look at my problem?" Some of these people became regular clients. In a couple of years I had all the work I could handle, and sometimes more. I have never asked for business nor have I gone looking for a client.

A Fulfilling Career.

Computer systems consulting satisfied me in many ways. It challenged me intellectually: there was always a new problem and something more to learn. It was a creative outlet: inventing new programs, testing them, seeing them do what I had dreamed of, and applying them to fill client's needs were genuine mountain top experiences. It fulfilled my desire (need?) to be of service to people. It provided stimulating and enjoyable relationships with energetic, vital people. And it brought in more money than I had made as a senior vice president of a Fortune 500 company!

An Exciting Venture.

Walter Chapin, my first boss at Minnesota Mutual, was a very creative actuary. While he was a consultant in Chicago he invented a new life insurance product (the Adjustable Life Policy), that required sophisticated computer programs to support it. These programs involved many actuarial formulas and concepts. Walter sought me out to write the programs. I was intrigued but felt I couldn't take the time. Walter persisted, "I don't know who else can do this, and it's so necessary to make Adjustable Life a success."

As a favor to Walter, I agreed to write the programs and charge him nothing. Instead of payment we formed a joint venture. He would sell the programs as he made his client calls to explain the insurance plan. I would receive three-eighths of the gross charge. He would call me in only when his client showed a strong interest in the programs. I put in many extra hours over the next year developing and testing the programs.

Soon we were contracting to deliver programs at $50,000 per client. Companies large and small bought. Among our customers were New England Mutual, Prudential, Equitable of New York, Minnesota Mutual, Northwestern National, and many smaller companies. A large software company in Dallas approached us with an offer we couldn't refuse:

They would market the programs for a percentage of the gross sales. They wanted exclusive rights to the package, but Walter and I declined. So we agreed on a nonexclusive basis.

The Threat of Riches.

The mere thought of what this project would do to the value of Digiplan's stock was a serious concern. It would create estate tax, gift tax and income tax problems that seemed horrendous. There was one solution: give away most of the stock before it became valuable. So I gave 15% of the stock to each of our five children and kept 25% and all the voting rights.

The Bubble Bursts.

Not long afterward the prime rate shot up to over 20%. This unprecedented development suddenly made the Adjustable Life Plan unmarketable. The sales of our program package dropped to nothing overnight. Walter was devastated. I was more relieved than disappointed. Happily, I had resisted Walter's entreaties to hire more staff to handle what he had felt was a potentially unmanageable burden. And I had never become emotionally involved. So it was a simple adjustment to return to the more routine consulting business. My share of the profits from the products we had already delivered provided a very gratifying return on the hours I had spent.

A More Flexible Life Style.

In 1983 our daughter Mary and her husband, Dave, took delivery on a 37-foot sailboat in Connecticut. They invited me to spend five weeks aboard. We were to watch the America's Cup races in Newport Sound for the first two weeks. Then I would help them sail it offshore to Panama. I was just completing delivery on a new program for administering health insurance claims. The client was almost desperately eager to start using it. So I agreed with Mary and Dave to skip the Cup races and join them the day before they sailed for Panama. (See chapter 31 for a brief account of this exciting trip.)

As I worked feverishly to deliver the claims program, I kept thinking, "What is this? I'm coming down with a bad case of indispensability!" I determined to change things when I returned from the sailing trip. Our son, Rick, and his wife, Satoko, had moved back from Pasadena. Rick was trying to establish his own computer systems consulting business and was finding it slow going. So I proposed to Rick and all of my clients that he would service them for a trial period. If they both found the arrangement satisfactory, they would become his clients. They all did. Everybody won.

New Activities, New Clients.

Doris and I began to do more travelling. I returned to teaching and took on considerably more community service work. I also developed more new clients than I had turned over to Rick. But they were of a different nature. In many of the small charities on whose boards I served I saw a crying need for automation. Because they had neither the expertise nor the budget to supply this need in any conventional manner, they became clients of mine. I serve them as faithfully and responsibly as I had served my paying clients, but I send no bills. There was one exception: a larger non-profit organization with a multi-million dollar budget. In nine years I took them from a totally manual operation through four generations of computers. I charged them about a fourth of the fees they would have paid in the retail market. They now have almost 40 work stations in a highly efficient local area network (LAN). By 1993 they were well enough established that they no longer needed my services.

The Joys of Serving Nonprofit Clients.

When I serve my small nonprofit clients, they win, I win, and no one loses. They become much more effective in their mission and feel satisfied that they are working more effectively. The computer systems companies lose no business, because my clients cannot afford their services. And I win in many ways: I enjoy the wonderful people with whom I become friends, the satisfaction of being of service, the opportunities to remain current in the rapidly changing computer world, and the marvelous effects on mind, body and spirit. So Digiplan remains alive and well from my viewpoint. It just doesn't make any money.

22. Programmed Business Systems

"If one does not fail at times,
then one has not challenged himself."
— Dr. Ferdinand Porsche

In November 1969 Bill Randall, then Ramsey County Attorney, made a private investment in a company, named Programmed Business Systems Company, that needed additional capital. (Ramsey County includes the city of St. Paul.) This company was going to process income tax returns on a computer. In only a few weeks it became apparent that things were not going well. Bill's personal attorney, John Vitko, asked me to investigate. It wasn't too hard to see that they needed new management. They asked me to manage the company. I was reluctant for several reasons.

First, they were badly undercapitalized. Raising capital, trying to sell this new product, and struggling to turn the company around didn't really look like as much fun as what I was doing. And it didn't look as if the computer equipment they were trying to use would do the job. Moreover,

I didn't need the additional income. But Bill was a charming, persuasive man. He took me to lunch and asked if I would do this for just a short time, until they could find a new president? I agreed and suggested that I work only for stock options to conserve the company's modest supply of cash. They also asked me to chair the board, whose other members were Bill and a retired revenue agent, Larry O'Connor.

Drastic Actions.

The company was sharing office space in St. Paul with its founder. The arrangement was expensive and otherwise unsatisfactory. My first action was to move them to a larger but less expensive office. Then I called the 10 shareholders together and told them, in effect, "If you ever hope to see any return on your hard earned money, you must invest three additional dollars for each one you put in originally. And there are no guarantees." Some were understandably reluctant. Others just didn't have the money. So we cut the price of the new stock to one third of the original issue price.

This action had two effects. It encouraged some of the more speculative shareholders to buy. It also reduced the value of the previous owner's shares to a number more nearly commensurate with the true worth of what he had sold. The principal investor, with whom I had become friends, took the largest share of the new offering.

Part-Time President.

I upgraded the computer equipment, hired a bright, personable young man, Mike Sauter, and trained him to sell our services by making joint calls with him. Tom O'Connor (no relation to Larry), our one programmer, needed help. We were also too vulnerable without some back-up for him. So Mike doubled as a programmer and salesman. I divided my time between running PBS and developing Digiplan's financial planning system.

Tom now had time to finish an accounting package that he had started before I came aboard. This additional service gave us badly needed year-round revenue. Mike was energetic and worked hard. He not only brought new customers for our tax and accounting services. He did custom programming for some of the customers and developed excellent relations with them.

Our Own Computer.

We had been buying our computer services from International Time-Sharing Company in Minneapolis. It was Mike who discovered a new mini-computer company called Prime. They had good hardware and an outstanding operating system on which it was relatively easy to develop and run our applications. It also served as an excellent time-sharing host. With this bold purchase we not only eliminated expensive time-sharing bills, we began to generate revenue by selling these services to our customers.

Expansion and Growth.

Soon we were operating at a modest profit. But I told the board that we were not going to meet our investors' expectations of growth without a more aggressive sales strategy than I had the time or the ability to provide. I proposed to hire a sales vice president. It would make us unprofitable for a while, but it would be a good investment. The board was reluctant. I finally said, "Look, I will hire this person with this understanding: If (s)he is not earning (her) his salary within six months, we will let (her) him go." On that basis we agreed to look for candidates.

Sales Vice President.

The man I found for the job had run the computer operations for Minnesota Blue Cross-Blue Shield. I was acquainted with him and his operation because of my activity as chairman of a committee to advise the downtown St. Paul Hospitals on automation. When he went with Blue Cross, the computer operation was struggling and unimpressive. He had turned that operation around and sold its services to hospitals representing half of the hospital beds in Minnesota.

We signed an employment contract and he went to work. He was a very democratic leader. He expected a lot from himself and his associates, and he got it. He also served as office manager, since I needed time to carry on with my original plans for Digiplan. Together we improved the product specifications, and I personally directed the efforts of our one programmer.

Investment in Growth.

Although our growth was gratifying and profitable, we needed more capital to do what seemed necessary to grow optimally. But the investment bankers didn't like to handle small accounts, and their charges would have been exorbitant. So we decided to do our own private placement. We were exempt from SEC regulations as long as we sold stock only to Minnesota residents. The Minnesota law permitted us to sell stock to as many as 25 investors without making a formal registration.

I drafted the Confidential Memorandum and had our attorney review it. This document contained most of the information you would find in a prospectus. We developed the prospect list, did the mailing, arranged and conducted the presentation to prospective investors, and issued the stock certificates. We sold our entire issue. Our total costs were about 10% of what it would have cost to work with an investment banker. We repeated the process two years later.

Stepping Down.

By 1980 we were high on INC Magazine's list of the country's 500 most profitable growth companies. We had over

500 accounting and law firms as customers and were grossing close to $4 million a year. Even though I was still nominally CEO, our sales VP was really managing all aspects of the operation. Digiplan had developed a substantial systems consulting business that consumed the major portion of my time. I told the Board that the company had been under "temporary management" long enough and that it was time for me to step down. They agreed. We elected the sales VP president and CEO, but I remained Chairman of the Board. I had continued all this time to take only stock options for my efforts.

The Last Stock Issue.

In the three years that followed, competition became much keener, and the computer world was changing rapidly. Our two Prime computers were serving us well, but the president felt the need to put our products on the better-known Digital Equipment Corporation (DEC) machines. He thought that by doing this we could sell these "turnkey" systems at a good profit. I was aghast at the large capital outlays required for new hardware, salaries for additional programmers, and the substantial increase in operating costs. But he insisted that, without these changes, the competition would "eat our lunch."

This decision would require much more capital than we had. It was time for another stock issue. This issue was too big for me to handle, so Dain Bosworth handled it on a "best efforts" basis. They also agreed to handle trades in the stock. Throughout the company's lifetime I personally acted as the company's transfer agent in order to keep our costs down. The stock was priced at $3.00 a share. This compared with a $1.00 original issue price and 35 cents when I took over the management. Although Dain didn't sell out, they came close enough to consider the transaction a success.

Disastrous Years.

As often happens, the expansion was more expensive and

took much longer than the president had estimated. Worse, the prime rate jumped to 21%, and our prospective buyers were reluctant to finance the purchase of these new systems. On top of that, the "microcomputers" (later called PC's) were making their presence felt in the marketplace. The president was reluctant to move to them: it would involve a third set of programs and more expense.

We lost over $2 million in the next three years, and went half a million into debt. The suppliers of capital had no more confidence in us. We were strapped. Our bank, one of the largest in St. Paul, was having its own problems. More than 20% of its loans, including ours, were "soft" (delinquent in principal or interest payments, or both). Its parent corporation and the bank examiners were leaning hard on them to clean up their act. The message to us was clear, firm and simple: "Pay up or we will liquidate you." I tried to tell the bank that I could sell the company any day for twice what we owed and that everyone would lose in a liquidation, but they were not interested in restructuring the debt.

A Friend in Need is a Friend Indeed.

It was an extremely muggy August evening in 1983 when I stepped off the plane at Logan Airport in Boston, expecting to take a cab to my hotel. To my surprise, there was my close friend, Hod Irvine. Hod is the most successful entrepreneur with whom I am closely associated. Starting with a handful of employees in 1965, he has built a business that has a market value of close to $100 million today. He asked me to join his board in 1980. His company, HADCO, is now the largest independent printed circuit manufacturer in the western world.

Hod said, "Stan, for the first time since I've known you, you look worried. What's the matter?" I told him the story: PBS was flat broke. Recently, I had put an additional $100,000 into the company at $1.00 a share. I had already exercised all of my options that had prices of not more than

$1.50 a share, which made me the largest shareholder, by far. In fairness to my family, I just couldn't do any more, and yet it wasn't enough.

Then Hod did something that will leave me forever grateful. He offered to match my purchase. I said, "Hod, you know that it is a euphemism to call this a highly speculative investment." He simply replied, "I want to do it anyway." It was with Hod's money that we met the payroll and kept the computers running for the last few months.

A Tough Decision.

We agreed that we had to find a buyer quickly. We were unable to do so. The best prospective buyer saw the president as the key problem, and I couldn't persuade him otherwise, but the buyer didn't want to be the one to have to fire him. I went to the Board with a bold plan. We would let the president go and I would groom the company for a quick sale. There was no objection: none of them wanted to throw their good money after bad. I can remember Sam Singer saying quietly, "Stan, you do what you have to do."

An Unpleasant Lunch.

It was February 29, 1984, leap day. What a leap! I took the president to lunch, and told him how extremely sorry I was that our once promising company had come to be in such desperate straits. He knew the situation as well as I did, except that our prospective buyer had not been as frank with him as he had been with me. He found it particularly hard to accept that his departure was the key to our salvation. He pleaded for more time. It wasn't a matter of money; his contract provided a year's severance pay and benefits. I told him we had no more time. The bank was ready to foreclose right then.

An Angry Ex-President.

He became extremely angry and accused me of all sorts

of things that are better left unsaid. It was obvious that his pride had taken a terrible jolt. I told him of the circumstances surrounding my departure from Minnesota Mutual and tried to let him understand that I had walked in the same moccasins. I tried to show him what a great favor Minnesota Mutual had done for me, and that I was better off in every way than if I had stayed with them. With his generous severance pay, he had excellent opportunities to start a business of his own, or seek whatever career he chose. He was not to be placated. After three hours of conversation, I told him again how very sorry I was. He left, still very angry.

He immediately retained one of the best trial lawyers in St. Paul, who demanded of us twice what the employment agreement called for. We, of course, responded that his claim was without merit and that we didn't have that kind of money.

A Successful Sale.

I thought it would take about six weeks to groom the company for sale. Those were long days: 5:30 in the morning until 11:00 at night. But after three weeks I had a call from Von Elbert, President of TLS in Cedar Rapids, Iowa. TLS was our principal competitor. Von had made two previous trips to examine us while the new president was still there. The call was brief as he began, "I hear you fired him." I replied, "You have good ears." He asked, "When can I come up and talk to you about buying PBS?" "When do you want to?" I agreed to meet him in his Minneapolis hotel room the following morning.

After a couple of hours of conversation, Von accepted my offer to sell the company for $50,000 in cash and one share of TLS stock for each four shares of PBS. TLS would assume all assets and obligations of PBS, including paying off the $500,000 bank loan as soon as the sale transaction was completed. I would go on the TLS board to represent the PBS stockholders. Von said he could not commit TLS without checking with his key officers and board members. He promised to do that the next day and express mail me a letter of intent with a binding check. I promised, in turn, not to talk to another prospective buyer for two days.

We Renegotiate.

Instead of a check I received a phone call the next afternoon from a very embarrassed Von Elbert. His board had pointed out that my price would be fair only if our optimistic projections became reality. Instead of four shares of PBS stock they wanted seven. They would issue additional TLS shares to our stockholders if, as and when, our projections became reality.

TLS stock was well regarded. Its price then made the sale worth about $1,500,000 on the one-for-seven basis. I felt that this was a fair price, particularly with the "dividend" of additional shares in prospect.

The Banker's Hot Breath.

I had been getting daily calls from our banker. The message was always the same, "Pay today or we will start foreclosure." My reply also was always the same, "If you are foolish enough to do that, you will have to explain to your superiors, and the bank examiners, why you queered a sale that would have brought you a half-million dollar certified check, and why you would be taking checks each for a few thousand in exchange for used office furniture and obsolete computers. And you can guess who will make it very clear to them what a foolish mistake you made!"

Von and I signed the purchase agreement in the banker's office and I endorsed his $50,000 check to the bank.

The Sequel.

Von and I became good friends. The sale went smoothly. I enjoyed the security of deeper pockets, which had been absent from PBS throughout all of its 14 years. The TLS board members were friendly and their board meetings were interesting. Because both companies were publicly held, we had to prepare a double prospectus and go through seemingly endless paper work.

Von's original dislike for the former president deepened as the latter's attorney made repeated demands. The attorney must have known all along that the demands were without merit, for soon the amount demanded began to decline. Von seemed to enjoy turning down these demands. Finally, when the amount was less than a fifth of the original demand, Von's attorney persuaded him to settle and dispose of this annoying nuisance. Von did, of course, honor the original employment agreement continuing the ex-president's salary and benefits for a year.

The Cash Out.

The honeymoon was over in about a year. The operation of PBS and a costly attempt to enter the difficult California market had overburdened TLS's capital, and it was forced to seek a buyer. The buyer was Pioneer Seed Corn, which had become a cash rich conglomerate. The sale was for cash at $6.10 a share. For PBS stockholders that amounted to 87 cents for each of the PBS shares they had exchanged for TLS stock: shares for which they had paid anywhere from 35 cents to $3.50. I heard no recriminations from any of them, and I received grateful thanks from a number who had become convinced they would never realize anything.

Points to Ponder.

- Although PBS was a business failure, I felt no sense of personal failure.
- My integrity and openness in dealing with people prevented recriminations and criticism.
- Although I was paid nothing for the time I had spent

over 14 years and received back less cash than I had invested, I felt richly rewarded in experience and in many new friends.

- Since I had not "put all my eggs in one basket," my losses in PBS did not seriously impair my estate.

- Since money is not as important to me as many other things in life, the financial loss left no emotional scars.

- A wise man said, "You can tell the size of a man by the size of the things that get him down." I feel a sense of triumph that the disappointments in PBS did not depress me. I am happier today than ever.

23. HADCO

I think it was 1978; Doris and I were vacationing in Kauai when I received an urgent telephone call from Hod Irvine in Salem, New Hampshire. You have already met Hod in the latter part of the previous chapter. He reported that he and his chief financial officer were completely unable to resolve their differences on how to automate the company. Could I come to Salem and help them resolve the dispute.

This type of situation was not new to me. I had flown to Miami a few years earlier to resolve a similar issue between the chairman and vice chairman of a very large family holding company. Emotions and egos always play a large part in these disputes. My formula is to get both parties to agree on their objectives and on a process for arriving at a solution. Once both of them have bought into those important aspects, we concentrate on the process of solution and the dispute is forgotten. The formula has never failed to work, nor did it fail at HADCO.

While I was there, I pointed out some modest computer applications on which the company could get a very quick payoff. Since their systems and programming staff were already over-committed, Hod asked if I would develop and install these routines. The answer was yes, provided we had the concurrence of their director of computer systems. I had already become his friend through my support of him and the chief financial officer in the original dispute. He readily concurred.

Board Membership.

Soon Hod asked if I would join his board of directors. At first I was reluctant, not being sure what I could contribute to a business I knew nothing about. I also teased him about wanting to save money since board fees were less than my consulting fees. Finally he said they needed me to head a board committee on human resources and management information resources. I said, "Hod, you already know my assets and limitations with computers. You must know before you appoint me chairman of this new committee that I will take my human resources responsibilities very seriously, all the way up to and including the chairman of the board." "That's just fine," he replied.

Thus began a process in which Hod thought very seriously about his own future role in the company. He decided that he would like to remain as chairman but bring in a new CEO as president. On our first hire we picked the wrong man and had to let him go within a year. The second one did wonders for the company, but had difficulty relating to Hod. My suggested solution was to use the executive committee as the forum for their exchanges and to have someone other than Hod chair that committee. Hod asked me to do this, so my trips to New England went from four to eight each year. The arrangement worked well, so the extra trips were worthwhile.

HADCO Stock.

In 1980 HADCO's stock was privately held. Hod said almost apologetically that the board liked their directors to own a little stock, and asked me if I would mind buying some. I asked if I could look at the company's financial statements. There I saw that their book value per share had been increasing by over 30% a year. I called Hod and said, "How much can I buy?" For the first time in my life I borrowed heavily to buy this stock. In 1984 HADCO went public and is now trading for 7 to 9 times what I paid for it. It is now a very important part of my estate. All this happened because some client of mine back in the late 70's must have told Hod that I was a good computer man who treated his clients well!

HADCO's Board.

The board members are a fascinating, brilliant, impressive and enjoyable group. They include a partner in one of the nation's leading investment banking firms and the CEO of an incredibly successful company that has a virtual monopoly in supplying germanium diodes to the world. Also on the board is a wealthy entrepreneur who sold his business interests and spends most of his time rehabilitating World War II bombers and exhibiting them around the country. The germanium man also has a great sense of humor, and his supply of good stories seems inexhaustible. Together they are stimulating and a joy to be with. The whole scene adds another dimension to my life for which I am very grateful.

Points to Ponder.

- More important than the wealth HADCO has brought me is the excitement, experience, stimulation, and joy of feeling needed and useful.

- This totally enriching experience came unsolicited because I had done a good job for someone. The survivors on the HADCO board are the "givers." The "takers," who were there for the money they hoped to make, didn't last long and usually left under a cloud of unpleasantness.

- I still feel I am making significant contributions to HAD-CO's continued success. When I feel that this is no longer so, I will resign.

24. Sho-Go and Field Control Systems

These two diverse companies have a couple of things in common. I became involved in both of them as a favor to the principals, who were friends of mine. And neither of them came close to reaching their potential. Sho-Go needed money and I bought their stock. Two years later the company went "down the drain." One problem was bad management; not by my friend but by his partner, who was the company's president. The other problem was their inability to hang on to the market niche on which their success depended. I lost all the money I had invested, but it was not enough to affect my estate significantly. And the friend who asked me to come in is still a friend. I continue to like him and respect him. He always "told it like it was." Of course we were disappointed, but I never felt cheated or taken advantage of.

In the other company my friend asked me to help him because of what he perceived as my financial expertise. I did what I could for him. When I could do no more, I asked him to accept my resignation. Time is just too precious to spend it in activities where I can't make a significant contribution.

Points to Ponder.

- You can lose money without losing friendship if honesty and understanding prevail.
- Don't invest in a speculative venture any more than you can afford to lose, both financially and emotionally.
- A relationship to which you're not making a significant

contribution is best terminated. You can terminate business relationships without terminating friendships.

- Time is an important and precious resource. It should be valued even more highly than money.

25. Life Rate Systems

I have known and respected Dave Haskin for over 30 years. Our first contact was at Minnesota Mutual, where he became the best director of human resources we had seen. He went on to bigger things, including a senior vice presidency at Northwestern National Life Insurance Company in Minneapolis, where his responsibilities included oversight of the management information systems. Dave was also a trustee of Metropolitan Medical Center in Minneapolis when they merged with United Hospital of St. Paul to form the original Health One. He was chairman of MMC about the same time I was chairman at United and we served on the Health One board together.

An Exciting and Challenging Vision.

In 1992 Dave called me. He had just become president and CEO of a new company called Life Rate Systems. They had a product and a vision that is both exciting and challenging. The product gave promise of providing the solution to a very complex and important problem in health care delivery. The problem is to measure the quality and cost effectiveness of a hospital or clinic in its treatment of a particular ailment. This measurement becomes useful only if it can deal with a variety of complex variables in a way that gives valid comparisons among institutions treating a great variety of patients. The process itself must also be cost effective.

There are several systems that claim to do this. None of

them has the flexibility or adaptability that is needed. We call this adaptability "open architecture." Life Rate Systems is truly an open architecture system. At Dave's request, I have agreed to serve as an adviser to Life Rate Systems. Both Dave and I see this project as an exciting business venture. What is more important, we see it as the most promising answer to a very perplexing problem that faces everyone dedicated to improving the cost effectiveness of our health care delivery system.

Five

Military Service

*"War challenges virtually
every other institution of society:
the justice and equity of its economy,
the adequacy of its political systems,
the energy of its productive plant,
the bases, wisdom and purposes
of its foreign policy."*
—Walter Millis

My five years of active duty in the United States Army and ten years of reserve duty were a very important part of my life. I learned a great deal about many subjects in many contexts. I experienced living in different parts of the country and the world in a wide variety of conditions. I learned how people react in times of great stress—I even saw generals cry in utter frustration. I met many people with diverse personalities and value systems and learned much about how to live and work with them.

Most of all, I learned much about myself. I found that I could survive in the midst of confusion, turmoil, physical hardship, separation from loved ones. I learned how to cope with stress and fears, and to free myself from worry. Among all the things I learned, the most important was this: Happiness depends largely on how we view things.

To state it briefly, I matured enormously as a result of my military service.

26. Active Duty

"*The tragedy of war is that it uses man's best to do man's worst.*"
—Harry Emerson Fosdick

Doris and I had been married exactly 13 months when Germany invaded Poland. As the clouds of war continued to gather in Europe, so did the clouds of uncertainty gather in our minds and hearts. As noted earlier, our thoughts and conversations were dominated by war-related questions: Would the United States enter the war? Should it? Would married men be drafted? Would men over 25 be drafted? How long would the war last? If I went in the army, what would happen to my job? Where would Doris live? How would a long separation affect our marriage?

These and other questions were major topics of discussion between us and among our friends. They filled our consciousness. They were no less real, nor less disturbing, than they are to young people today in time of war. The major difference is that the horrors of war are more vivid to all today because of television. But the casualty statistics, the separation, the upheaval in our lives, the sense of loss, the uncertainties were just as real.

The Fateful Call.

My draft board was the first one in Ramsey County to draft married men. I had the lowest draft number of all the men at Minnesota Mutual. One January morning in 1941 my telephone rang and a sweet voice said, "Is this James Stanley Hill?"

"Yes, it is."

"This is your draft board office, you will report to the

Armory at 8:00 AM on February 6th. Bring enough clothes for overnight."

I knew someone must be playing a practical joke on me, so I called my draft board: "This is James Stanley Hill; did you just notify me to report for induction?"

"Yes, we did!"

Fort Snelling.

Situated on high bluffs overlooking the confluence of the Minnesota and Mississippi rivers, Fort Snelling, the home of the Third Infantry Division, was much larger in 1941 than it is today. Stately rows of red brick buildings that had once been officers' quarters stretched for a mile or so on both sides of the parade grounds. Some of these buildings also housed the Third Infantry, a famous Minnesota regiment with a history going back to the Civil War. South of there sat a dozen or more large, two-story wooden barracks and several single-story office buildings, also of wood, that had been constructed to serve as the Fort Snelling Induction Station and Reception Center.

Army trucks took us to the Induction Station for our physical exams. As we arrived, my thoughts were in turmoil. Would I fail the physical exam and go back to a normal civilian life? Would I want that to happen? What would the doctor find? By the time I approached the final station, my initial ambivalence had been replaced by a powerful desire to pass the examination. I did.

At the Reception Center cheerful sergeants issued us clothing and bedding and assigned us to a barracks. The slacks that were part of the regular uniform were scarce, so we received surplus World War I breeches and puttees. The latter item is a rectangular piece of canvas, a kind of gaiter that is strapped on to cover one's leg between the ankle and the knee. We looked just as strange as we felt.

Headquarters Company.

As a part of the reception process we received an "aptitude" (intelligence) test, and a "classification" interview. The interviewer elicited information concerning education, work history, hobbies and sports, all of which he recorded on a 9 by 12 card, along with the test score. From this information draftees were classified in a military occupation that most nearly fit their civilian skills. I was classified as a clerk-typist.

The classification office needed additional interviewers. I was chosen as an interviewer and transferred to the Reception Center Headquarters Company. The pay was the same as that of any other "buck private" ($21 a month, no benefits). But there were many advantages to being in Headquarters Company: no guard duty, no latrine duty, no KP ("kitchen police"), no barracks police (janitor). In military parlance "police" is used both as a noun and as a verb to mean cleaning or straightening up.

New Friends.

Almost all the enlisted personnel in the classification were new inductees like me. The two exceptions were sergeants Bill Chapman and Elwood Turner. They were both "old army," long-service, line soldiers who had been transferred from the Third Infantry Division to form the "cadre" (core leadership) for this new project. They were all very intelligent and communicative. A number of friendships sprang up. The new inductees came in groups of up to 200. There was often time between arrivals of these groups to get better acquainted and cultivate these new friendships.

Morale in Headquarters Company was much higher than in the reception companies. The whole atmosphere was different and quite pleasant, in large part because the men who served there considered themselves the elite of the army, and conducted themselves accordingly. Another significant influence on morale, of course, was the news that we would remain at Fort Snelling for an indefinite period. That meant we could get weekend passes to be with our families. I have already recounted (in Chapter 13) the strenuous times that I experienced while moonlighting to pay for our house. It was worth it all to be "living at home" again.

No Hardship Discharge.

Lieutenant Misbach was the officer in charge of administering tests to recruits. He couldn't type, so he asked me to type his letters. This activity led to conversation, and the conversation led to friendship. When he heard about my tremendous efforts to keep my finances afloat and learned that Doris was pregnant but seriously ill, he suggested I apply for a hardship discharge. I did so, but my timing was unfortunate.

I took my application to the master sergeant in charge of headquarters personnel administration just a few hours after the Japanese had bombed Pearl Harbor. I asked him what he thought the prospects were for approval of my application. His reply was graphic and dramatic: Without a word he took the application, tore it in two and dropped it in his wastebasket. Word had already come down that almost all forms of discharge were suspended "for the duration."

Maurice Fitzharris.

First Lt. Maurice Fitzharris was in charge of the Classification Section of which I was a member. A hard-working bachelor officer, he took his responsibilities very seriously, as I did mine. He was quickly promoted to captain. We often discussed ways we could improve the classification process. This common purpose helped promote a strong affinity and mutual respect between us, despite the vast difference in our military status.

The relationship proved beneficial shortly after I received a second rejection (for lack of a college education) of my application to officer candidate school. Captain Fitzharris became highly indignant. He wrote an incredibly strong letter of protest, extolled my virtues and recommended that an exception be made to the college education requirement in my case.

His letter brought amazing results. Orders soon appeared to relieve me of my duties at Fort Snelling immediately and transfer me to Fort Washington, Maryland. There the next group of officer candidates, including me, would begin classes in just a few days, early in August 1942.

Mixed Feelings.

My feelings were a mixture of elation, sorrow and regret. On the one hand, my financial penury would soon end, and I was going on to new and exciting experiences. On the other hand, I would have to leave Doris, deprive her of emotional support during the birth of our first child and miss this precious experience myself. Finally, I would miss all the wonderful new friends I had made.

Fort Washington.

Located on high ground above a bend in the Potomac River, Fort Washington is 13 miles downstream from the nation's capitol. Built before the Revolutionary War, it played a strategic role in the defense of the capitol city during that war, but was abandoned after the war ended. Some time before World War II it was designated as a historic site and the ramparts were opened for public inspection. It also became a picnic ground and a campground for the Boy Scouts of America.

The Adjutant General Corps.

After the Japanese attack on Pearl Harbor the fort was re-commissioned and designated as the Adjutant General's School. This school was one of the many officer candidate schools (OCS's) hastily established to train the enormous number of officers needed to lead an army of over 10,000,000 men and women. The Adjutant General Corps is a group of officers who perform purely administrative duties in the U. S. Army. When I entered OCS, much tension existed concerning our curriculum. The traditionalists insisted that "every officer must know how to fight." Others argued that teaching military skills to men destined to work at desks was a waste of time and resources. The impass resulted in a compromise in which we divided our time roughly equally between traditional military training and the administrative subjects that we sorely needed.

Gentlemen by Act of Congress.

It took 90 days to complete OCS. Our training included courses on how an officer must behave and dress and so on. For example, we learned that an officer must return all salutes from enlisted men, must never carry an umbrella or packages, and must at all times be a gentleman. We referred to ourselves derisively as "gentlemen by act of Congress." The graduates of West Point, however, looked down their noses at us. How could we learn to be an officer in 90 days when it took them four years? They referred to us as "90-day wonders."

Regardless of how we got our commissions, what an exciting and gratifying experience it was to become an officer! As officers, we moved into a totally different environment: We had much more freedom, better food, better living quarters, better-looking uniforms, and more privacy. We had no inspections, KP, guard duty or other menial tasks. Best of all, we had much more money. With base pay, uniform allowance, and a married officer's living allowance, I was making close to three times as much money as I had ever made in my life. In short, "I'd never had it so good!"

Washington and Jefferson College.

Most of the graduates from our OCS class were assigned

to the G-1 (the army's term for personnel department) of an army installation. A few of us were picked to teach at the Adjutant General School for enlisted men at Washington and Jefferson (W&J) College in Washington, Pennsylvania. This historic old college was suffering the same fate as other colleges and Universities then. The draft had shrunk their enrollment to about half of its pre-war size. This left them with empty classrooms and dormitories—and empty bank accounts.

The army, on the other hand, needed unprecedented numbers of educational facilities to train millions of inductees in non-combatant specialized army skills. So they leased unused campus facilities from colleges like W&J and established army schools on these campuses. The rental income helped the colleges' beleaguered budgets.

It seemed ironic that my first experience inside a college was as a faculty member, not a student. As faculty members in a new army school, we faced prodigious challenges. Most of us had no teaching experience. There were no established curricula, no prior lesson plans, no examination policies and, worst of all, no grading standards.

A Short Teaching Career and a New Challenge.

After only two or three months of teaching I was aghast at the wide diversity in the quality of the exams. Even worse was the complete absence of grading standards. At a faculty meeting I tried to express my concerns clearly but tactfully. Apparently I was all too clear, but not very tactful.

The Dean was a fiery, excitable lieutenant colonel. He took my expression of concern as a personal criticism and became red in the face. He shot back angrily, "All right, Lieutenant Hill, effective immediately you are relieved of all teaching duties. You will report to the assistant dean as a full-time examination officer. You will be responsible for preparing weekly exams for all 15 courses, and for scoring and grading them!"

He was obviously punishing me for my brashness by heaping this seemingly impossible work load on me, and my first reaction was to protest. But, as I thought about it more, it seemed that I had an exciting challenge: to bring order out of chaos in this very important area.

A New Boss

Major Theophilus Christophil was my new boss, and he was a good one. With his handsome, swarthy face, black curly hair, flaring black mustache, and strong accent, he seemed to have moved from Athens just yesterday. He was upbeat, dynamic, friendly and helpful. He made a dramatic production out of everything, even an ordinary sentence. He realized the difficulty of the task I had been given. He also recognized that the new assignment put me in a delicate situation with the other faculty members, and he helped them accept it. He emphasized to them that I was relieving them of their most onerous task, but that it would work only if they gave me their fullest cooperation. He made generous amounts of his secretary's time available to me and urged her to help me in every way she could. I put my heart and soul and about 80 hours a week into this task. Soon we had an examination and grading system of which everyone was proud. Even the Dean expressed his appreciation to all the faculty for the great improvement they had all made. To this day, I suspect he did this at the prompting of Major Christophil.

A True Friend.

The major became a good friend. He helped me develop a greater degree of comfort with myself. He encouraged me to surmount the overdose of humility I had acquired in my boyhood. He asked for my advice about many things, and further strengthened my self-confidence. In short "he made a man of me." I owe him a great deal.

Hammond electric organs had just come on the market and they fascinated me. (All organs fascinate me!). The college had put one in its chapel. So the major helped me secure permission from the president of the college to play the organ any evening the chapel was not in use. I had no formal keyboard training, but when I was in high school I had taught myself to play popular music by ear. I spent many evenings teaching myself to do this on the Hammond. Other than writing letters to Doris, this was my sole diversion from work.

A Reunited Family.

The BOQ (Bachelor Officer Quarters) was a group of hotel rooms in the George Washington Hotel, a comfortable ten-story brick hotel on Main Street. Each of us had his own room; it was absolute luxury compared to the barracks I had lived in as an enlisted man.

My position looked about as permanent as anything could be in a wartime army, so I wrote to Doris and suggested that she and George, now eight months old, join me in "Little Washington." We rented a small "apartment" that the owner had carved out of the upstairs of a modest house. The house had only one kitchen, so we had kitchen privileges at certain hours each day. Our landlady, Rose Stein, was a very pleasant woman. She was excited about having "a real army officer" in her home. She was friendly and helpful to Doris, and she adored George. Her house was less than two miles from the college. I could walk both ways except when it was raining; then I took the streetcar, which ran right by the door. Best of all, we were a reunited family.

Reuben Horchow.

Less than nine months after my arrival at W&J, I received a message to report to the office of the Commandant, Colonel Main. I thought, "What have I done, now?" There I met Major Reuben Horchow, who was on special assignment in the Office of the G1 (personnel) in the Pentagon. The army was starting a new project; its purpose was to provide all army units with replacements who were better trained and more qualified to perform their missions than they were under the previous system. Major Horchow's mission was to determine the number of each type of military skill that would be required. He needed someone with both actuarial training and experience with the Army's personnel classification system. Would I agree to move to Washington, D. C. and work with him in the Pentagon on this new project?

This would require Doris and George to move back to St. Paul, and me to give up my new friends and the tranquil, pleasant life of a faculty member. But the new job did sound challenging, exciting and highly educational. And I didn't know if I really had much choice in the matter. I felt like a prisoner when I asked to be excused so I could make a phone call. Doris was understandably troubled by the prospect of separation; but, after weighing the pros and cons, we agreed that I should go.

The Pentagon.

Built as a perfectly symmetrical, five-sided figure, the Pentagon also had five stories above ground and five concentric rings of offices. It contained more office space than any other building in the world. The architecture was controversial, and a legend in its time. Because of its vastness and unique shape, people frequently became lost and disoriented in it. My favorite Pentagon story is about the Western Union boy who went there to deliver a telegram. At that time messenger boys wore khaki uniforms. Inevitably, he became lost—and he didn't emerge until he had become a full colonel!

The Army's Actuary.

The new job lived up to Horchow's billing, and it was exciting. I was given the top-secret manning tables for all of the units in the entire army. They were made up into a large book. The book was revised every month and the old copies were accounted for and burned. I also received reports of all the deaths and permanent disabilities that occurred in service. These were classified by branch of service: infantry, artillery, engineers, quartermaster (supply), signal corps (communications), etc. They were also classified by rank and military occupation. Most importantly, they were classified between battle and non-battle casualties.

Surprisingly, there were many more non-battle casualties than battle casualties, even in the theaters of operation (combat areas). This important fact was little known and less understood, and, as we shall see, it had a significant effect on my army career.

Moving to the Big Apple.

The BOQ for officers assigned to the Pentagon was in Arlington, Virginia, next to the famous national cemetery. About the time I began to think about inviting Doris and George to come live in Washington, we received surprising news. Some sharp-eyed attorney had discovered an old law that limited the number of military personnel in the District of Columbia to 30,000. The burgeoning Pentagon staff, added to other military units in the District, had exceeded this limit. Something had to be done.

The problem was solved by placing a number of small units, like ours, on detached service at locations outside the District. The unprecedented drain on civilian manpower had left many office suites vacant in New York City, so our unit occupied such a suite at 270 Madison Avenue. My BOQ was another hotel room, this time in midtown Manhattan, just a few blocks from the office.

Living the with Lockes.

Again it seemed appropriate to invite Doris and George to come live with me, and Doris agreed. I found a suitable apartment on Long Island between Flushing and Jamaica. (Recently, a new acquaintance described that area to me as "Archie Bunker land." In 1943, however, it was only partly developed and we were surrounded by a lot of open land.) George and Gloria Locke had remodeled the upstairs of their bungalow to form a snug little apartment with a small living-dining room, one bedroom and its own kitchen and bath. I moved in immediately and Doris and George followed in a week or so.

Suspicious Activity.

The office in Manhattan had no facilities for burning top-secret material. So I got the Lockes' permission to burn the old material in a corner of their garden. Every month I would go through my little ritual of building a small fire in the back yard and tending it patiently until every scrap was fully burned and the ashes pulverized. Later, after we had become better acquainted, the Lockes confessed their concern that I was a spy!

A Prophet Without Honor.

Before World War II the army replaced troops by unit. When a company or battalion had lost so many men that it was no longer effective, it was withdrawn from service. A new unit replaced it, and the depleted unit was sent back to a training camp. The Chief of Staff bought the idea that it was more efficient to replace individuals than units. It was our job to tell the Army how many replacements to train in each military occupational specialty.

Many of the commanding officers didn't accept the newfangled notion of individual replacements. Even more strongly, they rejected our "harebrained statistics." They thought the very idea that most of their losses didn't occur in battle was totally preposterous. (The reality was that many soldiers died in jeep accidents and non-combatant plane crashes, while many others died of infectious diseases—neither sulfa drugs nor penicillin was yet available.) So they insisted that most of their replacements be trained for battle positions, even though these men were commonly assigned to specialized non-combat positions for which they had no training.

A Sad Parting.

Major Horchow became completely frustrated. He decided there was only one way his ideas would ever bear fruit. That was to take them into a theater of operation where the commanding general would agree to try them. So we received orders to move our unit overseas.

So, again, I said good-bye to Doris and George as they moved back to our "home" in St. Paul. This time the parting was even sadder. We both knew that it would be "for the duration." Army officers did not take their families to combat zones.

An Exciting Trip.

In May 1944, commercial aviation was in its infancy. I had never flown on a commercial plane, to say nothing of flying across an ocean. We boarded a DC-4 (four reciprocating engines) at Washington National Airport, took off, circled the field, and landed because of mechanical trouble! Two hours later we re-boarded. This time we were on our way. The orders showing our destination were sealed. When we opened them, we discovered we were going to Casablanca. The trip took 19 hours, with refueling stops at Gander, Newfoundland and the Azores. The entire flight thrilled and fascinated me. I found the sunset and the sunrise to be particularly enthralling. Flying above the clouds across such a great expanse of water was also fascinating. I had read about the full circle rainbow with the shadow of the plane in the center, but it was exciting to see it for the first time.

The Short Snorter Club.

One of the interesting aspects of the flight was our initiation into the Short Snorter Club. To qualify, one had to fly across an ocean, and give two one-dollar bills to a member, Major Horchow in this case. He signed one bill and returned it as our certificate of membership, and he kept the other as his fee. He told us about the great return we'd net on our investment because of the many members we would initiate later. But, by the time I made my next overseas flight, air travel had become sufficiently common that the club had ceased to exist. We could have called it the "short life club!"

The Replacement Depot in Oran.

Oran, Algeria, was the smelliest, most depressing place I've ever been. The pilots claimed they could fly to Oran with their eyes shut, because they could smell it 30 miles out to sea.

Even in pleasant surroundings, the morale of men in replacement depots was low. There was no sense of organizational esprit since they weren't members of a permanent unit; and there weren't any meaningful duties other than KP, guard duty and latrine duty. The replacements were known as "casuals." I never envied the non-commissioned officers who had to keep these depressed, recalcitrant casuals in line. The common retort of a replacement, when asked to do something was FUBIC (F——— you bud, I'm casual). The whole atmosphere seemed like a very inauspicious place to start our noble experiment. Most field commanders did come to agree that the individual replacement approach did have its merits; and it was still in use at the end of World War II.

Saving a Life.

One Sunday an enterprising officer arranged to borrow a jeep in which several of us made a trip to the beach. Someone had found that if you soaked a mattress cover with water, it became airtight. Then, when you held the open end toward the wind, it would fill with air. Finally you tied off the open end and had a big float to lie on.

One of our group, Ted Koton, floated into water over his head. Then he fell off his float. He began to yell frantically for help. I was the first one to reach him and pull him back into shallow water. He was unharmed, but very frightened and extremely grateful. Having grown up by a lake, I found it hard to believe that a grown man couldn't swim.

Winter in the Volturno Valley.

We hadn't been in Oran many weeks when we learned that the Germans had retreated far enough up the Italian peninsula that we could move to Italy. We made the trip across the Mediterranean in a 300-foot freighter that had been converted to a troop ship. The trip was uneventful, but it was my first experience aboard any vessel larger than a small boat. Every aspect of the ship fascinated me as I explored it in great detail.

At the dock in Naples we climbed aboard army trucks that took us to our camp in the Volturno Valley, near Caserta, about 15 miles north of Naples. There we would spend the winter of 1944-1945. The temperature would drop into the 20's at night, and we slept in unheated tents. We had mattress covers and blankets but no mattresses or sheets, so we filled our mattress covers with straw and covered them with a shelter half. (Two shelter halves make a pup tent.)

We wore long underwear day and night, taking it off only to bathe. A little before bedtime we filled our canteens and put them on the office stove. When the water was hot, we slipped the canteens into their felt covers and ran for our tent. We slid into bed in a tight crouch and slowly pushed the canteen down with our feet. This operation drove the frost out of the shelter halves and body heat did the rest.

Hard Work.

The official title of our organization was Headquarters, Replacement Command, Mediterranean Theater of Operations (MTO). We were the first organization of its kind. We were organized like a regiment: We had a commanding general, a chief of staff, and the "four G's." G-1 deals with personnel; G-2 handles "intelligence" (information and communications); G-3 takes care of training and operations; and G-4 is the quartermaster, or supply officer. We had total responsibility for feeding, housing, training and assigning all replacements coming into North Africa, Italy and (later) Southern France.

Colonel Horchow, as assistant G-1, was still my superior officer. His desire for more and more analyses of the troop manning tables (organizational structure) and casualty statistics seemed insatiable. I had two lieutenants and half a dozen enlisted men grinding away day after day on hand-cranked portable calculators. Between this job and my duties as treasurer of the Officers' Club, I worked 70 to 100 hours a week, but I didn't feel burdened. The work was interesting and the time went fast. There was enough time left to eat, read a little, write a daily letter to Doris, and chat with the other officers. I was not the only one who felt this sense of dedication to duty. Several of us received the Bronze Star Medal in recognition of these efforts.

A Hot Mount Vesuvius.

Mount Vesuvius had erupted a few months before we arrived in Italy. Smoke was still curling from its summit when the American Red Cross began to run tours up the mountain to an area beyond which it was considered too hot and dangerous to continue. My tent mate, George Arms, and

I took the morning tour. At the top we decided to let the tour go back without us. We could explore on our own and go back with the afternoon tour.

We walked completely around the rim of the volcano. Much of the ash-covered ground was too hot to touch, but we managed to pick our way through areas that our heavy boots made tolerable. In many places there were "gas ports": holes two to four inches in diameter emitting gases. These gases were so hot that a scrap of paper, pushed into the port with a stick, would quickly burst into flames.

At one point we came across the remains of a British bomber that had crashed the night before and was still smoldering. The landing gear had been thrown clear of the flames. The "Eye-tyes" (Italians) had been there already and cut the tires off. They used the heavy rubber to make new soles for their shoes.

Rest and Relief.

The term rest and relief (R & R) is the army equivalent of vacation. George Arms and I spent our week at Albergo Vittoria Grande (Great Victoria Hotel) on the Sorrento Peninsula. This beautiful, mountainous peninsula forms the southern arm of the Bay of Naples. It gave its name to the famous Italian Song: *Tornerai Sorrento* (Return to Sorrento). Later, every time we'd hear this song, we would recall our wonderful R & R.

We could lie on the veranda of our hotel room and look across the bay at the Isle of Capri. It was on this veranda that I read that very moving novel, *The Robe*, by Lloyd Douglas. A good portion of the plot was laid on Capri. Being there, and later having a chance to visit this historic island by sailboat, made reading the book even more thrilling.

A Hazardous Journey.

Another memorable experience was bicycling over the mountains and along the scenic Amalfi Drive, which runs along the southern shore of the peninsula. As we coasted down the mountain grade my brakes failed. The only way I could control my speed was to drag my feet on the rough roadway. I wore the thick leather soles of my army boots almost completely through!

We were within a few miles of our hotel when I realized my military cap had slipped from under my belt and was lying untold miles up the mountain road behind me. I had no other cap with me, and being "uncovered" (without a cap or hat) was a serious offense. I was too tired to pedal back up the mountain, so I held onto the back end of a large, lumbering truck. As it pulled me up the mountain, I watched the road intently. A few miles up the mountain my search was rewarded. I finished ruining my boots on the final trip back to the hotel. No wonder there were so many non-battle casualties. Fortunately, I wasn't one of them!

Personal Communications.

The most common form of communication with our loved ones was by "V-mail" (victory mail). You wrote your letter on one side of a piece of very light-weight paper. The address went in a panel on the other side. When you folded the sheet correctly, it became its own envelope. Hundreds of thousands of these could be carried on a cargo plane. When there wasn't room on a cargo plane, the letters were opened and microfilmed. At the other end enlarged prints of the microfilms were placed in envelopes and delivered to the addressee.

For urgent messages, the Army Signal Corps would handle a special kind of telegram. The entire transmission contained only the recipient's name and address, the sender's name and 3 code numbers. Each number represented a stock phrase. Picking the appropriate phrase to convey a cogent, meaningful message was quite a challenge.

In November 1944 I received a 3-code telegram with the

news I had been anxiously waiting for. It read, "Daughter born — all well — all my love — Doris." My wry sense of humor got the best of me in my telegram reply: "Congratulations — many happy returns of the day — all my love — Stan." Doris didn't think it was that funny. That odd sense of humor runs in the family: My brother sent her a telegram from Panama with the identical first two phrases!

Those Fascinating Machines.

Whenever I could spare the time, I would visit my friend Lt. Dick Sindelar in the Machine Records Unit. These MRU's were a new development in World War II. Housed in large semi-trailers, they contained the latest models of IBM accounting machines — much newer than the ones we had at Minnesota Mutual. Dick and I became good friends as he showed me the intricacies of these machines and even allowed me to operate them. I dreamed of ways we could use them at Minnesota Mutual.

Dick was a happy-go-lucky, energetic young officer who could never decide whether to call me Jim (my first name is James) or Captain. After I was promoted to major, that settled it: He always called me Major. The night before we moved from the Volturno Valley the commanding general threw a party, complete with free drinks. I still remember Dick saying "I hope I pass out early; I need the sleep." He did!

Mussolini's Military College.

The Arno River separates Livorno (Leghorn) from Firenze (Florence). As our fighting forces crossed it, we moved our headquarters to Mussolini's abandoned military college, which was just south of Rome. The buildings had been strafed with mortar and small-arms fire, but they were still serviceable. Compared to our previous conditions, we felt very well off. Moreover we had a marvelous opportunity to explore the historic old city in our free time.

Bicycling in Rome.

A bicycle provides a wonderful way to see Rome—if you can deal with the traffic. I had never seen traffic like this! The major streets intersected at large open areas where street vendors set up their stands. The cars and stands all seemed to converge in one chaotic gridlock. The drivers lay on their horns while they exchanged obscenities with the street vendors and each other. The driver with the loudest horn and the least concern for his vehicle, property or human life seemed to prevail. The "carabinieri" (police who carried carbines) looked on calmly, interceding only when the disputes erupted into physical violence.

We quickly learned to avoid these areas in favor of the quieter streets. The latter were more scenic anyway. Little parks, gardens, fountains and statues made marvelous resting places. We practiced our Italian by trying to read the inscriptions on the statues.

A Sense of History.

One cannot spend much time in Rome without being deeply impressed with the city's ancient history. Tours of the Coliseum (half in ruins), the early churches and the Catacombs were the most impressive.

The most moving experience we had was attending an evening performance of the opera *Aida* (complete with elephants, cannons and fireworks) in the Termi di Carricola (baths of Carricola). These baths had served as recreational areas for the wealthy Romans. Built in the shape of a large open amphitheater, they contained concentric rings of flat rocks that served as benches for the ancient theater. We allied soldiers sat on these benches, just as the Romans had done 19 centuries earlier, to watch and hear this magnificent modern performance.

Flying Over the Alps.

Our headquarters had one small plane assigned to take

us staff officers to inspect the replacement installations and stockades (prisons) that were part of our command. Our pilot, Gerry Gerg, had been a bomber pilot who was shot down. His injuries removed him from combat duty, but they didn't keep him from noncombat flying. He complained that the L-4 (Piper Cub) they gave him was so under-powered it was dangerous, so it was exchanged for an L-5 (Aeronca). The L-5 carried one passenger in a seat in front of the pilot. Both pilot and passenger wore helmets with headsets so that they could talk to each other.

One day, while we were flying from Rome to Florence, Gerry asked, "Want to fly it?"

"Sure," I replied.

He started to instruct me, "Left rudder, left aileron ..."

I interrupted him, "Let me try it without instruction."

After I had made a few banks and turns, he said, "You've flown before."

"No," I replied.

"Then how did you know what to do?"

"I read a book."

After a while we began to lose altitude. I pulled the stick back slightly. We lost speed, but we continued to lose altitude. I pushed the throttle forward. We gained back some speed, but still we lost altitude. I was about ready to call for help when we began to gain altitude just as rapidly as we lost it. Suddenly it dawned on me: we were encountering huge downdrafts and updrafts caused by the mountains below us. After that discovery, I set the controls for level flight, relaxed, and enjoyed nature's roller coaster.

A Difficult Takeoff.

The L-5 could take off and land in a very short distance. When the installation we were visiting was some distance from an airport, Gerry would land in a bare field next to the installation. One day he chose a plowed field on which it had been raining. He said, "We'll have to take off early before this field thaws."

We arose at daybreak to find that the ground had not frozen! But Gerry had to get back to headquarters that day to take the CG (commanding general) somewhere. So, against my better judgment (and his, I think), he taxied right up to the trees, turned around and gave it full power. I can still see the landing wheel on my side dragging through that thick, sticky mud as we gained speed much too slowly. Far down the field, with the trees at the other end approaching, I felt we must surely abort. Just then we hit enough firm ground for the landing gear to pull free of the mud. The small plane surged forward, lifted off and became airborne just in time to clear the trees! I'm not sure which of us heaved the louder sigh of relief!

Assistant G-1 of MTO.

It was September 1945, four months past V-E day (victory in Europe), when V-J day occurred. Our replacement command was no longer needed, and I was transferred to Headquarters of the Mediterranean Theater of Operations. My office was in the Royal Palace in Caserta. Built in a traditional large hollow rectangle shape, this beautiful limestone and marble building had seen much history. Garibaldi had made it his headquarters in the 19th century. The German High Command took it from Mussolini in 1941, and lost it to the Allies in 1943.

The American people were already putting great pressure on Congress to "bring the boys home." Congress pressured the President and the Pentagon officials who, in turn relayed it down the line. As assistant G-1, it was my duty to see that the selection of both officers and enlisted men to be sent home was done equitably, without regard for rank or unit. We used a point system: one point for each month of active duty plus another point for each month of service out of the USA. With almost five years of active duty and 15 months overseas, I was a "high pointer," but not quite high enough to go home right away.

A High Priority Courier.

Army regulations required endless paperwork. We used to say, "The Army that runs out of paper first will win the war." Much of the paperwork that had been neglected during battle operations had to be caught up now in order to complete the many forms needed to fulfill the legal and logistical requirements for discharge. A special Address-ograph (a trade name for a mailing list system in common use before computers) plate was prepared for use in preparing these forms at the separation centers "back home." Embossing these soft metal plates with printed information was a slow, noisy job that could be done in our office while the troops were waiting for transportation. Doing it in our office reduced the amount of time a soldier would have to spend in the separation center. These plates were precious, since the loss or misdirection of a batch could delay the separation of thousands of servicemen. We put 110-pound batches of them in a mail sack, and sent them home by plane with highly trusted couriers.

Top Priority.

Every available ship and plane was commandeered to take men back to the states. Most of the troops went home on slow freighters, which could take a couple of weeks to make the trip across the Mediterranean and the Atlantic. The luckier ones made it in a week on passenger ships. Planes were reserved for the hardship cases, the seriously ill, wounded, high ranking officers on "official business," and the inevitable congressman or Administration official on a junket.

The Military Air Transport Command used an elaborate priority system to determine who would fly on the next available plane. Congressmen and couriers had top priority. By mid-December "my number was up." I had become friendly with the Regular Army master sergeant who chose the couriers. One morning he stuck his head in my office and asked, "Major, how would you like to be the courier tomorrow?" The answer was obvious!

The Best Trip of All.

My heart sang as the DC-3 took off from Naples, "I'm going home, I'm going home!" I was in Casablanca only an hour or so before I boarded a DC-4 for the trip to New York City. It gave me time to see the huge crowd of men (5,000, I was told) with lower priorities, some of whom had been waiting for days for an empty seat.

New York City looked beautiful to me, but I didn't spend much time there. I found the officer who was waiting for my heavy bag of plates, got a receipt from him and hurriedly took a taxi to Penn Station. My orders were to go to Camp McCoy (in south central Wisconsin) and go through the two-day separation process.

I called Doris, explained the separation process, and told her to expect me home the following Wednesday. She told me of her plan to spend the weekend with her parents in White Bear Lake. The overnight train trip to Chicago and the transfer to The Hiawatha (the fast day train to St. Paul) were familiar and pleasant routines.

Going AWOL.

As the train sped from Illinois into southeastern Wisconsin, I couldn't get the thoughts out of my head. This train is going to a station within 12 miles of my beautiful wife whom I haven't seen for 18 months. Why am I getting off at Camp McCoy? It's Friday afternoon. Separation centers don't work on weekends. Technically, I will be absent without leave; but who is going to know? Even if they know, who is going to care? Even if I were called on the carpet for it, how could an officer fail to understand my human desires?

By the time the train reached Camp McCoy I had thoroughly resolved to stay aboard. When I called Doris from the Union Depot in St. Paul, she was a very surprised lady. When I convinced her that I wasn't joking, she told me she would come immediately to pick me up. Her mother told me she had never seen anyone fly out of the house so fast and into a car!

Getting Reacquainted.

Doris and I had no trouble picking up where we had left off. Our almost daily letters had kept us close in spirit. But we still had much catching up to do. The physical closeness seemed heavenly. I don't remember any difficulties in adjusting to civilian life, even after almost five years of army life. Of course, I had experienced none of the terrible stresses and psychic trauma of battle conditions.

At almost two-and-a-half, George wasn't quite sure how to react to this strange man in a Major's uniform. It was several days before he could really accept me as a member of the family.

Everyone else was glad to see me, particularly my parents. It was over three years since I had last seen them. They seemed much older than I had remembered them.

Because of my very early entry into the service, I was the first of my friends and business associates to come home. It would be months yet before I would see some of them, including my brother. My early return was a great boon to my business career, as you have already learned.

By the way, I made it back to Camp McCoy early enough on Monday that my absence was never noticed.

Points to Ponder.

- Almost all of life's situations, including military service, offer rich learning experiences, if you are attuned to them.

- Marital fidelity has great rewards, which far outweigh the brief pleasures of alternative lifestyles.

- Absence does not necessarily make the heart grow fonder, but bonds can be strengthened through good communication.

- As in civilian life, so it is in the military: Doing the best job you can in every situation pays two great dividends. The greatest of these is the good feeling you have about yourself. The other is, of course, the material rewards.

- Life is much more interesting if you are willing to take some risks. You must weigh each risk carefully, however, to make sure that it is not foolhardy or overly dangerous.

- Military service builds and tests character. It can also exhibit weakness of character.

- As in most of life, mental outlook is the real key to happiness in military service.

27. Reserve Duty

> *"He who escapes duty avoids a gain."*
> —Theodore Parker

When we were separated from service we had two options. One was to receive an honorable discharge. The other was to remain as an officer on reserve status. Reserve officers had three obligations. The first was to accept possible recall to active duty in times of national emergency. The second was to serve two weeks a year on active duty with your reserve unit. The third was to attend two meetings a month with your reserve unit. There were no reserve Adjutant General units, so I had no meetings to attend. This also meant that my active duty would be with Army Headquarters or higher units.

Reserve status sounded logical and held the prospect of interesting assignments. There were also several material advantages. One was full pay and allowances for active duty. Another was full years of credit toward the 20 years required for a military pension. There were also service credits which would increase the pension. We were also eligible for promotions. I had no idea how adequately I would be able to support my growing family with a civilian job. So these material benefits were a strong incentive in my decision to remain in the reserves.

Going to Jail in Chicago

One active duty assignment took me to 5th Army Headquarters in Chicago. Army Headquarters were located in a hotel at 30th and State St. South. Doris, George, Jan and Mary took the train to Chicago and spent the last few days with me. I had planned the last morning very carefully; I loaded our luggage in the car and parked it on State Street, just half a block south of the hotel. I would finish my work at headquarters, then my family and I would walk to the car and start our drive home to St. Paul.

Extra paperwork delayed me until after noon. When we walked out on State Street there were no parked cars to be seen. Then the horrible realization struck me: that side of State Street became a tow-away zone at high noon! We took a taxi to the police station, paid a stiff fine plus a large towing fee to redeem our car and finally began our belated trip home. Next week, during show-and-tell time at her school, Jan reported on our trip to Chicago. When her teacher asked what was the most exciting part of the trip, Jan replied simply, "When Daddy had to go to jail!"

Watching TV in Washington, D. C.

Another active duty assignment I recall was in the Pentagon. This looked like a good opportunity for my family to see Washington. So I rented a house for the month that covered the two weeks we would be there. We had planned that Doris would take the children to one or two places of interest each day. The house had a TV. We hadn't yet installed TV at home. After about three days of sightseeing, the kids said, "Mom, do we have to go sightseeing? Can't we just stay home and watch TV?" So much for educational trips!

Eighth Army Headquarters.

My last active duty assignment was at Eighth Army Headquarters in Minneapolis. I worked regular office hours and went home every evening. I don't recall the nature of the work, but I do recall receiving some publicity in the weekly newsletter. Each week the newsletter contained a safety slogan. The commanding general picked these slogans from submissions by the staff. My only submission was selected while I was still on duty there, and was published with suitable plaudits from the CG:

"Here lie the bones of Jonathan Gay; he died defending his right of way.

"He was right, dead right, as he sped along; but he's just as dead as if he'd been dead wrong."

Doris and I found it a challenge to explain to the children the changes in my daily routine. One question was, "Why is Daddy going to work in that funny suit with all the gold and ribbons on it?" We had moved to Mahtomedi and had only one car. I normally rode the bus to and from work so that Doris could get to the stores, school and other necessary places during the day. Since it wasn't practical to ride the bus to Army Headquarters in Minneapolis, I used the car for those two weeks. One morning Jan asked,

"Where is your car, Mommy?" Doris replied, "Daddy took it to go to the Army." The next morning, it was not a question but an indignant outburst: "Mommy, Daddy took your car again!"

Honorable Discharge.

After I was promoted to Lieutenant Colonel, the Army found that they had more reserve officers in these higher ranks than they would ever need. In the mid-1950's the annual letters concerning active duty took on a different tone. They contained an added paragraph offering me the alternative of honorable discharge. My life had changed considerably in the previous decade. I had acquired much heavier responsibilities at the office. Family obligations and community service obligations were taking much more time. And I was earning much more money than I had ever dared to dream of 10 years earlier.

Consequently the discharge alternative looked just as attractive and logical now as the option to remain in the reserves had looked originally. And so my army career came to a close.

Points to Ponder.

- Circumstances change the desirability of decisions. It was just as logical for me to resign from the military reserve in 1955 as it was for me to enroll a decade earlier.

- Every decision we make affects the future course of our life, many times in unexpected ways.

- Most good decisions enrich our lives and give us additional learning experiences.

- Properly viewed, "duties" become positive, enjoyable learning experiences.

- By grasping opportunities for service we enrich our own lives as well as the lives of others.

Six

Sports for a Lifetime

"Old age doesn't cause inactivity;
inactivity causes old age"
— Stan Hill

The scene is a high school gym in 1926. The compulsory gym class is about to play its first game of indoor softball. A scared 12-year-old freshman boy goes to the plate. A 17-year-old senior throws a fast ball. The batter starts his swing about the same time as the ball smacks into the catcher's glove: "Strike one." The scene is repeated twice more: "Strike two," "Strike three." The batter walks dejectedly to the bench. Shortly after that, the coach assigns him to the catcher's position. Moments later an enthusiastic batter takes a mighty cut at the ball, follows through and connects firmly — not with the ball but with the catcher's forehead! After a period of total unconsciousness he is revived and sent home: a not-so merciful end to a very short baseball career.

Since I was small for my age as a youngster and was only 14 in my senior year, high school team sports were fraught with failure and trauma, both psychic and physical. So I avoided them wherever possible. Grade school team sports had not been introduced yet, at least not in White Bear Lake, Minnesota. When I was eight, my MD uncle wouldn't let me run because it was "hard on the heart"!

The Aerobic Pioneers.

When my family lived on the East Side of St. Paul (1937-1938), I did walk to work and back (about 3 miles each way); but the purpose was to save money. Most people did not consider exercise to be healthful until I was in my early 40's.

After President Eisenhower had his heart attack, Dr. Paul Dudley White sent him out on the golf course. Everyone thought he was crazy. About then I read a book by Major Kenneth Cooper, an Air Force surgeon who was a pioneer proponent of aerobic exercise. He was the first person (to my knowledge) to quantify the amount of exercise needed to maintain a good aerobic capacity. He also quantified the amount provided by each type of activity and sport.

His book inspired me to take a businessmen's membership in the St. Paul YMCA. Norm Strom (then one of my actuarial students at the Minnesota Mutual Life Insurance Company) and I used to play handball there and do a bit of running. But the "Y" was five blocks from the office and many days we didn't feel we could take the time, so it didn't work out too well.

Saint Paul Athletic Club.

In 1951 I decided I could just barely afford to join the St. Paul Athletic Club, which was right across the street from the office. There was a two-year waiting list, which was fine with me, since I was making only about $6,000 a year as an assistant actuary. Two years later we moved to our lake-front home in Mahtomedi, and money was really tight when a cheery voice on the telephone said, "Congratulations, Mr. Hill, your name has come to the top of the list, and we have an Athletic Club membership for you!" I gulped twice, decided to take it and was never sorry.

I jogged on the indoor track for a couple of years. I gave it up when my doctor advised me that it would exacerbate my cervical spondylosis (an arthritic condition of the vertebrae just below the neck). Besides, I found much more enjoyment in competitive sports, such as squash, racquetball and water volleyball.

Around 1960 I bought a life membership in the Athletic Club. It required a substantial investment (perhaps $15,000 in today's dollars), so I considered carefully my chances of surviving and staying in St. Paul long enough to make it pay. The Club filed bankruptcy and closed its doors over 3 years ago, and I'm still in St. Paul and going strong!

"I'm Getting too Old to do This."

Far too often I hear younger people saying "I'm getting too old to do this." I wonder if they realize what a great disfavor they are doing themselves when they even hold such a thought. Some of you will say "Active sports in your 80's? You must be kidding!" I'm not. Part of it must be good genes, but I believe a great deal of it is a mind set. This mind set encourages me to continue these activities just as long as I'm able. They give pure enjoyment and play a major part in keeping body, mind and spirit alive, vibrant and vital. Read on . . .

The Modern View.

Aerobic exercise at least 3 times a week is one of the cornerstones of good health. Listen to Susan Johnson (Director of Continuing Education at the Institute for Aerobics in Dallas):

> *"We've discovered that it's never too late to improve on fitness. There are plenty of studies on 80- and 90-year-olds, and they all show improvement. . . . We can slow down the aging process. We see a 20-year advantage between those people who are fit and those who are not fit. That is, the 60-year old fit person has the body of a 40-year old unfit person."*

My Preference.

I much prefer to get my exercise through sports rather than workouts. Not only are sports more enjoyable, but they often offer people contact, more relaxation, and generally more uplift to the spirit. Not all continuation sports are aerobic, but they do have the other benefits just mentioned. For outdoor sports, sun block, a cap, and sun glasses with certified UV (ultraviolet) protection are essential — see the chapter on "Aging."

28. Bicycling

The four rules for perpetual youth:

1. Eat sensibly.

2. Exercise regularly.

3. Drink only in moderation.

4. Lie SHAMELESSLY about your age!!

> *A 13-year-old boy had saved up $15 (about $150 in today's dollars) by walking 3 miles each way to work on a vegetable farm for a dollar a day. He dearly wanted (and needed!) a bicycle. A man he knew only casually sold him one for the $15. He told him the wonderful merits of this bike: Gears and a drive shaft connected the pedals to the back wheel, so there was no chain to come off, etc. The boy realized too late it had no brakes and couldn't coast, but these deficiencies didn't plague him long. He then discovered that the gears were badly worn. A week after he bought it they stripped completely; and left him with a piece of useless junk. He told the man he felt cheated; the response: "you bought it, that's your problem!" There were no small claims courts in 1927 . . .*

My bicycling career was not resumed until Doris bought me a Columbia 10-speed touring bicycle for my 50th birthday. Only then did I learn the true joys of biking. What a wonderful way to explore the neighborhood, the community, and the surrounding countryside! What a marvelous way to get your aerobic credits, clear the mind, and raise the spirits.

The bike is an ideal way to go to the grocery store, library, post office, marina, hardware store, hospital (as a visitor!), a friend's house, construction sites — the list goes on and on. When a car needs servicing, I stick the bike in the trunk and have a pleasant way to get home from the service station or auto dealer. When the car is ready, I reverse the process.

The Health Span Bike Classic.

In 1988 Health One (now Health Span—a group of upper Midwest hospitals) and a local TV station (KARE, Channel 11) sponsored their first annual 150-mile bike classic. These classics motivate me to ride more: I train by riding at least 500 miles in the 10 weeks preceding the classic.

They are also a fun way to raise money for your favorite charity. I have consistently raised $5,000 to $7,000 each year, which has been enough to win the grand prize.

Although my prime motivations have been exercise, fund raising, and the joy of the ride, the prizes have been fun too:

- 1988: Two weeks in New Zealand for two. Doris went with me for a delightful trip which we extended to three weeks.

- 1989: A week of sailing in Tahiti for two including airfare. My daughter, Jan went with me and we had a ball! *Windsong* is a 440-foot motor sailer with half an acre of sail. We sailed mostly at night. Some time during every morning we would anchor in some beautiful lagoon. The transom (stern end) would swing down on big hinges to become a water sports platform. From this platform we could swim, sail, windsurf, snorkel, scuba or water ski.

- 1990: Round trip for two to anywhere Northwest Airlines flies. Doris went with me to Maui where we were guests of Jan and her husband, Loren, as Doris' 75th birthday present.

- 1991: Same as 1990. This time Doris flew to Hawaii on Senior Ultra-Fare coupons. On the trip back we split up; Doris flew east (home) and I used one prize ticket to fly west to Tokyo. Our son, Rick's wife, Satoko, used the other prize ticket to fly from Minneapolis-St. Paul to Japan, where we spent 10 wonderful days with her as my guide and interpreter. I lived, ate and slept in three different Japanese homes. I was not surprised to be treated with courtesy, respect, and generosity, but the warmth and love I felt as I was treated as a member of the family totally overwhelmed me.

- 1992: Same as 1990 and 1991. This time our daughter Bev and I flew to London and spent nine marvelous days in Edinburgh, London, Oxford, Stratford, Cambridge, Canterbury, Folkstone and Dover.

How the Money is Raised.

Many pledges come without asking. The rest "just happen" during conversations with friends interested in the same charity — United and Children's Hospitals of St. Paul. I don't even mention the subject to anyone unless they have a strong interest in the hospitals or me.

Immediately after the classic I use my word processor to write an individually addressed letter to each of my sponsors. Usually two full pages, it describes in some detail the conditions and experiences in the ride (these are sagas in themselves). They are all individually addressed and laser-printed originals. Many sponsors have expressed their gratitude and extreme pleasure in becoming "part of the event" through these letters. The letters are also a signal to send a check, although many send theirs before they receive the letter.

A Third Bike.

The 24-year-old Columbia had over 10,000 miles on it and seemed inadequate for the Classic challenge. So I gave it to George and treated myself to a Peugeot (an impressive French name for a machine made in Taiwan!) mountain bike with city tires. These tires have a heavy tread on the shoulders for safer riding in sand and gravel. But they also have a smooth rib in the center. When the tires are inflated to 65 pounds of pressure, you ride on this rib, almost as easily as on small diameter tires — and much more safely.

Safety Considerations.

Safety considerations are paramount: A good helmet, carefully fitted by an experienced sales person, is essential. Mount a large (2" x 4") rear view mirror on the left handle bar and use it. When riding on the shoulder, I watch every car approaching from behind to make sure (s)he will give me adequate clearance. The inattentive, drunk, incompetent, or malicious drivers are a small minority; but it only takes one to put you in the hospital or the morgue.

Study the routes available to you and pick them for safety features: a separate bike path, wide smooth shoulders, wide traffic lanes, multiple lanes, low speed limits, and low traffic density. Remember that you are subject to the same obligations as a motor vehicle.

Comfort.

Comfort is also important for serious riding. A wide seat with a lamb's wool cover is a good investment. Bike pants are a great source of comfort for rides of more than 10 or 15 miles. They eliminate the chafing experienced with other shorts; and slacks are too warm for summer riding. A fanny pack is a great convenience since bike pants have no pockets.

Health.

And now let's look at some health considerations. A water bottle is important. Be sure to take it on rides of 5 miles or more. Use it at least every 15 minutes if the weather is hot. Dehydration occurs before you feel thirsty and can be a serious health hazard. If you're just starting a cycling program, or if you're planning your first ride of 20 miles or more, tell your doctor and listen to what (s)he has to say. Ride 10 miles or more three times a week on non-consecutive days. This will maintain your aerobic fitness. Keep a cadence of 60 to 70 pedal revolutions per minute and shift down for even the smallest hills, when riding against the wind, or if you get short of breath. This takes the pressure off your knees and keeps them from getting sore or injured.

Points to Ponder:

- Aerobic exercise can be enjoyable.
- Exercise clears the mind.
- Enjoyable exercise lifts the spirits
- Exercise dulls (or eliminates) pain.
- Health and safety considerations are important.
- You can start bicycling when you're older — but check with your doctor first.

29. Skating and Skiing

A 10-year-old boy, whose all-wood skis have only a leather strap across the toe for a harness, cuts a cross section from a discarded inner tube. Slipped around his heel and under the toes of his boots, it keeps the boot from sliding out of the strap: the forerunner of the cable harness! His few skiing experiences are not happy ones. He attempts to tag along with his brother, who is 4-and-a-half years older, and the other older boys. He has a hard time keeping up and feels very unwanted.

A 13-year-old high school junior, desperate for spending money, takes a part-time job selling tickets for public skating. It pays 50 cents for 2 hours work. There is still an hour of skating time after he closes the ticket window. So he spends 3 evening's pay on a pair of used skates — and finds the first sport he can really enjoy.

It's early November. An-80-year-old-man climbs into the overhead closet in the garage of his condominium. He has already stored his Windsurfer and sailboat for the winter. It's time to get down the ice skates, the cross-country skis and the downhill skis.

Skating.

One of the great advantages of living in Minnesota is the ready availability of these exhilarating, aerobic sports. When the roads get snowy, or the daytime temperature fails to reach 40°, I hang the bike up for the winter. A few weeks later White Bear Lake freezes over. We are fortunate: Right in front of our condo, White Bear Lake has a wide, shallow shelf. This shelf acquires the two inches of ice needed to support an adult on skates long before the rest of the lake freezes over. There is a unique thrill and exhilaration in skating on this clear, smooth ice. But many people consider it dangerous, so it has few devotees. What a pity to miss this fantastic experience! The worst you'd suffer if you broke through—I never have in 70 years—would be some cold, wet legs and perhaps a few bruises.

In 1992 Doris and I went to a luncheon open to all alumni of White Bear High School. There were about 100 of us there. As I talked to various women, it seemed as if half them said "I used to skate with Stanley"—perhaps that was a bigger part of my life than I had remembered!

Cross-Country Skiing.

The skating lasts until the snow comes. That's the signal to get out the cross-country skis. This highly aerobic sport exercises the whole body—as mildly or as vigorously as you want. What a fabulous way to view the winter countryside close at hand! Crosscountry skiing is enjoyable at almost any temperature (down to about -10° wind chill) because you generate more than enough body heat to keep you warm. Wear light, well-ventilated, layered clothing to help avoid generating so much body heat that you perspire. If that happens, hurry home and put on dry clothing.

Many people put their skis in the car and head for groomed ski trails. I am fortunate in having two golf courses within two miles with a lake between them and our condo. So, most of the time, I just put the skis on in the front yard and take off from there. Cross country skiing almost cost me my marriage— before it had occurred! I had met Doris in September 1934, and we saw much of each other for the next 4 months. One Saturday in January of 1935 I was trying to think of something we could do together that didn't cost money. I skied to her house (about a mile) and asked her if she would like to go skiing with me. Somehow, the very idea struck her the wrong way and she slammed the door in my face! I was so hurt that I didn't go near her house for a year.

Downhill Skiing.

Downhill (Alpine) skiing is not aerobic when done in Minnesota, where a typical vertical drop is about 300 feet. I regularly make one trip a year to Vail, Colorado with a group of doctors from United Hospital. Some of them are experts; but many are intermediates like me. Although the area is very large (several square miles), I can ski it all without a map. It is great fun to be the guide for those in the group who have skied it less often or not at all. Most years I find time to work in another trip, usually with Bev and her family, or with Jan and Loren. At one time or another I have skied with all of my children, mostly in Colorado. These trips have brought close associations and fond memories. Skiers over 70 receive complimentary lift tickets at Vail and many other ski areas (one of the many compensations of age!). I have skied most of the Colorado areas, but Vail is my favorite.

Sheer Terror.

When George was in high school, in 1958, he asked me to drive him to Trollhaugen (a ski area about 30 miles from St. Paul). I decided I wanted to be more than a chauffeur, so I bought some used ski equipment at a church auction. Not willing to spend money on lessons, I tried to teach myself. Looking down from the top of the 300-foot hill terrified me! Through a series of falls and traverses (going diagonally across the face of the hill to make the descent more gradual) I managed to get to the bottom. It was not a particularly enjoyable experience. I had no sense of being in control and couldn't seem to turn where I wanted to.

After a few such tense outings, a friend sold me a pair of very short skis. They were about 30 inches long. What a marvelous feeling to go down the hill and know that I could go where I wanted — not where those darn long skis wanted to go! Later that winter George lent my beloved short skis to a friend who lost them. But by then I felt ready for something longer and rented a pair of 6 foot metal skis. With the confidence and turning skills I had gained on the shorties, I found these most enjoyable. My Alpine skiing career had finally begun. For a period in the '70's some ski schools taught using skis of graduated length, but that approach has gone out of style.

How Wrong Can Fathers Be!

The following season I bought new skis. George had his driver's license and was off on his own, so I began to take the rest of our children to local ski areas. Rick became an expert skier without ever having a formal lesson. Mary and Jan quickly became comfortable on skis, but it didn't seem to be the sport for Bev. I can remember suggesting that she didn't have to ski: there were tennis, horseback riding, and other enjoyable sports. Some time later George invited her to go to Afton Alps, where he was then on the ski patrol. There she met a young instructor named Tim Kohl who gave her more lessons than I could ever have afforded, and she became the most beautiful skier in the family. How wrong fathers can be!

The Mountains.

We began to make annual family skiing trips to Colorado around 1960. The first one was to Aspen where we skied with a friend, Ed Childs, and his son Rick. I vividly remember taking my first look at those huge mountain slopes and feeling the return of the terror I had before my first run at Trollhaugen. A lesson helped; but I was still quite tentative. The tension and the effort of trying to keep up with my family were exhausting. The pain in my thighs was excruciating. I could hardly wait until evening to climb into a hot bath (hot tubs were to come later). Some fun!

It was Bev who finally persuaded me to let the skis run a little faster, so that the turns came more easily. Between her sophomore and junior years at the University of Colorado Bev spent two years as a ski instructor at Vail. She was the first female member of the Rocky Mountain Ski Instructors Association, and a marvelous instructor. She used to get the VIP's for private lessons. She was, by far, the best instructor I ever had. She could diagnose and articulate my problems, and do it in such a constructive, encouraging way that it made the process enjoyable and rewarding. (Is this the same little girl I thought would never learn to ski?!)

With Bev's help, mountain skiing became a relaxed, exhilarating experience. There are few experiences that can match the sheer joy and beauty of being on a snow-covered mountain at 11,000 feet in bright sunshine and clear air under an incredibly deep blue sky. Cruising down an intermediate slope in wide, sweeping turns with the wind whistling past your poles and your ears is a transcending sensation that is well nigh incomparable.

I still ski as well as I ever did, although I may stop more often on the way down the mountain to enjoy the scenery (and to let my legs recover!). I know this won't last forever, but I'll surely enjoy it while it does!

Points to Ponder

- It is never too late to start your skiing (or skating) career — but check with your doctor first.

- Lessons are a good investment.

- The best way to survive winter is to enjoy it.

- If your health is reasonably good, you can enjoy skiing and skating, regardless of your age.

- The more aerobic sports you enjoy, the easier it is to stay fit.

30. Racquet Sports

> *"The secret of winning at tennis*
> *is in the choice of one's opponents."*
> —Stan Hill

A-12-year old boy goes to a school tennis court with his father. Their racquets are old and in poor shape. The balls are dead. The boy knows nothing about the game and the father very little more. Neither finds it very enjoyable. None of his (few) friends play tennis. The experience is not repeated.

Sometime in the 1950's I started playing squash and racquetball at the St. Paul Athletic Club. Then, when I joined the White Bear Yacht Club (in the mid-60's), I started playing tennis regularly. I would go to the Saturday morning men's opens. In this format you change partners and opponents after each set of doubles. The pro marks individual wins and losses on the score board. At first, if I was not the poorest player, I was close to it. The pros were good at matching us up so that the scores were usually fairly even; and the better players were good sports about it. The same was true at the Friday evening mixed doubles sessions. There you kept the same partner all evening. One memorable evening the pro matched me with Dorothy Sanborn, who was rated as the best woman player in the group. That tells you how I was rated! We won the event. Dorothy must have been good!

Improvement.

Gradually my game improved until it was respectable, and I no longer felt self-conscious about the quality of my play. With that improvement came relaxation, more victories, and a much higher level of enjoyment of tennis.

The St. Paul Athletic Club was right across the street from my Minnesota Mutual office. After I left Minnesota Mutual in 1969, it became much less convenient to play squash or racquetball. So I joined the White Bear Tennis Club, which had 5 indoor courts then. Playing tennis year-round did wonders for my game.

Like my skiing, my tennis has never been better. I play regularly in a weekly group and substitute frequently in several other groups. In the summer, sailing and biking cut into the tennis time, so I play only about half as much.

31. Sailing

"There is simply nothing half so important
as messing around in boats"
— Author Unknown

A 9-year-old boy has just moved to White Bear Lake (a suburb of St. Paul, Minnesota). He has no friends and is too poor to own a bicycle. A frequent summer pastime for him is to walk a mile and a half to Johnson Boat Works and watch everything that goes on. Watching the sailboats, as sails were hoisted and they glided silently away, particularly enthralled him, even though he knew in his heart he would never have enough money to own one. . . . . .

The smell of new cedar and spruce lumber still brings back powerful memories of those pleasant hours. Sailing has brought so much joy and sharing to our family that you will find three chapters devoted to it. Once considered a rich man's sport, it is now available to almost anyone with any discretionary income.

Our First Sailboat.

It was the summer of 1953, just a couple of months after we had moved into our lake-front home in Mahtomedi (on the East shore of White Bear Lake). I came home towing a 16-foot sailboat behind our small fishing boat. When Doris saw it, the conversation went something like this:

"What's that?"

"It's a sailboat."

"We don't need a sailboat with an expensive house to pay for."

"But it's a family sport — something all of the children will enjoy."

"I bet — it's something for you to enjoy."

Our children will have my everlasting gratitude; all five of them became sailors and racing skippers. For a number of years we owned two sailboats as well as a motorboat for water skiing, watching races and towing sailboats home when the wind died. After a few years, the novelty of water skiing seemed to wear off for most of our children, but their strong interest in sailing continued as long as they lived at home. Many summer evenings I would go down to the dock to make sure the boats were secure. I knew the sailboats had been out for hours; there would be cobwebs on the motor boat hoist.

The Mystique of Sailing.

As anyone who sails will tell you, there are elements of mystique and fascination with sailing that don't exist with any other sport or pastime. It's hard to explain, but easy to describe. The quiet movement through the water, the fascination of trimming the sails to be properly in tune with the wind, the satisfaction of harnessing nature's energy, truly brings peace to the soul.

Ocean Sailing.

In 1962 Archie (Mac) McCauley (President of the North American Reassurance Company of New York) introduced me to the joys of salt-water sailing in keel boats. Mac had a 25-footer which he kept at the American Yacht Club in Rye. It was my first experience with a sailboat that had a motor. My first few trips in this boat in the western end of Long Island Sound excited and fascinated me. Mac used to call me a "crazy sailor" because I would take the boat up to the dock with sails alone (if the conditions were right). He had never seen a boat brought alongside the dock with the mainsail up and the motor turned off.

The America's Cup Races.

In 1964 Mac invited George and me to watch the America's Cup Races with him from his boat. We left the American Yacht Club early in the morning three days before the first race. The east wind was blowing right down Long Island Sound, in precisely the opposite direction from where we wanted to go. That meant we had to "beat our way" (sail a zigzag course, since you can't sail directly into the wind) all the way up the sound. By evening we were only as far as Port Washington — about 30 miles from our start! The second day the wind was stronger; but still on the nose (blowing from the direction we were headed). The 40-mile-an-hour head wind and the 5-foot waves made progress impossible; so we went back into the harbor and waited for the wind to abate. By noon it had subsided a little, but progress was still slow and uncomfortable. Mac and George were both seasick, so I was on the tiller until dusk — and enjoyed every minute of it! That night we made harbor at Nattituck, a small inlet on Long Island, still less than two thirds of the way to Block Island, our destination. The third day was beautiful; but the wind grew quite light. By afternoon we had to use the motor, and still didn't make Montauk harbor (on the eastern tip of Long Island) until almost midnight. Motoring across a glassy Atlantic under a full moon was totally enchanting.

An Incredible Sight.

The first race began at noon the next day. We left Montauk at daybreak and sailed directly for the race course (some 10 miles southeast of Newport, Rhode Island) arriving there well after the race had started. What an absolutely incredible sight! There were thousands of beautiful spectator yachts, both power boats and sailing craft, ranging up to well over 100 feet in length. They made a line to the horizon as they cruised in close formation and watched the progress of the two contenders. That spectator fleet makes up a boat show that has no equal, and virtually upstages the contenders for both excitement and beauty. It was only when we approached that spectacular convoy that I realized how small and slow we really were. There were no other sailboats as small as ours.

The races usually finish by 4:00 PM. At our cruising speed of 5 knots it would take us until dusk to return to the Block Island harbor. Then we'd have to be up at daybreak to make it back to the race course for that day's noon start. They were long days; but the novelty and excitement of it were worth it.

Bare Hull Charters.

In 1967 I did my first bare hull charter (you rent the boat with no captain). It was an old but fast 41-footer. We made it from City Island Yacht Club (the extreme western end of Long Island Sound) to Point Judith Harbor of Refuge (just across Naragansett Bay from Newport) in one day. It was a tremendously exciting two weeks for me. But you don't just decide to captain a yacht and go do it. Thirteen years of sailing on White Bear Lake plus dozens of hours of study plus several trips with Mac McCauley were a bare prerequisite. The best book on this subject is Chapman's *Piloting,*

Seamanship and Small Boat Handling[11]. This preparation enables you to avoid embarrassing, costly, and even serious, mistakes in navigation, as well as to minimize the risk of damage to your boat—or others—and injury to yourself and your passengers.

Each America's Cup series (about every 3 years) from then through 1980 found me as captain of my own charter. My family always had first choice to crew. When they couldn't go, I would invite friends to fill out the crew — usually six including the captain. Daughter Mary made three of the trips and her husband Dave made two. They both developed a great love of the sport and bought their own yacht in Panama, where they have lived since 1973.

The Caribbean.

In 1973 a group of men from Control Data chartered a beautiful 43-foot ketch (a two-masted sailboat) to sail in the Virgin Islands. None of them had any ocean sailing experience. Through a strange set of circumstances I became their captain, even though I didn't know any of them. I had never sailed the Virgins, but I picked the brains of several people who had. We had a delightful 10 days sailing and snorkeling around these beautiful islands. We brought scuba gear along, but the water was so clear you could see down 100 feet, so we forsook the scuba gear in favor of snorkeling. Among the most memorable sights were the incredible beauty and profusion of fish and coral in Dead Man's Cove on Peter Island; the wreck of the Rhone (a British mail packet that sank in 60 feet of water in the 1860's off the north coast of Salt Island); the baths (underwater caves) on Virgin Gorda; and the perfect white sand beaches along the north coast of St. Johns.

Offshore Sailing.

In 1983 Mary and Dave took delivery in Connecticut of a new 37-footer in time to watch the Cup races in mid-

September. They invited me to watch the races and then help them sail the boat to Panama. Unfortunately I came down with a "bad case of indispensability" a week or so before I would have had to leave. I was just installing a health claim administration system for one of my clients; and it didn't seem right to absent myself for four or five weeks during that critical time. So I skipped the Cup races and arrived just in time to set sail for Bermuda with Mary, Dave and my neighbor Tom Gunderson.

Seasickness.

Not getting my "sea legs" before we started that seven day off shore trip (sailing 24 hours a day on the open ocean) was a serious mistake. I was seasick the whole 7 days — my first-ever experience with this most unpleasant and disabling illness! We were on the heels of a hurricane; the sea was still rough, and every night we would have brief squalls. The helmsman could hear them coming and would yell "all hands on deck." The wind would blow 40 to 50 miles an hour, seemingly from every direction. Then, almost incredibly, within 5 minutes after we got the sails down the wind would abate. We would put up full sail and be on our way again.

These nightly interruptions, the constant noise of waves breaking against the hull, and the rough motion all conspire to put much stress on the body. We were all wrung out by the time we reached Bermuda and ready for a few days of rest and relaxation.

Two Ways to See Bermuda.

The most hazardous part of our trip was riding mopeds in Bermuda. Keeping to the left took constant concentration, particularly when making right turns at busy intersections. One of the local men told me 12 tourists had died on mopeds in the previous 10 months. But it was an excellent way to explore the interior of this fascinating British Island.

There was a safer and more delightful way to explore the coastline of the harbor we were in. With Dave's permission I had bought a sailboard in Connecticut and brought it aboard with us. With it we could visit parts of this fascinating and beautiful harbor area that were inaccessible in our larger boat. There was no concern with running aground in shallow water or getting in and out of tight places.

The Turks and Caicos Islands.

The next seven days offshore to South Caicos Island (about 110 miles north of the Dominican Republic) were a little easier. The sea wasn't quite as rough, and I wore a scopolamine patch. This patch gave me a bad taste in the mouth and a general feeling of discomfort, but that was preferable to the seasickness. I learned later that many people my age cannot tolerate these patches.

Again it was time to break out the sailboard. Cruising along the shoreline just before sunset, I realized that the shadow below my board was not from the sun. It was brown and about six feet long! I sailed back to our boat and described it to Dave. He said, "Oh, that's a nurse shark; they don't bother humans." My reaction was: "You know that, and now I know that; but does he know that?!"

The following day we sailed to Grand Turk Island (about 20 miles) and picked up Ross Robertson, an Australian friend of Mary and Dave who replaced me as crew. It was time to go home. I was glad to have had the experience, but I find coastal sailing much more enjoyable.

Offshore Racing.

The next year, 1984, Dave invited me to crew for him in the race from Colon (the Atlantic end of the Panama Canal) to San Andres Island (about 250 miles northwest). San Andres Island is due east of Nicaragua, but is part of Colombia. The local yacht club members had only Sunfish (a 14-foot sailboat with just enough cockpit to put your feet in). They loved our big yachts and treated us like royalty. We took them sailing, and many of them got seasick!

Becoming a Licensed Captain.

In 1985 Fred Brewster, a wealthy St. Paulite, gave his beautiful 43-foot ketch to the St. Paul YMCA. They used it to begin a sailing program on Lake Superior. Unfortunately, they had only one captain for a 100-day program—a classic burnout situation. So I volunteered as an alternate captain. Then I learned that the Y's insurance contract required the captain to have a Coast Guard captain's license. The exams one must pass to obtain this license require hundreds of hours of study and a great deal of memory work. Many people try more than once before they make it. For example, for the navigation exam, you must learn the meaning of over 150 light patterns, and dozens of whistle codes. I burned a lot of midnight oil that winter!

Taking the exams was an experience in itself. A Coast Guard ensign came up from St. Louis to administer them. We had to take the toughest one (all the memory work!) first. If we failed that one, we didn't even get to take the rest. It contained 20 multiple-choice questions, of which 18 had to be answered correctly. As often happens, four or five of the questions seemed to have more than one right answer, and I was a very concerned guy. While I sat waiting for the ensign to score it, I found myself huddled in a chair with both my arms and my legs crossed: eloquent body-english testifying to my fear and anxiety! The other exams concerned the practical aspects of navigation, boat handling and seamanship and were a piece of cake. For my first voyage the Y had no passengers, so I recruited five of my friends as paying guests: Larry and Jackie Klopp, Stan and Wiz Fiorito and their 16-year-old son Stan. I also invited my 16-year-old niece to join us. If you want a boy of 16 to enjoy a sailing trip, invite a girl the same age — and vice versa! What a great way to cruise the beautiful Apostle Islands

—at no expense—and to feel you are doing a service at the same time!

After I had made four such trips, the Y found they could afford to have another paid captain and split the duties evenly between them. They would have made the same arrangement with me, but I wasn't willing to devote that many hours.

My Very Own Keel Boat.

In 1989 I bought a 22-foot Capri (a model made by Catalina yachts) to sail on White Bear Lake. It is a great boat in which to take out friends and family. It has a large, comfortable cockpit, and it can be safely and enjoyably sailed in breezes as light as 4 miles an hour up to winds of almost 35 miles an hour. The jib (foresail) is roller-furling: You can rig it for sailing merely by pulling on one line (rope) and furl it by pulling another. It sails well on the jib alone — or even part of the jib — when there's too much wind to raise the mainsail.

The cabin is laid out very efficiently and can sleep four adults in comfort. Rick, Satoko, and grandsons John and Enoch and I have spent more than one pleasant night on it on White Bear Lake.

In October 1989, after a busy summer on the lake, I took the boat to the St. Croix River near Stillwater and launched it there. Each day, for the next 4 days, different members of the family joined me for a day of sailing down the St. Croix and the Mississippi. On the fourth afternoon we hauled it out at Wabasha (about 80 miles down-river from St. Paul). Everyone had such a good time we repeated the trip in 1990.

The Pleasure Continues.

The pleasure in sailing this beautiful, versatile boat continues. It's a great experience to share with friends and family. They enjoy it whether they are experienced sailors or novices. Even the first-timers quickly lose their apprehension, and seem to relax and enjoy it. It's a great way to return a favor. I have even invited prospects for substantial charitable contributions as guests. Rick and his family (Satoko, Enoch and John) are my most frequent guests because they enjoy it so much. One or two nights during the summer we go aboard after dinner and sail until long after dark. Yet it isn't really dark, even on a moonless night. One's eyes adjust miraculously as the light fades to blackness, the stars shine brilliantly, and the surroundings take on a new beauty. The mystique and quiet make these hours a precious time for closeness and peaceful contemplation.

32. Sailboat Racing

On a sunny, breezy June Saturday a 13-year-old boy sits alone on the shore of White Bear Lake. Scores of sailboats glide quietly in a stately dance as they await the starting gun for their afternoon race. The boy knows nothing of the intricacies of racing, but he is quietly fascinated by the mystery and beauty of the starting procedure. How wonderful it must be to take part in such a wonderful event — but that is another world of which he cannot hope to be a part.

In 1954 George became our family's first racing skipper, using the old Class X (16-foot) sailboat that I had towed home the previous year. The following winter we discovered quite a bit of dry rot in the hull. I had neither the skill to repair it nor the money to have it done. So the following spring I attempted to put a layer of fiberglass cloth over the exterior of the wood. In trying to make a smooth finish, I used about three times as much resin as I should have.

The result was the heaviest boat in the X fleet! We had named the boat *Zephyr*; but it quickly acquired the nickname *Old Ironsides*. It wasn't very competitive except in the heaviest winds; but we declared it to be the safest boat on the lake, and George stuck with it for two more years.

A Brand New Boat!

By then George had learned a lot about racing and, not surprisingly, was lobbying strongly for a new boat. In 1957 I felt we could afford to take this great step. George and Hurricane justified our investment. He and his sailing friend Harvey Mills became the two best skippers in the White Bear X fleet (a class for skippers 16 years old and younger). Harvey seemed to have a slight edge in the local competition (he had started racing when he was 9), but George had the better record in national regattas. One year he brought home a national fourth place trophy and made us all very proud.

Once a week a parent became the skipper with the regular skipper as crew. Starting in 1954, George and I did well in this series and brought home more than our share of trophies. The thrill of competing (and occasionally winning) added a whole new dimension of enjoyment to an already enjoyable sport. Unfortunately this series lost its popularity and was abandoned about 1958—before I had the privilege of sharing it with our younger children.

A Succession of Skippers.

We made it a family rule that, if you wanted to earn your coveted place as skipper of Hurricane, you had to crew for your next older sibling. Although this created some tension, it worked well in many respects: It provided readily available, reliable crew, simplified the logistics (and reduced expenses!) of regatta trips, and provided the best available training. White Bear Yacht Club had no sailing school then, and private lessons were out of the question financially. Jan and Mary each took their turn, first as crew and then as skipper. Bev was not that interested in sailing, so Rick got an early start.

Another Sailboat.

I became hooked on racing through the parent-child series, but I couldn't justify buying another boat until George turned 17 and could no longer compete in the X class. That year, 1959, we bought a new Class C (20-foot) boat with the idea that I would be the skipper and George would crew for me. I had crewed for a friend, Dr. John James, for a few years on his C, and felt I was ready to join the ranks of the regular skippers. After his illustrious career as an X boat skipper, George didn't find crewing for me to be a mountain top experience, but he did stick it out for one summer. Then he had a chance to be the skipper of Mandy Moles' C boat (Mandy was a girl about his age who lived on Manitou Island); that was an offer he couldn't refuse. After that, Jan and Mary both crewed for me, but we never set the world on fire.

Judging.

By then I was on the board of directors of the Yacht Club's Sailing Division. For many years Gene Markoe, a long time White Bear resident, had been our head judge, and a wonderful one he was. Gene was now in his 80's; we were concerned about his doing the job alone, but didn't have the budget to hire an assistant. So I volunteered to become his unpaid assistant and continue until he was ready to retire. This commitment involved Wednesday evenings and most of the day every Saturday and Sunday. The two years I spent on the lake with Gene were very enjoyable and educational. I learned the fine points of setting a course of the proper length for each class of boat, correctly oriented with the wind direction, and so arranged so that the three different classes of boats didn't interfere with each other. In addition a judge must know how to set the start and finish lines with careful regard for the wind direction, fire the sequence of starting guns, and display the proper starting flags and course signals. Then (s)he must record the finishes, hear and rule on protests, and know when and how to postpone, cancel or discontinue races in the event of adverse weather conditions. Finally the judge must be able to drive and care for the motorboat used for judging, and take care of the starting gun, signal flags and the buoys used to mark the course.

After Gene retired we hired Bob and Doug Zak as judges, and I had the privilege of training them. They had both been outstanding Class X racing skippers and became excellent judges.

Scorekeeping: A New Career for Doris.

Gene had also been our scorekeeper. Keeping track of how every boat finished in six different classes totalling over 100 boats, each racing three times a week from the middle of May until Labor day, is quite a task. The scorekeeper must also assign points for each finish position, total these and rank the totals to determine the final positions in each of six series into which the season is divided. There are numerous other complications that are beyond the scope of this book.

It seemed to me that Doris had everything it took to be an ideal scorekeeper. She had a keen interest in the sport, dedication to any commitment she made, a facility with numbers, and an ability to keep neat, meticulous records. So she consented to try it, in about 1963, I believe, and continued to do so for the next 30 years! Until 1987 she would cover the entire wall of our back porch all summer with score cards filled out in her neat hand. The outer door was always unlocked, and the sailors would stop by to see how they were doing.

Automation Strikes Again.

When we sold our house, a cabinet was built on an outside wall of the sailor house to display the scores. To make the results more compact we had to computerize the scoring process. So I became the assistant scorekeeper in charge of pushing the keys on the computer.

Although Doris never was a skipper, she crewed for me in a special race each year (appropriately called the "Mr. and Mrs. Race"). She is listed in the White Bear Yacht Club 100th Anniversary History for having won this race one year. She became a keen spectator of the sport. During regattas she would invite visitors to share our front lawn. Many of them have remarked to me on the clarity of her running commentary.

When she retired from scorekeeping in 1992, she received very generous recognition at the annual awards dinner in September. This recognition included a standing ovation and the gift of a beautiful, large, framed, colored etching of the schooner America.

George has succeeded Doris as scorekeeper, and so this important function continues into the second generation.

Our Class E: "The Queen of the Scows."

One day in the fall of 1965 George announced excitedly that he had found a wonderful buy on a used Class E boat. These beautiful 28-foot boats are the top racing class on many inland lakes, including White Bear. I had admired their sleek speed for many years, but never really thought we could afford one. Jan and Mary had lost interest in racing our Class C, so after a great deal of thought and family discussion, we decided to sell the C and buy the E.

The Family Crew.

It became evident very quickly that George's keen mind and ability to make lightning-fast decisions were what was needed to make a competitive racing skipper. Rick gave up his X boat career a year early to "hold jib" (tend the forward sail), and I agreed to "fly the 'chute." That involves tending the two lines that control the big spinnaker that we hoist when sailing downwind (in the same direction as the wind is blowing). This position also "flies the reacher" (controls a smaller spinnaker used in going crosswise to the wind), and "works boards." These boats draw just a few inches of water, and they have a large aluminum-alloy board built into each side of the hull to keep the boat moving forward instead of sideways. Every time you tack (turn so that the wind strikes the sails on the other side), you must raise one board and lower the other.

Since these boats have no keel, the crew must "hike out" to keep the boat from capsizing: They extend their upper bodies outside the windward side of the heeling boat, putting their ankles under a strap to keep from falling overboard. In the heavier winds either Jan or Mary would be our "fourth."

Jib Men

Jib men are very important. The jib sail must be trimmed (pulled in or let out) just the right amount. This amount changes quickly and frequently as the wind and the boat change relative positions. When heavy gusts hit, it must be released quickly to prevent a capsize. Rick ended his career as jib man after one season, partly because he didn't like the tensions that can arise in a crew during a race (especially when the skipper is your brother). We recruited our good friend Rod Weddell to replace him. He had a wonderful sense of humor and could often break the tension with a light remark. If he couldn't, he would seemingly ignore it. Rod was a great jib man for 14 years, until 3M transferred him to Europe.

We were equally fortunate to find John Taylor, his successor. Of John, his mother says: "If I were stranded on a deserted island, John is the person I would like to have with me." Conscientious, bright, analytical, helpful, and easy to get along with, are the words that come to mind. John knows most of the many fine points of racing and is a real delight to have aboard. When I miss a move, he will quietly perform it for me without saying a word.

Now that John is the father of two small boys, he finds racing three times a week too time consuming. After Rod returned from Europe about four years ago, we had a wonderful arrangement in which he and John share the races. In 1993 illness overtook Rod and, for some little time he had been unable to sail. Rod died two days before Christmas 1993. He was a wonderful husband, father and friend. We all miss him. In the winter of 1992-93 George acquired new neighbors, Jim and Nancy Hertel. They came from Lake Minnetonka (a beautiful lake west of Minneapolis) and had been bemoaning their separation from the Class E Scow on which they had sailed there. Great was their excitement in April of 1993 when they saw George turn into his driveway towing an E-boat. Now Jim is the alternate jib man and Nancy is a marvelous fourth.

Tension Aboard.

Most racing skippers become very tense during a race and tend to yell at their crew. Being yelled at by my son was a new experience for me. At first I found it extremely difficult to accept. I would become angry and yell back, particularly when I felt I was criticized unfairly. Gradually I realized that I couldn't control George's yelling, but I could control my emotions. The yelling was worst when George had made a mistake that cost us our competitive position. By understanding his frustration, and recognizing that he obtained relief by venting his feelings, I could make my anger disappear.

"Not in My Contract"

Occasionally, however, I felt that the criticism became

riding, and that accepting this was "not in my contract." After the race I would tell George quietly that I sailed for pleasure, his actions had taken the pleasure out of it, and he could find a buyer for my half of the boat. He would say he didn't want to do that, and things would be better for the rest of the season. Fortunately this happened only three times during the early part of our long racing career. Recently, each year has seen less tension than the year before. I think we are both mellowing . . . . .

National Records.

George and I raced a Class E scow together for 26 seasons. We believe this is a national record for a father-son team, since these combinations seem to be particularly fragile. We also have a national record for the age of the spinnaker man. In 1991, with a new boat, new sails, good sailing, and a bit of luck, we managed to place second in a national regatta. This achievement brought us an invitation to the Blue Chip Regatta (held each year in Pewaukee, Wisconsin) to which only top-flight sailors are invited. Buddy Melges (an Olympic Gold Medalist in sailing) attended regularly before he got into America's Cup competition. Another regular attendant is Gordy Bowers, America's Olympic Sailing Coach in 1989. In 1991 Gary Jobson was the special guest skipper. Gary made a name for himself as a successful ocean racing skipper, but he became a household word when he was a color announcer on ESPN for the America's Cup races in 1990.

A Standing Ovation.

We were badly outclassed at the Blue Chip Regatta and ended up last, but it was a great experience. Besides the usual fun, excitement, and fellowship of a regatta, the awards dinner was something special. Gary Jobson gave a most entertaining talk and presented an exceptionally fascinating film of Americas Cup sailing. A group of sailors had raised a couple of thousand dollars and presented Bob

Allen with a beautiful memorial to his son, Kenny. Kenny had died the previous year in a tragic boating accident on Lake Minnetonka. It was very touching. Bob has raced scows since he was eight or nine. Bob's parents, Ken and Barb, are marvelously warm-hearted people. They have opened their lovely home on Lake Minnetonka to sailors ever since our children were small. All of their sons are champion sailors. One son, Bill, crewed for Olympic Gold Medalist Buddy Melges. Ken and Barb were there for the presentation to Bob. Following that, to my total surprise, I was given a standing ovation for being the oldest (by far) active sailor in the group! I was overwhelmed.

Early Retirement.

George and I continued to race three times a week every summer until 1992, when I took "early retirement." I had done plenty of pelvic curls during the winter to keep the stomach muscles in shape for the "hiking out." But there are other physical demands that I found myself less and less able to meet fully. One of these demands occurs after the occasional capsize: raising myself almost 6 feet vertically from the lower projecting leeboard to the upper one. Other requirements include a general quickness in hooking the control lines to the spinnaker, and in pulling the spinnaker down as we approach the next racing buoy, and the ability to raise and lower the lee boards in the split seconds available. I never wanted to put George in the position of feeling he would like a younger crew, and being hesitant to say anything, so, in May 1992, I told him I felt he should have a younger, stronger gorilla in my place.

Points to Ponder.
- Sailboat racing combines the pleasures of sailing with the excitement of a competitive sport.
- Sailboat racing can now be a relatively low-budget sport.
- The upper age limit is much higher than most people

think. As long as you are healthy and have the physical strength, keep doing it.

- Sailboat racing is an absorbing, character-building sport for children, and teaches them many physical, mental and social skills.

- Under expert supervision (i. e. good sailing schools), children can start sailing as early as age five or six.

33. Windsurfing

A visitor to Newport in 1973 sees some athletic-looking young men scooting around the harbor on surf boards. They are not propelled by the surf but by a sail whose mast and wishbone boom they hold in their two hands. He thinks, "What a fascinating sport, but only for the young and muscular." The following year he sees the same performance on White Bear Lake and has the same thought.

In 1980 I helped a neighbor, Pete Santee, move a boat hoist across White Bear Lake. To thank me he invited me to use his windsurfer. My first thought was similar to those I'd had in 1973 and 1974, but I didn't want to refuse Pete's kind offer. After much falling and experimentation I managed to get a few short rides. What an exhilarating experience it was! I was hooked!

My 66th Birthday Present.

In July 1980 I said to Doris, "I know what you can get me for my birthday." She assented. I got not only the windsurfer, but a book on how to windsurf[3]. It was late that summer before I could stay on the board in heavy winds. In the meantime I spent scores of hours falling off the darn thing, clambering back on, and getting the mast and sail up out of the water. But with the practice came confidence, longer rides and the marvelous feeling of having mastered a difficult sport.

Learning to Sail Dry.

The numerous falls and dunkings exacerbated an existing allergy to the algae in the lake water. A malaise like hay fever followed each windsurfing session. By 1981 I had developed sufficient skill that I could go for an entire session without falling. I thought, "If one session, why not all summer?" To increase the motivation to stay dry, I began to sail in leisure clothes instead of a swim suit.

One day I carried some business papers across the lake to my friend Hod Irvine's summer home. This incident developed into a rumor that I windsurfed in a business suit. That rumor resulted in:

Unexpected National Publicity.

In August 1988 I answered the telephone to hear:

"This is Tom Hollyman, I'm a photographer from New York doing a project for *Town and Country Magazine.* I hear you windsurf in a business suit."

"I have a hard time living up to my image!"

"Would you do me a favor? Put on a white shirt, a black bow tie, a dark blue blazer, slacks and a yachting cap, and sail out on the lake. I'd like to take some pictures."

"Do you really want me to do that?!"

He did, so we arranged a time and an area of the lake for the photo shoot. When Doris saw me starting out in my outfit carrying my windsurfer, she exclaimed, "I hope no one sees you!" As I approached the chosen area Tom approached on a pontoon boat with his assistant:

"I don't believe it!"

"Well, you asked for it!"

An hour and a half and scores of pictures later Tom exclaimed,

"That's great! What can I do to thank you?"

"Take this cotton-pickin' blazer for me. I'm dying of the heat!"

The best of the pictures appeared as a full page in the July 1989 issue of *Town and Country*. The issue sold out in the Twin cities because of the eight pages of beautiful pictures of White Bear Lake and some of its better known residents. Doris and I received scores of comments about the picture. All I could think of was Doris' hope that no one would see me.

A Frank Exclamation.

I get numerous reactions about windsurfing at my age. Late one beautiful August afternoon I sailed by one of the many sailboats on White Bear Lake. The skipper asked,

"Aren't you a little young for that sport?"

"Yes, but I'm getting older."

Another similar evening I sailed under a small bridge that connects a beautiful residential island in White Bear Lake with the rest of the city. As I came out the other side into the bright sunlight, I startled an 18-year old man who was fishing from the bridge. As his eyes widened in startled surprise, he exclaimed,

"Shit, what an ancient dude!"

Points to Ponder.

- You can learn to windsurf at any age if you're in reasonably good health, weigh at least 65 pounds, and have enough motivation.
- Windsurfing is a great toner for the upper body.
- Don't try to learn without assistance: read a good book and/or take lessons.

- Women, as a rule, learn more readily than men. They seem to have a better sense of balance.

- Most states require that you wear a life jacket (Personal Flotation Device). Minnesota law considers the board itself to be a PFD.

- Because of the moderate difficulty, mastering the sport will give you great satisfaction and improve your self image.

34. Water Volleyball and Other Continuation Sports

A 10-year-old boy with no friends or other boys in the neighborhood finds the summers long and lonely. To amuse himself he finds a discarded wheel from a coaster wagon, nails a short stick across the end of a longer one, and learns to roll the wheel with the stick. He has heard the boys in school talk about the fun they had playing kick the can, capture the flag, cops and robbers, and other games. But he does not feel a part of these groups, and has no idea of how to become a part.

In 1953, shortly after I joined the St. Paul Athletic Club, I discovered the joys of water volleyball. A group of businessmen gathered in the shallow end of the swimming pool every weekday noon to play this zany game. You stand in waist deep water and play volleyball with a referee enforcing the regular rules. At that time the club was all male. So we played in the same clothes we were born in. The feelings of freedom, abandon, hilarity and teamwork combined to produce many new friendships.

After each session we would go to lunch together. I made many new friends through this very enjoyable sport. But, as I became more conscious of the need for aerobic exercise, I played more squash or racquetball and less water volleyball.

Golf, Horseshoes, Mountain Climbing, Volleyball, Hunting, Fishing, Archery.

Most people (including me) class these activities as non-aerobic. As you can readily see, I chose more aerobic sports for my own exercise. As I become unable to pursue some of my present activities, I expect to do more walking. Is sailing aerobic? Hardly, but it provides such great pleasure!

Jazz Exercise, Swimming, Water Aerobics.

These are certainly aerobic activities that can be performed as a regular activity as long you have reasonably good health. I have a definite preference for the activities described in the previous six chapters. But if you prefer one these others, go for it!

A few years ago I came home and announced:

"I just joined a jazz exercise class at Lakewood (Community College)."

"Do you realize you'll be in a class with a bunch of young girls?"

"Yes, but that's your problem!"

My interest in the class was largely the novelty, and I haven't repeated it.

Points to ponder:

- Regular (three times a week) aerobic exercise is a must for good mental and physical health at any age. It also makes weight control much easier.

- If you take your exercise in a form you really enjoy, it's much easier to do it regularly.

- Exercise is more enjoyable if you do it with someone else. I also believe it's more beneficial because of the companionship that we all need.

- Almost any continuation sport can be started at any age. But be sure to check with your doctor first and tell him what you plan to do.

- In competitive sports, look for people with about the same skill level as yours—not necessarily the same age level. My best tennis singles matches are with considerably younger people.

- The same principle applies to non-competitive sports.

- If your schedule permits, have regular times for your exercise. If not, put it on the calendar a week in advance for whatever time is appropriate.

- Try hard to maintain your program when you're out of town. Put it into your travel plans.

Seven

The Arts

"*Nature is a revelation of God;*
Art a revelation of man."
—Henry Wadsworth Longfellow

The arts have played a significant part in every civilization throughout the recorded history of humankind. Even before that, artifacts and cave drawings give mute testimony to the presence of arts in prehistoric times. I confess to a relatively late awakening to an interest in the arts, an interest that still isn't fully developed. My father had absolutely no interest in any phase of the arts. He considered them a waste of time and felt he could better spend his time and money elsewhere. Unless you included her exquisite needlework, my mother's only interest in the arts was in playing the piano. Our extreme poverty may have contributed to the absence of the arts in our life.

As in sports, interest in the arts may be either active or passive. Again, as in sports, my own interest is largely active and is currently limited. As a consequence, this section will be quite short. I included it to affirm my own appreciation of the importance of arts in our lives.

35. Music

> *"I listened, motionless and still;*
> *And, as I mounted up the hill,*
> *The music in my heart I bore,*
> *Long after it was heard no more."*
> —William Wordsworth

A six-year-old boy sits restlessly at the keyboard of his mother's square grand piano. She tries to teach him to finger the scale. He seems much more occupied in scratching his head than in playing the scale. She loses patience and explodes in a tirade of recrimination. He protests that his head itches intolerably. Her investigation reveals a bad infestation of head lice. The head lice are banished, but the piano lessons are not continued.

An eight-year-old boy is practicing the violin. The scratchy sounds that emanate are not pleasing to him, to his teacher or to his uncle, who is paying for the lessons. After a few more weeks of uninspired practice and unpromising results, the lessons are discontinued. Everyone is relieved.

An eleven-year-old boy and his 16-year-old brother play their cornet and clarinet together as they practice their band music. Both of them enjoy their participation in the school band.

A thirteen-year-old boy is disappointed in and frustrated with his best friend, who has refused to play chopsticks with him on the piano. He resolves to play the piano by himself.

In the 1920's, White Bear High School was one of the first schools in Minnesota to have a band. It was led by Harry Hauglie, who also gave group lessons to 7th and 8th graders as a kind of "farm club." Apparently I showed some promise on the cornet. In an unusual move, he suggested to my parents that they allow me to play in the High School band. They consented, and I became the youngest member of the band at age eleven, trading the borrowed cornet for a trumpet which my parents bought for me.

Playing in the band was a great source of both inspiration and enjoyment for me. I also received a good music education in the process. In the summer time the former students joined us, and we played weekly concerts in the downtown park. In 1932 I reluctantly sold my trumpet because playing it aggravated my inguinal hernia.

Playing the Piano by Ear.

My musical education in the band, together with my resolve to play the piano, started me on a long and varied career with keyboards. I made an interesting discovery. Any tune I heard, I could play on the piano. I also found that I could put the right chords with the tune, so that the result began to sound presentable. By playing in only one key I developed a fluency that made playing a new song on the piano as easy as whistling or singing it. The key I chose was six sharps (or six flats), F# (or G^b) an esoteric key rarely seen in written music. The reason for this odd choice seemed logical to me: all the black keys are in the major scale. They were easier than the white keys for untrained hands to find. Many years later I learned that Irving Berlin had made the same choice. When he had made enough money, he had a special piano built for him. It allowed him to crank the keyboard to the right or left, across the strings. That way he could play in any of the 12 keys while still pressing the piano keys as if he were playing in six sharps (flats).

After high school, I found a demand for this talent. I could play scores of popular songs for dancing, sing-alongs, or just background music. Our low standard of living did not allow the proliferation of record players we see today. Hi-fi, stereo, tape cassettes and CD's were not even in our vocabularies. I have continued to play the piano and other keyboards by ear to this day.

Piano Lessons.

While visiting the Red Cross Officers' Club in Rome, I had heard a marvelous pianist. He played Chopin's *Polonaise Militaire* magnificently. I was so inspired I resolved to play that beautiful, but difficult number. I would take piano lessons until I learned to play it, perhaps not as well as he did, but at least passably.

After I finished my actuarial exams, I sought out a piano teacher known for his success in teaching adults and told him my goal. He was intrigued. Apparently no student had approached him previously with such a specific goal. I also told him, somewhat apologetically, that I played the piano by ear. To my surprise he said, "That's wonderful! Playing by ear is a sign of musical ability."

Three years later I had achieved my goal. In addition to learning a great deal about music, I learned that playing by ear produced much more enjoyment for much less effort. Moreover, I wasn't finding the same relaxation in playing by note. So I discontinued the lessons.

Choir Singing.

When I was 9 years old I starting singing soprano in the choir of the First Presbyterian Church in White Bear Lake. I sat in the front row of the choir loft, which was separated from the pulpit and congregation only by a curtain, three feet high. I was subject to fainting spells at the time. On two different Sundays over the next two years I fainted and rolled under the curtain onto the pulpit. Two choir members carried me into a side room and revived me.

Both episodes occurred during the sermon. I never did find out just how well the sermon went over after these dramatic interruptions. I suspect there were serious discussions between the choir director and the minister as to whether I was more of a liability than an asset to the morning service. Happily, there were no more fainting spells, and I remained a choir member.

In the late 1940's Doris and I joined the First Baptist Church of St. Paul, in which she had grown up, and I joined the choir. In 1954, when we transferred to Lake Drive United Methodist Church in Mahtomedi, we both joined the choir. We continued to sing in church choirs until just a few years ago. We quit only because our heavy travel schedule makes it impractical for us attend regularly.

Choir singing has had many benefits. It is a very meaningful form of personal worship. It builds stronger lungs. It contributed greatly to my musical education. It is enjoyable and inspiring. And we acquired many good friends through this activity.

Concerts and Opera.

As a way of saying "thank you" for the computer systems service I provide, the St. Paul Chamber Orchestra gives me two season tickets to 16 concerts every year. Doris and I enjoy these concerts when we don't have a conflicting obligation. Among our family and friends, we always have happy users for the others. Currently, I have little or no interest in opera and Doris has even less.

Hooked on Ragtime.

I became fascinated with ragtime music after seeing the movie, *The Sting*. I bought a couple of ragtime records, but I couldn't seem to make the music sound right on the piano.

So I bought a large book with over 100 rags in it, and learned several of my favorites. My musical memory is better than my sight reading. By the time I can play a piece decently I have it memorized. So these numbers have now joined my large repertoire of pieces that I can play without sheet music.

The Digital Ensemble.

In the late '80's a new type of electronic keyboard came on the market, known generically as a sampler. My particular instrument is a Panasonic Technics Model 100 Digital Ensemble. This amazing instrument contains the CD-recorded notes of 36 different instruments. You can split the keyboard at various points to play a different instrument with each hand. It also has a solid state memory in which I have recorded rhythm and chord patterns for almost 80 different songs.

It is almost every pianist's dream to play with his own "combo." This new toy allows me to do this, choosing from almost 1000 combinations of rhythm patterns and chords. The instrument has many other options, of which I'll mention just one. The transpose key gives me the same facility that I've just described on Berlin's special piano! This purchase has added a whole new dimension to my musical life.

36. Painting and Sculpture

Drawing, sculpture and painting were my worst subjects in school. I always felt that when my teachers gave me a D, they were being very charitable. My handiwork never decorated the classroom wall. A number of friends find pleasure and relaxation in these activities; but I have never taken the time even to try them.

My passive interest has not been much better. When our children were younger, we would dutifully take them to art museums. I suspect our lack of interest was evident and was transmitted to them. When Doris and I decorated our condo, we enjoyed picking out quality registered prints of good contemporary artists. We chose those that pleased us and harmonized with our colors, with no thought or knowledge of the more technical aspects.

37. The Stage

Doris and I have bought four season tickets to the Lake Shore Players in White Bear Lake for many years, and we have supported them regularly with additional contributions. We attend other regional playhouses and an occasional Broadway production when it tours the Twin Cities.

As a teenager, I played supporting roles in a couple of community stage productions. I enjoyed this a great deal. Occasionally I have thoughts of resuming this activity. In all reality, I don't have the time until some of my present commitments are concluded. I did consider auditioning at Lake Shore Players for a part in a recent production; but I had conflicts on all of the audition nights.

Points to Ponder.
- The arts play an important role in all civilizations.
- Participation requires a dedication of both time and money for the purpose. It can bring important personal rewards.
- As in other aspects of life, active participation is the most rewarding.
- Our children are most apt to find interest in the things that interest us.

Eight

Beliefs

"The clock of life is wound but once,
And no man has the power
To tell just when the hands will stop,
At late or early hour.
Live, love, work with a will,
For tomorrow the hands may then be still."
— Author Unknown

The little girl could not resist the allure of those delicious, aromatic cookies. Her mother had already provided generous samples, along with the usual admonition to eat "no more until dinner." But temptation overcame the girl. The unmistakable sound of the cover against the jar carried clearly to her mother's ears in the dining room:

"Doris, keep out of the cookie jar," she called out.

The girl appeared in the dining room doorway, hands on hips eloquently attesting to her indignation, "Did God tell on me?" she demanded.

Everyone has a belief system. Some systems are good: They contain much wisdom that leads the believer to do and think those things that make her (him) happier and more fulfilled. Some are bad: They can leave the believer unhappy and unfulfilled at best. If bad enough, they can

lead him (her) into severe difficulties, prison, or even un-
timely death. Most belief systems are a mixture of good
and bad.

The Important Thing.

The important thing is to work continually to strength-
en and increase the good parts of our belief system and
remove the bad. Neither is easy, but the effort is enjoyable
and extremely rewarding. Eliminating the bad parts can
be extremely difficult, particularly if they came from someone (such as parents) who had a great influence on our lives.
In many cases professional help is needed. It is no shame
to seek such help. In fact, it is a great virtue to have the
courage to do so.

Religious Faith.

The church school teacher asked a boy to define faith.
His answer was, "Faith is believing something even though
you know it ain't so!" Many cynics believe this is true of
religious faith. But faith isn't really a stubborn belief in
something one knows to be false. Rather, it's a belief in
something one knows in the depth of one's soul to be true
despite a lack of "objective" or scientific evidence of the
belief's veracity. Belief and faith are the cornerstones of our
personal religion. One cannot be truly religious without having both. You will find religion of sufficient importance to
me that I have devoted a separate chapter to it. It is inter-
twined in all the chapters of this section.

Profound Changes.

My own beliefs have undergone profound changes over
the years. Many of these changes are reflected in other
chapters. Some which aren't or which are worth repeating:

- I used to love a good argument. I now find it very important to understand other people's point of view, even

if I don't agree with it; and it's much more fun than an argument.

- I have quit trying to convert people to my way of thinking. (It never did work!) Understanding the other person's belief system, point of view, and feelings is where acceptance begins. Accepting people as they are is the cornerstone of a good relationship and an essential part of love.

- It is no longer very satisfying to try to impress people in conversation. Being a good listener is not only an important social grace, it can be great fun. It's always rewarding, however.

- I once thought that physical surroundings weren't very important. I now know they have a strong effect on our emotions. Beauty and light are strong contributors to a positive outlook.

- My parents were very private people. I don't ever remember them sharing their feelings with me. Consequently I learned to keep my feelings to myself. I now realize that openness strengthens a relationship. A certain amount of openness is essential to understanding. But it shouldn't be pushed to a point where either party is uncomfortable.

- In the past, I gave very little thought to the effect of my words on other people. I have learned that, if saying something will affect another person negatively, it's important not to say it. Conversely, if it will affect that person positively, it's important to say it.

- Doing things to gain people's respect is not as important as I once thought. It's more important to do things for the good that results. The respect follows naturally.

- At one time I thought I could be a hermit. I now realize that loving relationships with people are vital to my happiness. The poem *No Man is an Island* expresses great wisdom.

- "That's interesting — can you tell me why you feel that way?" is much more apt to bring understanding and agreement than "I can't agree with you."

- For a long time I didn't appreciate the many different ways in which we talk to others. The differences include speaking logically vs. emotionally, seriously vs humorously, respectfully vs. disrespectfully. Other differences in conventional style include a distant vs. an open approach, caring vs. uncaring, critical vs. accepting, egocentric vs. other-centered, concerned vs. detached. Nor did I realize the importance of using the way that is most appropriate for each situation.

Many of these things I'm still learning and trying to apply — it's great fun to grow and change!

38. Religion

A small group of ten-year-old boys sit facing a calm, 60-year-old farmer in the front pews of a small-town church. They listen quietly while he reads reverently from the Bible. They don't understand it all, but his fervent sincerity keeps them strangely still. When he finishes, they beg him to say the Lord's Prayer in German. As he does so with his eyes closed, the tears stream down his face. The boys are profoundly moved.

A 14-year-old boy leads the singing and conducts the opening worship service for the Sunday School of a small non-denominational church. The words of the "gospel hymns" do not impress him, but the music and the enthusiastic singing make him feel good.

A 23-year-old man is sitting close to his fiancee in the partially darkened, beautiful sanctuary of a large downtown church in St. Paul. They are listening quietly to sublime music coming from the great pipe organ. He feels enraptured, and senses a Presence...

A 28-year-old-army 1st lieutenant is flying in a C-47 (DC-3) from Oran to Algiers during World War II. Married only four years, and despondently lonesome for his beloved wife, he pulls out the pocket Bible his mother had given him. Reading the words of Jesus, he feels powerfully moved and very close to Him. He genuinely believes he has found a whole new meaning to his religion, and writes his wife about the experience. She is moved to tears.

Religion is defined as the expression of our belief in, and reverence for, superhuman power(s) regarded as responsible for creating and/or governing the universe. I think it is more than that: Our own beliefs are the cornerstone of our lives and deserve much more attention than they usually get. There are many religions, and the range of individual religious beliefs is incredible. Even within a denomination or sect the range of individual beliefs is amazingly broad, ranging far beyond the differences in beliefs attributed to different nominal religions.

My Own Beliefs.

My own beliefs appear to have undergone many changes through the years. Perhaps it has been merely a process of sifting and sorting what I really believe from what I have been urged to believe. I have had difficulty accepting much of the doctrine expressed by most religious authorities or implied in the worship services of almost all churches. It has taken me a long time to feel OK about rejecting these doctrines. I now see many of these doctrines as ordained by man, not by God. This section of the book is largely devoted to sharing what I do accept and do believe. I can accept all of these things with a whole heart. They provide me with a structure that gives life real meaning, inspires, motivates, comforts and guides me every day of my life — and that is what religion is all about.

Your Beliefs.

Please understand, I am in no way saying you should believe what I believe. If you are totally comfortable with your present beliefs, and if they give you the guidance and strength to live a happy, fulfilled life, that's great. If you can believe, and accept with a whole heart, what your church tells you to believe, that's great. If you can't, or if some of those things trouble you, it's important to do something about it. First, tell your minister, pastor, priest, rabbi, or guru what's troubling you. Most likely (s)he will respect you for your frankness, and welcome the opportunity to discuss it.

Time for a Change.

If such discussions don't satisfy you, it's time for a change. In the unlikely event that your religious leader becomes upset with you for questioning official doctrine, you have the wrong religious leader. Such people are really telling you that they have problems with their own beliefs. So it's time for a change. For many years I resisted such change. I felt that change would have been upsetting for my family. I now feel that they could have handled it as well, or better, than I could. The original motivation for this book came from a desire to share more fully with them these and many other portions of my life and thoughts. Hopefully it will help them—and you—with your own struggles and doubts (if any) about your beliefs.

39. Churches

It is a beautiful Sunday afternoon in October 1925. Out of a cloudless blue sky the bright sun is highlighting the brilliant colors of the half-fallen leaves—it's a gorgeous day to be outside. It is "Every-Member-Canvass" Sunday. The First Presbyterian Church of White Bear Lake is attempting to underwrite its budget. A humble, church-going, devout woman in her mid-fifties sits miserably, quietly crying in the living room. She has pulled the shades down tightly in all the rooms and has commanded (no, begged) her eleven and 15-year-old sons to be quiet. This is to complete the appearance that no one is home. The father, as usual, is out of town. A heavy sense of apprehensive waiting pervades the house. A caller finally knocks at the front door. The mother urgently signals her boys to be completely silent. A louder knock is followed by utter silence. A third and final knock is answered like the others — with utter silence. The caller gets in his car and leaves.

Years later I understood this annual ritual: My mother had no money to her name and was too ashamed to say so. Each week she would carefully hoard a dime from the grocery money, and slide it quietly into the collection plate on Sunday morning. It did nothing to assuage her guilt or shame.

Are church leaders still this insensitive? I suspect some are, though many of them lack the vigor to carry out the "Every-Member-Canvass" so literally.

Psychic Trauma

Occasionally a church creates more severe psychic trauma

for a member. Doris had served her church as office manager and secretary for almost 30 years. I assured each new pastor that I would try to persuade her to retire gracefully should he desire to make other arrangements. But none did. She was too valuable, and the price was right. She worked about 20 hours a week, and was never paid a cent.

After all those years of service, however, a dark cloud appeared when a kooky pastor directed her to pad the membership rolls to hide the fact of declining membership in his annual report. She refused, and told him she thought it was wrong. He did it on his own. This and other un-pastor-like acts disturbed her greatly. She "blew the whistle" on him, and he became extremely angry with her.

The Firing.

Getting Doris to retire was not enough to assuage his anger, so he decided to fire her. To do that, however, he needed grounds, so he told the personnel committee a preposterous lie: He said that she couldn't keep the confidences needed to conduct the pastor's delicate business properly. Since people generally believe that ministers don't lie, he led the committee to believe she was a gossip and they approved the firing. That hurt worse than the firing itself.

To Doris' great credit, she did not brood about the incident or become bitter. Instead she is performing vital volunteer service for a battered women's advocate organization. On the other hand, the pastor's misdeeds became so flagrant that he was fired. Things got so bad at home that he ordered his wife out of the house, and one of the daughters attempted suicide.

Feet of Clay.

Unfortunately, this pastor didn't have a monopoly on unseemly actions. His predecessor had an extremely warped personality. When the authorities assigned him to our church, he was recovering from a nervous breakdown, a fact they carefully concealed from our local congregation. This pastor's principal delight appeared to be saying negative things about people and attempting to play one individual off against another. When this began to tear the church apart, the lay leadership insisted that he be replaced. He left extremely embittered and threatened retribution against the church. We learned of many instances in which he spoke critically and falsely of our church. How I pity that man!

Another pastor in the same church harbored a lot of bitterness and anger in his soul. It would surface in his sermons and leave the congregation confused and even angry. Shortly after his father died, he left the ministry and bought a small trucker's motel in Denver. I visited him there and found an incredibly relieved and happy man. It was then he told me he had realized very early that entering the ministry was a mistake. He stayed in it only because his father was so proud to have a son who was a minister. But all that time he felt a prisoner of his father's pride, and that made him very angry.

These three pastors served our church consecutively. No wonder the church nearly died during their tenure. Those few members of the faithful congregation still remaining after the third had left sold their building and made a new start in another community. They were doing very well with a new minister until he retired. His successor was another kook who did incredibly stupid things. The congregation succeeded in ridding themselves of him, but not until he had driven away a number of badly needed members. Even so, the congregation felt it only courteous to give him a farewell reception. But he was not content to leave peaceably: At the reception he proceeded to rip the congregation up one side and down the other until good, decent members became so upset that they said things they were sorry for. No one needs that, particularly in church. Understandably, they are now suffering from burnout.

In the first church my family joined in White Bear Lake, one minister left his wife and children and ran off with the choir director. Another was emotionally unstable to the point where he had spent extended time in a mental hospital. He was a powerful and persuasive preacher, but some of his doctrines were "off the wall," (e. g. a literal interpretation of the apocalypse) and the church elders forced him to resign. A dozen or so families (including mine) left with him and started the Community Church. This church later changed its name to the Church of Christ and is still in existence (under better ministry, I hope).

The Problem with Ministers

Being a good minister (priest, rabbi, or pastor) is a difficult and challenging job. Many church members have unrealistic expectations of their minister and are quick to complain when he or she doesn't meet these expectations. These church members don't realize that a minister is human and needs praise and moral support, just like the rest of us, to do his (her) job well.

Also like the rest of us, a minister needs a decent standard of living. Ministers are notoriously underpaid. Traditionally, their dedication to the cause and its spiritual rewards were supposed to make up for this. This principle has also been applied to teachers and nurses. It has now been questioned for teachers and nurses and they receive (more nearly) market rates. I believe churches must also abandon this archaic principle for ministers if they wish to attract women and men of adequate ability and potential who have suitable personalities.

Faulty Selection Processes

I have observed closely the ministerial selection process of a mainline Protestant denomination at all levels: from the local church through the state headquarters. When I was on the board of an ecumenical seminary, I probed carefully its role in the process. From this research I concluded that, with a few exceptions, the process is seriously flawed. Denominational officers praise local churches for the quantity of ordination candidates they produce, with inadequate emphasis on moral quality and emotional suitability. These officers say they depend on the seminary and the local church to judge these characteristics since they "know the candidate better."

The local churches rarely even inquire into the moral quality or emotional suitability of their candidates for three reasons. They don't wish to disturb or offend the candidate or her (his) family. They depend on the denomination and the seminary to weed out the poor candidates, since they "are more skilled in these matters." Both minister and congregation enjoy the praise they receive for increasing the body count.

For their own reasons, seminaries usually accept students who simply meet the academic standards and graduate those who complete the course requirements. They are struggling to keep their enrollments sufficiently high to balance the budget. They say it is up to the denomination officers and the local churches to screen out candidates who are emotionally unsuitable. They don't wish to offend either of these entities since they are the best source of student applicants.

And so the circle, or triangle, of buck passing is complete. As a result, congregations and the potential of their churches are severely limited by inadequate ministers. A high percentage of these ministers are emotionally unsuitable and incapable of meeting the heavy personal demands that the ministry places on them.

The weakness of the selection process is further exacerbated by a phenomenon called adverse selection, which also plagues the professions of psychiatry and psychology. The phenomenon refers to the tendency of larger than proportional numbers of people with emotional problems to enter these professions. They do so in an attempt, conscious or unconscious, to solve their own problems. I have already described the three ministers who served my church consecutively, and who caused serious problems for the church and themselves. All three were, in my opinion, grossly unsuited for the ministry because of their emotional make-up. At least two others were marginal. It was the experience with these five ministers that caused me to research the subject.

The Back Door is Too Small.

In business and industry the policies and processes relating to the termination of unsatisfactory employees are often referred to as the back door. In the denomination I studied, the back door was too small. In other words, the processes for terminating unsatisfactory and inadequate ministers were woefully lacking. There are a variety of reasons for this:

- Ministers are quick to blame criticism of them on church members who are "too picky." The occasional shred of truth in this tends to make these statements credible with denomination officers.

- Denomination officers are glad to accept this explanation because it relieves them of a difficult and possibly unpleasant task.

- For the same reason, these officers tend to rationalize that the problem is "bad chemistry" between a minister and a congregation. They "solve" the problem by reassigning the pastor to another church where the same problem develops.

- Some local churches are more assertive in demanding the replacement of unsatisfactory ministers than others. Such ministers are often glad to assist their denomination officers in branding these congregations as "chronic complainers," and those congregations lose their credibility still further. Ironically, the process often stifles the churches with the greatest potential: In reality the chronic complainers usually are congregations with an abundance of an essential element for growth: strong lay leadership.

- Denomination leaders are reluctant to deal with the fact that some ministers cannot succeed in any church, at least without expensive remedial processes. The very nature of the ministry makes them more charitable toward their brethren; and their budgets won't cover the needed remedies.

And so the weak selection processes are exacerbated by an unjustifiably low rate of involuntary termination. There is an unwholesome reluctance to terminate a minister for even such serious anomalies as low ethical and moral standards. We see ample evidence of this in the histories of ministers whose misdeeds make the papers because someone finally blows the whistle on them. Accounts of the tolerance of denomination officers toward these ministers' misdeeds and the failure to terminate them from positions where they continue to do great damage are shocking.

Widely Prevalent?

Since I researched only one denomination in one state, I cannot speak with authority about others. But there are two reasons why I believe these problems may prevail elsewhere. First are the public accounts to which I alluded in the previous paragraph. If heinous misdeeds are tolerated in various denominations, how much more prevalent must be the failures to deal with less serious shortcomings that can still make a minister ineffectual. Second is the recognition that the human failings that cause these shortcomings are not restricted to one denomination or one state.

On Balance, a Force for Good.

This is not a diatribe against churches. Rather, I want to acknowledge reality. As someone has said, "The church is not a community of saints, it is a spiritual hospital for sinners." Ministers and denominational officers are no exception. This reality has not dimmed my appreciation for churches as a strong force for good in their communities, both historically and currently.

Community of Worshippers: A Great Value.

Many religious writers have emphasized the value to the individual of worshipping with a community of believers. I heartily agree. This is one of the many values which churches bring to their community and the world at large. Here are some of the others I see:

- Helping individuals to formulate and strengthen their religious beliefs, their personal theology, and their philosophy of life.

- Strengthening the moral fiber of individuals, and consequently the family and of the community.

- Enhancing individual value systems. This, in turn, strengthens the family and the community.

- Ministering to individuals' emotional needs and problems. This includes, but is not limited to, the bereaved, the recently divorced, single parents, caregivers, shut-ins, people with serious financial or legal problems, and the unemployed. These individuals can then become more effective family members and more productive people, not only at work but in their communities.

- Motivating and training people to be good volunteers, outside of the church as well as within, and teaching the great rewards in being givers rather than takers. Encouraging them to reach out into their communities and the world, and giving them organized outlets to do so.

- Teaching and encouraging individuals to be better citizens, to take a more active role in our government and, as a minimum, to vote more intelligently.

- Providing religious training and enhancing the value systems of children and young people.

- Providing a wholesome atmosphere in which youths can spend their free time and socialize.

- Enhancing the cultural backgrounds of individuals by exposing them to the rich heritage of drama, the arts, and both sacred and secular music.

Note how all of these processes begin with the individual member. I believe that direct attempts by the organized church at political action are largely ill-advised and counterproductive when measured by the broad aims of our society.

Our Best Hope but in Need of Strengthening.

Most serious students of the ills of our society recognize that no particular political system or party can deal effectively with these ills at present. This will be so until far greater numbers of individuals have a much deeper commitment to work vigorously toward making their community a better place for all of its members to live. Who is going to teach these individuals and motivate them to change their paradigms and their lifestyles to the great extent needed for this to happen? I believe the best answer in sight is the organized churches.

But the churches cannot and will not accomplish this unless certain conditions are present. Here is a list of these requirements as I see them:

- Churches must quit trying to compete with each other, both intra- and interdenominationally. This is not a new idea, but it is essential if the churches are to perform their missions effectively. I believe the most effective way to do this is through the super-church, a concept I will describe a bit further on.

- Individuals must support the church in their community that best performs its fundamental jobs as outlined on the previous pages, and help it to become the super-church. This means providing the impetus for their church to become part of the super-church.

- Individuals must insist that their minister emphasize the commonality of important beliefs and elements of worship that make us a great body of common believers. Conversely, he must play down, but not deny, the differences.

The impetus for all of these important requirements must come from individuals. It is not likely to come from pastors and denominational officers who have too much vested interest in the status quo.

The Great Body of Common Believers

The essential beliefs and worship elements are common not only to the different branches of Christianity, but to all other major religions of the world. Do you believe that God, in infinite wisdom, gave understanding of the Divine Will to only the minority of human beings represented by one denomination, religion or sect? I don't. I believe it is much more likely that the common elements are ordained by God and the differences are ordained by man.

When I listen to people of different religious beliefs, I hear the same tune. Only the words are different. This tune contains all the elements that are, in my opinion, necessary to the salvation of the individual, our community, our nation and our world. These elements are described in later chapters of this section. Which of you cannot, in good conscience, accept these common elements?

So you want to believe other things, as well? Fine, go right ahead, and I will respect you for your sincerity. But don't let the fact that others believe differently keep you from joining the Great Body of Common Believers. You and your loved ones will not benefit by clinging to those differences if you fail to support the Great Body of Common Believers. For then our civilization will continue to crumble.

The Super-church

A few super-churches exist in various parts of the country already. They exist in various denominations, but have many qualities in common:

- They have at least one minister who is a powerful preacher capable of preaching to people's emotional and spiritual needs. These ministers have strong personal charisma, and are people of great vision, energy, enthusiasm and outreach. They tend to stay in the same church for their entire careers because their congregations are delighted with them and because they reach personal fulfillment in their highly successful endeavors. Personal income is of secondary importance to them, but their church is financially able (and willing) to see that their material needs are well provided for.

- They attract and motivate outstanding and dedicated lay leadership. These people interact strongly with the minister to create bold, far-reaching programs. Together they motivate the rest of the congregation to carry out these programs in a highly effective manner.

- Their congregations are large, numbering from a few thousand to over 10,000 in a few cases. These people are attracted to the church because their spiritual, emotional and social needs are met to a much higher degree there than they are in ordinary churches. So they are willing to ignore the doctrinal differences between the super-church and the church(es) in which they were brought up, and to forsake their former church. In many cases they had already forsaken the church because their needs were not being met.

- The large number of people provide an adequate financial base to pay quality staff, provide and maintain superb physical facilities, and fund highly effective programs to fill a wide variety of special needs. Serious budget shortfalls are rare and much less emphasis and energy is needed to raise money. Because people are more satisfied with and enthusiastic about their church, the church has fewer financial problems.

- Large numbers provide the "critical mass" needed to form smaller groups that can minister effectively to a great variety of special needs.

- The church leaders insist vigorously on achieving and maintaining top quality and effectiveness in the church's programs. They conduct national searches to obtain outstanding youth and music ministers. The results are programs so effective that they attract young, energetic families and individuals from a wide geographic area and with diverse religious backgrounds.

We are fortunate in having a super-church only five miles from us in a neighboring community: St. Andrews Lutheran of Mahtomedi (a town already described earlier in this book). Its membership, rapidly approaching 6,000, exceeds the entire population of the community in which it is located!

Their senior pastor, Roger Eigenfeld, is the epitomy of the super-church pastor I described just a few pages ago. If the great Lutheran denomination established a hall of fame, Roger would certainly be a charter member. His theme, adopted in 1992, is "Out to Change the World." That says it all, and he has made a significant start in his own community, in Jamaica, and more recently in Czechoslovakia. Sunday after Sunday I say to Doris on the way home, "That sermon was another keeper." His 1992 sermon on financial commitment was the best of its kind I've ever heard in my long association with churches. There is only one problem: There aren't enough of him.

The Super-church of the 21st Century.

Dream with me of a church of the future that can fulfill its destiny as the great force that can and will enable us to deal with the problems of our modern world. It will change the minds and hearts of the majority people so that they will become givers rather than takers. These people will then insist that their political leaders do likewise. Graft, corruption, greed and pork-barrel politics will no longer dominate our governments. Strong, selfless, inspired leaders can then emerge and direct their energies and our resources to addressing the real needs of our community, the nation and the world.

A fantasy, you say. Perhaps, but what alternative do we have to alter the self-destructive direction in which our society is headed? Until the majority of people truly have not only the desire, but the will and the commitment to serve others as well as themselves and their immediate families there can be little hope. I prefer to think of this as a vision rather than a fantasy. It will take only a small number of people with this vision (and dedication, and courage) in each community to bring the dream to reality.

Bear with me while I paint a scenario:

- The scene is a community or suburb with a population of approximately 20,000 people. The majority of people in the community gather on Sunday in a huge sanctuary. There are several of these services at different times to accommodate various preferences and plans and the logistics of the building. The worshippers join in triumphant hymns of praise and thanksgiving to a Bountiful Creator who gave us the many beautiful and wonderful blessings we enjoy on this earth. The sound of their rejoicing rises up in a great chorus that stimulates and inspires all of them. This mood is reinforced with psalms and prayers. An inspired and gifted minister speaks for 10 to 15 minutes. He addresses people's emotional and spiritual needs. He emphasizes the important part that love of, and service to, others plays in our own well-being. The service ends with a prayer of commitment to our Bountiful Creator and to each other. The commitment is to set aside at least three time periods during the week when the people will serve others outside their own families. All elements of the service have been carefully chosen and prepared so that they recognize only those beliefs that are common to all the people. The whole service takes only 45 minutes.

- Those who wish, adjourn to their former churches or to small sanctuaries on the superchurch campus for brief services to celebrate their traditional distinctive liturgies and religious beliefs.

- Religious education of children, youths and adults and preparation for church membership follow a similar pattern: The core curriculum deals with only the common elements of belief and worship. Optional courses are available for those who wish to have their children learn the traditional beliefs of the parent's religion. Young people and adults can avail themselves of courses in their traditional religion and courses in comparative religion.

- All youths and adults are urged to attend study groups that focus on societal problems. They discuss organizations that are currently showing the greatest promise of dealing with these problems effectively. They talk about the specific ways they as individuals can support and enhance the work of these organizations. Their group leaders are carefully selected for their own high energy levels, dedication and infectious enthusiasm. These talents will be further enhanced by intensive training conducted by a paid leader whose own great skills and high energy levels energize those being instructed and focus them on the vision. Such people are rare, but every community has some, and the super-church will be a magnet that will draw them irresistibly. Where such an organization is missing, members of the superchurch organize to create it.

- All other activities and ministries follow the patterns of the existing super-church, which have been described already.

Transition: a Long Road, but Achievable.

The road to the new church's full destiny is clearly a long one, but the only obstacles are our lack of vision, commitment and faith, coupled with indifference and unwillingness to change. During the transition there will be some disruptions and inconveniences; but people have endured more to obtain lesser ends.

Ministers must be re-oriented and challenged. Some will be slow to accept change. But when they see the rewards of service to the new church and its vast potential, they will be more inclined to work with it. Those ministers who cannot, or will not, adapt to the changes will find themselves playing a lesser role in their community than they do even now. Or they may have to move to communities where the superchurch is not developing, or seek other forms of livelihood. Buildings will be used for different purposes than at present. Some that now exist may have no function in the new church. The money saved by not maintaining them will help finance newly needed structures. Large auditoriums or civic centers may be rented until a large enough sanctuary can be built. When the owners of these buildings realize the far-reaching, positive effects of the new church they may be glad to make the buildings available without charge.

As in the case of today's super-church, financing the ongoing operations should not be a problem. Raising up-front capital outlays will present more of a challenge. When they see the broad positive potential impact of the new church, city officials may be willing to make their bonding authority available, much as they now do for new industry.

The Seminary of the 21st Century.

There is a strong interdependence between churches and their seminaries. The church looks to the seminary to train its leaders, both lay and ordained. The seminary looks to the churches for its life blood, the students without which it cannot exist. They also provide a significant portion of the additional, much needed financial support. Like other institutions of higher learning, seminaries derive only a minor portion of their needed revenue from tuitions.

Because of this heavy dependence on the traditional churches, the seminaries hesitate to be an agent of change for fear of alienating their supporting churches. In reality, they can only change as their constituent churches change. They must, therefore, seek out the emerging super churches wherever they can be found. The latter will see the former as an important source of its super-pastors who are already highly energized with the vision of their mission to change the world.

It will take a rare combination of elements to effect this necessary change and free the seminary from the shackles that prevent it from reaching its full potential. These elements will include professional leaders with courage and vision, a board willing and able to take some risks, and a strong ecumenical culture. Many seminaries will be unable to change in this way because of their unbreakable bonds to a single denomination.

I know one seminary that already has this potential: United Theological Seminary of the Twin Cities, on whose board I served for several years. In a typical year the students there represent almost two dozen denominations. The school's president, Dr. Benjamin Griffin, is a dedicated leader and a man of courage, wisdom and vision. He has strengthened the seminary's administrative staff tremendously and is a strong agent for change on its faculty.

My opinion of UTS's potential was reinforced by no less

an authority than Dr. James L. Waits, Executive Director of The Association of Theological Schools in the United States and Canada. In his eloquent and inspiring address at the seminary President's Dinner in 1992, he challenged the school's leaders and its major donors with just such a vision. He spoke of the desperate need in this world for a "public voice" that would lead the people to espouse a fundamentally sound value system, the lack of which is at the root of most of the world's problems. Many churches now seek to be such a "public voice," but their voice is too weak to be heard amid the clamor and confusion.

40. Philosophy

"Philosophy, when superficially studied, excites doubt; when thoroughly explored, it dispels it."
—Francis Bacon

The word philosophy literally means "loving wisdom." A philosopher isn't necessarily a learned scholar. You and I are philosophers if we live and think according to a particular belief system. I believe that everyone can improve his or her life by reading philosophers, sifting and sorting, keeping what really seems to work, rejecting that which doesn't. Philosophers don't have to be ancient. Here are excerpts from some of my favorite moderns:

Rabbi Harold S. Kushner*

"I am convinced that it is not the fear of death, of our lives ending, that haunts our sleep so much as the fear that our lives will not have mattered, that as far as the world

When All You've Ever Wanted Isn't Enough
COPYRIGHT © 1986 by Kushner Enterprises, Inc.
Reprinted by permission of Simon and Schuster, Inc.

is concerned, we might as well never have lived. What we miss in our lives, no matter how much we have, is a sense of meaning." (page 20)

"Religion focuses on the difference between human beings and all other species, and on the search for a goal so significant that we make our lives significant by attaching ourselves to it." (page 22)

"You don't become happy by pursuing happiness. It is always a byproduct, never a primary goal." (page 23)

"The need for meaning is not a biological need like the need for food and air. Neither is it a psychological need, like the need for acceptance and self-esteem. It is a religious need, an ultimate thirst of our souls. And so it is to religion we must now turn to look for answers." (page 29)

"There is nothing wrong with being successful. Churches, colleges, museums and medical research all depend on the generosity of successful people sharing the fruits of success with them. There is nothing wrong with having enough power to influence events. On the contrary, people who feel powerless and frustrated are more dangerous to society than people who know the effect of their influence and use it wisely, because they may do desperate things to compel us to take them seriously. But there is something very wrong with single-minded pursuit of power and wealth in a way which shuts us off from other people. It may put us in a position where the only thing worse than losing is winning." (page 58)

"My objection to the 'looking out for number one' philosophy is that it does not work. Take advantage of other people, be suspicious of everyone, and you are liable to be so successful that you will end up far ahead of everyone else, looking down on them with scorn. And then where will you be? You will be all alone." (page 59)

"When you have learned how to live, life itself will be the reward.

"The person who has discovered the pleasures of truly human living, the person whose life is rich in friendships and caring people, the person who enjoys daily the pleasures of good food and sunshine, will not need to wear himself or herself out in the pursuit of some other kind of success." (page 151)

"There is more to my life today than there was five or ten years ago because of all the ways in which I have grown and been enriched in that time." (page 171)

H. Jackson Brown[8]

". . . deciding whom you marry is the most important decision you'll ever make." (page 11)

". . . most things I worry about never happen." (page 11)

". . . money is a lousy means of keeping score." (page 17)

". . . if you really want to do something positive for your children, you should try to improve your marriage." (page 97)

"If you pursue happiness it will elude you. But if you focus on your family, the needs of others, your work, meeting new people, and doing the very best you can, happiness will find you."

Murray Banks[4]

"Many of us take care of our physical health: regular exercise, medical checkups, weight control etc. But how many of us do the same for our mental health?"

A. H. Maslow[9]

". . . we need the truth and love it and seek it. . . We are also simultaneously afraid to know the truth. For instance, certain truths carry automatic responsibilities which may be anxiety-producing." (page 40)

"The people I selected for my investigation were older

people who had lived much of their lives out and were visibly successful." (page 43)

"Self-actualizing people are, without one single exception, involved in a cause outside their own skin, in something outside of themselves. They are devoted, working at something which is very precious to them . . ." (page 43)

"People [who are self-actualized] go about it in these little ways: They listen to their own voices; they take responsibility; they are honest; and they work hard." (page 50)

"My feeling is that the concept of creativeness and the concept of the healthy, self-actualizing, fully human person seem to be coming closer and closer together, and may perhaps turn out to be the same thing." (page 57)

". . . the most wonderful good fortune . . . is to be paid for doing what [one] passionately loves to do. The salary that such a [person] gets is only a small part of his 'pay'. Self-actualizing work . . ., being its own intrinsic reward, transforms the money or paycheck into a byproduct." (page 305)

41. Regrets

> *"Regret is an appalling waste of energy;*
> *you can't build on it;*
> *it's only good for wallowing in."*
> —Katherine Mansfield

I heartily agree with Mansfield. The expression "I wish I had. . ." isn't in my vocabulary any more. Instead I think or say, "Next time I'll do it differently."

Things I Would have Done Differently

For some things there may be no next time. A good example is how we dealt with our children. I've already covered that in Chapter 11. Some other things:

- I would have taken myself a little less seriously. This applies particularly to my approach to my job and to my fellow workers. I remember my friend Clem Oliver at Minnesota Mutual saying, "Stan, you're so sincere you scare people." At the time I thought is was an odd statement. How could one be too sincere? But now I know what he meant. If something went wrong, I would go into high gear to "get to the bottom of it," often frustrating and annoying fellow workers in the process.

(For those of you who tend to do likewise, the following quotation will be enjoyable—don't take it literally:

I am one of those people who never go anywhere without a thermometer, a gargle, a raincoat and a parachute. If I had my life to live over I'd try to make more mistakes next time. I would relax, I would limber up. I would be sillier than I have been this trip. I know of few things I would take seriously. I would be crazier, I would be less hygienic. I would take more chances. I would take more trips. I would climb more mountains, swim more rivers, watch more sunsets. I would burn more gasoline. I would eat more ice cream and less beans. I would have more actual troubles and fewer imaginary ones. You see I am one of those people who live prophylactically and sensibly and sanely hour after hour and day after day.

Oh, I have my moments, and if I had it to do over again, I'd have more of them. In fact I'd try to have nothing more or less. Just moments, one after the other, instead of living so many years ahead of each day. If I had it to do over again I would go places and do things and travel lighter than I have. If I had my life to live over again I would start going barefooted earlier in the spring and stay that way later in the fall. I would play hooky more: I wouldn't make such good grades, except by accident. I would ride on more merry-go-rounds. I'd pick more daisies.

- I would have been more open with people, as I am trying to be now. The rewards are great for both parties. Openness strengthens friendships and increases mutual trust and understanding.
- I would have expressed my admiration and affection for people more freely.

Oh, there are many other things, most of which are expressed or implied elsewhere in this book. But mostly, I did what I thought was right at that time. Most of us have done a few things we knew were foolish at the time. For these we should forgive ourselves, ask God to forgive us and, where appropriate, ask others to forgive us.

"I'll Never Forgive Myself"

The person who says, "I'll never forgive myself for what I . . ." is condemning him(her)self to a life of remorse and carrying a load of guilt, and probably causing greater harm than the original act did. How much better to obtain forgiveness, then use all of our energies in positive, productive and triumphant living!

We need also to examine our thoughts about what might have been and ask ourselves "Isn't it still possible?" Oftentimes we tend to think or say "it's too late now", when the real problem is our unwillingness to make the effort or take the risk needed to do it now.

42. Sin

"Sin is that which hurts ourselves or others."
— Murray Banks

This is the most concise and workable definition of sin I have come across. If we test each of our actions and thoughts against this definition, and act accordingly, it will take us a long way toward being the kind of person we want to be. But you say, "How can we tell whether a certain action is (or will be) hurtful?" If you're in doubt, ask someone in whose wisdom and judgment you trust on this particular subject. And seek help in prayer and meditation, if you can. After discussing it thoroughly, make up your own mind.

The Negative Emotions.

If we want to be healthy, happy and truly fulfilled, there is no place in our lives for the negative emotions. They truly meet Murray Banks' definition of sin. Let's look at them:

Worry.

Someone once said "Worry is the misuse of imagination." I believe there are only two groups of things to worry about: the kind you can do something about and the kind you can't. If you can do something about the thing you're worrying about, do it as quickly as possible—even getting up in the middle of the night, if it's keeping you awake. You'll sleep so much better afterward. If you can't do anything about it, there's really no use worrying, is there?

Anger.

Let's dismiss the sudden flares that subside as quickly as they came. I don't know anyone who isn't subject to them.

The important thing is not to do or say anything until they subside (some people count to 10). The real killer is the lingering, or chronic, anger (often called resentment) which continues to smolder in our hearts. It's usually due to the action, or inaction, of some person—perhaps even long ago.

There are two cures: understanding and forgiveness. They work well together. When we understand someone, we are much more likely to be able to forgive them. When we forgive someone, we truly put out of our minds any further thought of the hurt that we felt. We feel relieved, "released," from that fire that has been consuming us. You say, "That's easier said than done." You're right! That's where understanding comes in. Perhaps you've said, "I wonder why Joe did (or Mary said) that terrible thing to me." Did you really wonder why or was it only a rhetorical question? If we really wonder why, we will look behind the act, and see a person who was frustrated, envious, or otherwise upset. If we can really (in our imagination) walk in that person's shoes and understand the state of mind that caused the hurt, then we are ready to forgive — and our anger goes away.

The Folly and Irony of Seeking Redress.

The folly is that seeking redress never brings us what we're really looking for: happiness, respect, and a better self-image. The irony is that the efforts of seeking redress usually create more anger and resentment (in both parties), and the fires build rather than subside.

Should We Say, "I Forgive You"?

Now true forgiveness can only be born of understanding and acceptance. Some people can say "I forgive you" in a tone that says "I'm really condemning you for your stupid acts." I think it's unwise to voice forgiveness unless someone asks for it and you're sure you are truly ready to forgive. As in most other situations, our actions speak louder than our words. If we say "I forgive you," but continue to harbor our resentment, neither party is benefitted. One continues to have his(her) soul eaten away by the negative emotion. The other is either bewildered, or convinced that the forgiver is insincere. On the other hand, if we have truly forgiven someone in our hearts and our resentment or anger has melted away, they will know it by the way we act, talk and look.

The Joys and Rewards of Forgiveness.

Anyone who has truly experienced the joys and satisfactions of feeling genuine forgiveness toward another can relate to this paragraph: The feeling of relief, release, calm, inner peace is truly a marvelous experience. The biblical admonition to forgive "70 times 7" is not mere hyperbole; it's the prescription for a soul-cleansing liturgy based on sound psychological principles. When this burden of anger and resentment is lifted from us (more accurately when we lift it from ourselves), our mood brightens, our spirits are lifted, we look more radiant, everything about us and around us takes on a happier aspect. It's well worth the effort to understand and accept, yes?

Look in the Right Place.

We often say, "(s)he made me so mad!" That's a lie. No one can make us feel any emotion, unless we allow them to. We are (or can become) in control of our own emotions. It takes practice. Why did Jesus, under the worst imaginable physical and mental torture and torment say, "Father forgive them for they know not what they do?" He had learned how to control his own emotions. Only by understanding and forgiving his tormentors could he "keep from cracking up," as we would say today. Now few, if any, of us can achieve control to this degree. But through practice we can move in the right direction. As in many other endeavors, we learn best by trying the easy tasks— and succeeding. The slight hurts from people we already respect and love are the easy ones. You've probably experienced true forgiveness there already. The same principles apply to the tougher ones. Try them. . .

What if We Can't Forgive?

Probably you have heard a person say, for example about a spouse's infidelity, "I'll never be able to forgive!" That's a tough one, made tougher by our unmistakable monogamous instincts. Yet we may also know of such cases where there was true forgiveness. What was different? If you could look deep enough into the latter cases, you would find: (1) a strong motivation to forgive, (2) an understanding of the circumstances that motivated the infidelity, and (3) acceptance of the action. Now accepting is not condoning. Nor is it agreement. Nor is it permission to repeat the grievous act. More nearly it is a recognition that the spouse (1) is not perfect, (2) may have harbored some bad emotions that need to be dealt with, (3) is truly contrite, and (4) understands that repetitions may not be so easily forgiven, if at all. The same principles apply to other sources of anger and resentment.

When is Forgiveness Not a Solution?

Forgiveness is necessary, but not sufficient, when the offender is totally incorrigible and worthless—which is not often the case. But if it is, we have the additional obligation to banish that person from our lives. Otherwise the continued relationship will destroy both parties. Such a decision is a drastic one. It should be made only after careful counselling with friends who know this person and whose judgment you respect. The forgiveness can still be achieved only with understanding and acceptance. But you are not condoning the person's actions, nor are you accepting them into your life. You are merely accepting the reality that this person has no place in your future life.

Fear.

So many wise people have expressed themselves on fear that I can do no better than quote some of them:

"If a man harbors any sort of fear, it percolates through all his thinking, damages his personality, makes him landlord to a ghost."
                    —Lloyd Douglas

"He who fears being conquered is sure of defeat."
                    —Napoleon Bonaparte

"Nothing is so much to be feared as fear."
                    —Henry David Thoreau

"Fear is the tax that conscience pays to guilt."
                    —George Sewell

Greed, Envy and Jealousy.

*"The covetous man pines in plenty, like
Tantalus up to the chin in water,
and yet thirsty."*
                    —Thomas Adams

*"Jealousy is ... a tiger that tears
not only its prey
but also its own raging heart."*
                    —Michael Beer

Greedy and covetous people are takers and not givers. They condemn themselves to a life of perpetual slavery to obtain a goal, and deny themselves any chance of real happiness and fulfillment.

Notice what all of these negative emotions have in common: They are the egocentric feelings that prompt the selfish acts of a taker. If we fill our minds and hearts with thoughts of others and our days with loving acts of kindness and unselfishness, we assume the role of a giver. Life immediately becomes more satisfying.

Of course there are many other ways of sinning: No need to name them. We need only to give each of our thoughts, feelings and acts the litmus test of Banks' simple definition of sin already quoted.

43. Theology

> *"Theology is but our ideas of truth*
> *classified and arranged."*
> —Henry Ward Beecher

> *"The best theology is rather a*
> *divine life than a divine knowledge."*
> —Jeremy Taylor

Many of us have been told that we should never discuss religion with others because it is such a sensitive and disturbing subject. I would modify this statement. Not only is it OK to discuss *the common beliefs and elements of worship,* but such discussions strengthen the bonds of love and friendship and the faith of the discussants. On the other hand, you can undertake a discussion of *beliefs that are not common to all major religions* only with people who are very comfortable with, and secure in, their own beliefs. Many people are not. And so I confine my discussion of theology to the first group.

God

God is a supreme being with powers beyond our ability to comprehend or understand. This supreme being created not only the universe, but also the laws that govern its operation. God's laws are universal in operation and apply to all elements and all people equally at all times.

God's Will for Us

When we seek to understand God's laws and apply them in our daily lives, we are doing God's will for us. Salvation is the process of doing God's will and realizing the fulfillment that follows. There are many paths toward this common goal, and they all lead to the same place. As I said earlier, the words are different, but the tune is the same. Some words are more attractive to some people, different words are more attractive to others, thus the existence of so many different religions. We must respect all of these religions that truly help their adherents to a better understanding of themselves and help them become more fulfilled individuals.

When we concentrate on the differences in our theologies, we tend to drive ourselves apart. When we concentrate on the common elements of our theology, we strengthen each other and develop a strong feeling of community.

It is only in this latter activity that theology and religion can really help us in our quest for a better community, a better nation, and a better world.

44. Love

> *"If there is anything better than*
> *to be loved it is loving."*
> —Anonymous

> *"Love gives itself; it is not bought."*
> —Henry Wadsworth Longfellow

"I never knew how to worship
until I knew how to love."
—Henry Ward Beecher

"There is a Law that man should love his neighbor
as himself. In a few years it should be as natural to
mankind as breathing or the upright gait; but if he
does not learn it he must perish."
—Alfred Adler

The word love is used to describe a wide variety of qualities. To avoid confusion it is helpful to list the various meanings:

The intense affectionate concern we may feel for another person.

An intense sexual desire.

God's benevolence and mercy toward man.

Man's devotion to, or adoration toward God.

The benevolence, kindness or brotherhood that we should feel toward others.

An expression of one's warm feelings.

A strong fondness for or enthusiasm toward something.

An open-minded, charitable attitude that gives others the benefit of the doubt.

All of these forms of love play a part in our happiness and fulfillment. It is important that we understand them, accept them into our belief system, and make them a fundamental part of our lives.

We have often heard that we must love ourselves before we can love others. Jess Lair[6] says it better when he stresses the importance of accepting ourselves.

Most of us learn at a fairly young age that love is much more than a physical attraction. Some of us are fortunate enough to have learned true love through our marriages (Chapter 10). But how many of us have learned to practice this love continually in our daily contact with our spouses?

In love, as in all other aspects of life, it is truly more blessed to give than to receive, and in many situations giving is a condition precedent to loving. But don't make the mistake of believing that you are entitled to demand love in return for having loved. On the contrary, when you make such demands, you become very unlovable. The same is true of friendship. There will be times when these overtures are not returned.

Conditional Love is not Love.

Occasionally we hear people say, especially to their children, "I will love you if . . ." That is not real love. What's more, the statement sends the wrong message about love, and it will confuse a child. The converse is even worse: "I don't love you because you were naughty." For a child to hear that a parent doesn't love him(her) is an emotional disaster that may entail a long and difficult recovery. Far better is, "I still love you, but I sure don't love what you just did!"

My county library system lists 391 titles under the subject of love. Lengthy as the list is, it represents only a fraction of what has been written about this all-important subject. If you have any doubts or questions about its importance in your own life, I suggest that you start with the 13th chapter of First Corinthians, and continue your readings on the subject until your questions are answered and your doubts melt away. (If you use the King James version of the Bible, substitute "love" for "charity.")

45. Pride vs. Humility

"One of the best temporary cures for pride
and affectation is seasickness; a man who
wants to vomit never puts on airs."
—Josh Billings

"Pride is an admission of weakness;
it secretly fears all competition
and dreads all rivals."
—Fulton J. Sheen

"There is this paradox in pride—
it makes some men ridiculous,
but prevents others from becoming so."
—Charles Caleb Colton

"Pride goeth before a fall"
—Proverbs

"I feel coming on a strange disease—humility."
—Frank Lloyd Wright

"Without humility there can be no humanity."
—John Buchan

"Humility: the first of all other virtues
—for other people."
—Oliver Wendell Holmes

How can we accept ourselves and take our place in the
world if we have no pride? How can we assert ourselves
and affirm our destiny if we are humble? This is one of life's
seeming paradoxes. It is evident in the apparently conflict-

ing quotations I have chosen. I believe that, as in many other aspects of life, the answers lie in balance and moderation.

We all know people who make such a virtue of their humility that they are insufferable. We know others whose pride makes them equally so. There is a happy medium. At times in my life I have swung to both extremes. My mother gave me an overdose of humility that caused me to be too timid for my own good. I was in my late twenties before I overcame this. In my forties I went through a stage in which I felt superior to other people. This damaged my relationships with other people.

We can be sufficiently proud of our own accomplishments and abilities to maintain a good self image. We do not need to articulate them to others: they will be apparent. At the same time we can recognize the abilities and accomplishment of others and articulate them. This, I believe, is the true balance.

46. Aging

> *"Old age isn't for sissies"*
> —Millicent Fenwick

You can tell you're getting old, when . . .

- you get in your rocking chair and it won't start;
- your back goes out more than you do;
- you don't care where you go as long as you're home by nine o'clock;
- the most exciting thing in your life is nap time;
- your bowling score is lower than your golf score;
- you can't remember what it was you forgot;

- you see an attractive person of the opposite sex and your pacemaker opens the garage door;

- your telephone answering machine can't remember who called;

- you turn on your Macintosh and instead of saying "ready" it says "hello gramps;"

- you can tell which way a storm is coming from by which knee hurts most;

- you can tell it's lunch time because you're ready for your Geritol;

- the high school graduating class looks like a bunch of eighth-graders;

- you look at the new bank teller and wonder what happened to child labor laws;

- you wonder who babysits the theater ushers.

I can see and feel the symptoms of getting older: diminishing muscular strength; graying, thinning hair; reduced sex drive; corneas thinning out; hands, arms and face showing the ravages of the sun. There are also temporary memory losses, speaking of which, my daughter-in-law Satoko told me a delightful story:

> *Three aging people were discussing their problems.*
> *The first person said, "I'm getting a terrible problem, I can't remember anything. This morning I was halfway upstairs and couldn't remember why I was going upstairs."*
> *The second person added, "Me too, I go into the kitchen to get something, and forget what I went for."*
> *The third person responded, "I sure hope I don't get like that (knocking on the wooden table)—who's there?"*

In June 1993, I also had a couple episodes of transient ischemic attacks (TIA). These attacks result from a temporary insufficiency of blood to the brain. The symptoms may be any combination of numbness, paralysis, loss of one or more of the senses, or loss of consciousness. My first episode produced a numbness and paralysis of the fingers of the left hand, which lasted about 20 minutes and cleared up completely.

Two weeks later the same hand became numb up to the wrist, and I couldn't speak clearly. All I could think of was, "Omigosh, I've got to give a two-hour seminar tomorrow morning." After about 25 minutes of bewilderment, wondering what was happening, it occurred to me that this could be TIA. So I put my head down almost to my feet and, in less than two minutes the symptoms were all gone!

After a neurological exam, an MRI scan and an ultrasound exam of my carotid arteries, the neurologist pronounced me to be in excellent shape for my age. He put me on a ton of anti-oxidants (25,000 units of Beta-carotene, 1000 mg of vitamin C, and 1000 units of vitamin E) plus 4 aspirin a day. He also told me not to smoke (I never have), get plenty of exercise (which I have for years) and eat right (which I have for years).

Rather than feeling depressed, I am elated by how little I have had to change my life style in the last 20 years or more. My tennis game has never been better (that's not saying much!); the same is true for my alpine skiing, windsurfing, long distance bicycle riding, cross country skiing, and most other continuation sports. And, of course, it helps when people marvel at my continued activity. When people really want to know how things are with me (not just "How are you?"), I can honestly tell them, "It gets better every year. I don't know how long that will last, but I'll enjoy it while it does."

The Secrets.

What are the secrets to enjoying the aging process and staying active? One is to pick activities you truly enjoy and keep on doing them as long as your body will let you. I hear people in their 40's, 50's and 60's (sometimes even in their late 30's!) say: "I'm getting too old to do this." What a terrible thought! Sure, as you grow older, you won't be able to run as fast, or lift as much as you could in your youth. But you'll be pleasantly surprised at the number of qualities that persist: stamina, hand-eye coordination, quick reactions and sense of balance. Many qualities actually improve with age: competitive strategies, relaxation, enjoyment, exhilaration and a sense of humor about the game.

Another secret is to adopt compensating techniques: substitute improved strategy for strength, and increased accuracy for power (e.g. in tennis shots). Learn techniques that put less strain on the weakening muscles: pick up a tennis ball with the racket rather than stooping over and straining your back.

Useful techniques for adapting to age aren't limited to sports, by the way. For example, when rising from a chair, toilet seat or bench, push down on any convenient object (chair arms, chair seat or adjacent table) with your hands or elbows. This takes the strain off your knee ligaments. If no other object is available, push on your knees. You can learn to do these moves quickly and smoothly so that they look graceful and relatively effortless. Plan ahead by looking for the most advantageous place to sit down.

In competitive sports, seek out opponents of the same skill level or just slightly better. You will be pleasantly surprised to see that these people are often quite a bit younger than you. If you always play with people your own age whose game is poorer, your own game will deteriorate. If you play too often people who are much better than you are, you will spoil their game and become discouraged or even depressed. Worse yet, you might become convinced that you're getting too old for the sport!

Be Pro-active.

Be pro-active: Organize a game if one doesn't exist; call a friend to share your bike ride or ski outing. But if one isn't available, don't let that stop you. Pick sports your spouse can share, if possible. Don't take the sport too seriously; have fun! In non-competitive sports, exult in the fact that you're still able to do this. If you're tempted to "just stay home and relax," remind yourself, "If I quit doing this, I will get old and stiff faster."

"But," you say, "I gave up that activity (tennis, alpine skiing, sailing, etc.) years ago." Why not take it up again? First, make sure your doctor believes that healthy older people should be athletically active (if he or she doesn't, change doctors!) Then ask if there's any reason you shouldn't resume your favorite sport(s), or take up a new one.

"But," you argue, "my muscle tone is gone; I can hardly walk to the grocery store." Studies have shown that the most common reason people need help in nursing homes is (unnecessary) loss of muscle tone: they can't even get up out of a chair without help. There are now weight-lifting programs for 90-year-olds that have been marvelously successful in restoring muscle tone. If they can do it, so can you, provided your doctor concurs.

Dealing with the Inevitable.

Of course, sooner or later, we all come to that inevitable time when we can no longer engage in a cherished activity. How will we react? Too many people view that change as a loss. Instead, make a list now of enjoyable and stimulating activities that you will still be able to do but don't have time for now. My list includes a number of things, such as reading the classics, reading more philosophy, watching more good TV programs (e. g. public broadcasting programs and C-Span). It also includes visiting friends and shut-ins, and solving mathematical puzzles. It's a long list.

We should also plan substitutes for our physical activities. When I can't play tennis any longer, I can ride my bike more. If I can't do that, perhaps I can swim. If I can't swim, I can do exercises in my chair, on the floor, or even in my bed.

Overcoming Losses.

One of the potentially most disruptive inevitable events is the loss of one's driver's license. We need to plan for this traumatic loss: The reduction in driving expense may be enough to pay a grandchild or high school student to drive us to places not accessible by public transportation. Or the sale of the car and the consequent savings in operating costs will pay for many cab rides. Or perhaps a friend with more time than money would welcome the additional cash, and you would have the additional companionship.

The greatest loss one can face is, of course, the death of a spouse. During the intense period of grief that follows, many people lose their own desire to live. But, after the grieving is over, it is crucial to throw oneself vigorously into planning a new life. Two of the most serious obstacles to be overcome are loneliness, and the tendency not to eat well. Invite a friend who understands those problems to share a meal with you every other day. Make it a festive occasion. Celebrate your friendship. When the friend reciprocates, you have the cornerstone of good nutrition and an antidote for loneliness.

If the friend doesn't reciprocate, try another friend. The friend may be of either sex. An association with a friend of the opposite sex may lead to a romantic interest. In either case, other common interests may emerge: going to plays or movies, joining a card club, accepting social engagements together for gatherings where singles are out of place. The list is almost endless. The best part is that you can take the initiative.

Bad Influences: Is This Loss Necessary?

Many of the losses people endure are not really necessary. They are the result of societal beliefs that old people "naturally" become inactive, lonely, and unable to do things for themselves. The most insidious of these beliefs is that older people can no longer be of service to others and to society.

A Triple Tragedy.

This prevalent belief is a triple tragedy: It harms the individual, those whom he or she would have reached, and society itself. The individual loses opportunities for outreach and service that can enhance her(his) quality of life. That loss hastens the debilitating process and increases the need for more care and service. So society must spend more resources both on that individual and on those he or she would have helped.

Society is also denied the productive services of individuals who might have been motivated to do wonderful things for someone in real need. Instead they are conditioned to think of themselves as people in need, and they soon become so. Multiply this situation by the increasing millions of older people and one begins to see a serious national problem. This problem would diminish significantly if we could only get people, both young and old, to realize one simple fact: It is tremendously beneficial, both personally and to society, for every one of us to remain active and productive as long as we possibly can.

What the Experts Say.

Listen to what some other experts on this subject have to say. Stanley Jacobson[14] writes:

> *"To Emory L. Cowen, Ph.D., a University of Rochester psychologist, psychological wellness means having a sense of control over one's fate, a feeling of purpose*

and belongingness, and a basic satisfaction with oneself and one's existence.

"Unfortunately, tragedy may result when others do for us what we can do or learn to do for ourselves. One pair of researchers calls the effect infantilizing— learned helplessness."

Don McLeod[15] writes (in *Parade Magazine*) about Matilda White Riley:

...now, at 81, [she is] senior social scientist at the National Institute on Aging (NIA).

Society's views of older people are extremely outdated, Riley feels.

She says the same rigid structures that tend to force older people into idleness also lock younger people into school, jobs and other responsibilities with enormous pressures to accomplish everything early in life—and then get out of the way. The result, Riley says, is a waste of older talent at one end of the spectrum and a smothering of younger talent at the other.

I see a society where the structural revolution has provided more choices and more varied roles for older people, she says. A society where lifelong learning replaces the lockstep of traditional education, a society where the burdens of the middle generation are spread over the life course.

Earl Ubell[16] (in *Parade Magazine*) writes:

[Scientists] have much good news...which boils down to this: You can age successfully, and keep your body young and your mind alert into your 90's.

In the absence of disease, many of your body's powers decline very slowly if you maintain them with proper diet, exercise, brain stimulation, and good social support. Moreover, you can recover lost function.

Scientists have singled out these major ingredients for a long, good life: lifelong, high-level mental and physical activity; an adequate low-fat diet; emotional stability; and good luck, which includes healthful heredity.

[lung] Capacity drops 40 percent between ages 20 and 80, Dr. James Fozard says...[but] you can improve your lung function with special diaphragm exercises.

[Dr. Fozard's study for the NIA]...shows, when heart disease is absent, the amount of blood pumped is the same, independent of age. In fact the heart seems to get stronger...and the capacity increases with age.

We have built up myths about the aging brain, says Dr. Zaven Khachaturian, another NIA researcher. Without disease, we do not find dramatic losses of thinking ability from aging by itself.

Paul Costa, Jr. [head of] the NIA's Laboratory of Personality and Cognition [says] healthy and mentally intact older men and women show the same emotional and personality characteristics—the same ways of coping, the same responses to psychological therapy—that younger people do. Personality itself may contribute to successful aging. Usually that means an optimistic, friendly outlook. Young or old, crabbiness cuts your ability to cope with life.

What Others Think.

Philip Berman[17] has written a best-seller called *The Courage to Grow Old.* When I showed the title to Doris, she said, "Why does it take courage? It just happens!" It is interesting that a number of people from whom Berman requested essays said the same thing. Berman and Connie Goldman[18] wrote a similar book, called *The Ageless Spirit.*

Both books are enjoyable and inspiring. Both of them reinforce almost everything I have said in this chapter. But I don't agree with everything they had to say. For example, two or three women grew to hate the sight of their bodies. My body would do no credit to a man of 25 years, but I am proud of it because it's in about the best shape it can be for a body its age. That pride inspires me to take the best care of it that I possibly can.

One woman says in Berman's book that every woman who can afford it should have a face lift. I believe that a woman who is happy and tranquil becomes more beautiful with age, and that there is a great charm to that natural beauty. I think Doris is an excellent example of this.

A couple of the men tell how frustrated they are with the physical limitations of growing old. But I find it quite challenging and rewarding to compensate for these increasing limitations. And I believe that meeting this challenge is an important secret to extending the period during which we retain and enhance the quality of life.

47. Integrity

"I would give no thought of what the world might say of me, if I could only transmit to posterity the reputation of an honest man."
—Sam Houston

"Honesty is the best policy: I have tried both ways."
— Mark Twain

"The greatest test of courage on earth is to bear defeat without losing heart."
—Robert Green Ingersoll

*"Loyalty means nothing unless it has at its heart
the absolute principle of self-sacrifice."*
—Woodrow Wilson

*"He who lives only to benefit himself confers
on the world a benefit when he dies."*
—Tertullian

*"That man who lives for self alone, Lives
for the meanest mortal known."*
—Joaquin Miller

Integrity is more than a moral virtue. When viewed from the cold test of pragmatism, it is, far and away, the most successful way to live.

Many business studies have asked what characteristic executives value most in a key employee. In all of those studies that I've seen, integrity was at the top of the list.

I believe there is as much truth as humor in the words of Mark Twain quoted above. Sooner or later, lying and deceit get us into trouble. When—almost inevitably—we are found out, the consequences are invariably bad. Someone is disappointed in us, and probably upset. We have lost our credibility. People lose respect for us. What's worse, we lose respect for ourselves.

Tact vs. the White Lie.

Integrity does not require us to express an opinion on everything. Unsolicited expressions of opinion, if negative, are a sign of bad manners and may cost us friendships. If they are positive, of course, they are always welcome. They may well bolster a self-image or brighten someone's day. In fact, it's a good habit to develop. Just be sure the compliment is sincere.

Of course, many opinions are solicited, as when someone says to you, "How do I look in this dress (suit)?" You think she(he) looks terrible. What do you say? Do you tell them what you think? Not wanting to hurt their feelings, you might be tempted to say "OK," or even "fine." That would be what some people call a white lie. I believe there are very few, if any, situations where lies—white or otherwise-can be justified. Not only will you be uncomfortable: You have done your friend a disservice by not supplying the help requested.

A better alternative exists. Tell the truth, but express it in a positive way: "I really like your blue one better." Or, "You have other dresses (suits) that I think are more becoming."

A Sin.

Recalling our earlier definition of sin (that which hurts ourselves or others), I conclude that lies—even the white ones—must be classified as a form of sin.

The Broader Meaning.

In its fullest sense, integrity involves strict adherence to a code of moral values, which in turn involves such other things as courage, adherence to principle, unselfishness, loyalty, and other virtues. I hope it is evident from other parts of this book that I subscribe heartily to this broader concept as the cornerstone of successful and fulfilled living.

48. Humor

> *"Good humor isn't a trait of character,*
> *it is an art which requires practice."*
> —David Seabury

To Seabury's excellent quotation I would add just one thought: The practice pays off handsomely. My dictionary defines humor as the quality of being laughable or comical. This quality is a great asset in almost any situation. It makes people laugh, and laughter is truly good medicine. It aids healing, relieves pain, and promotes wellness. It can relax a tense situation, and it can often head off confrontation, recrimination and other unfortunate developments.

Humor is a great icebreaker when you are with strangers. It relaxes everyone and encourages them to talk. They will often respond in a similar vein.

The ability to laugh at ourselves is a great quality. It makes us more approachable and shows that we don't take ourselves too seriously. Of course, we must avoid laughing at others or making them the butt of our humor.

The Anatomy of Humor.

Books have been written on this subject. However, I don't think we have to become experts to improve our own ability in this area if we just keep two or three thoughts in mind. There are two general kinds of humor: situation humor and jokes. The first involves the ability to see the comic side of everyday situations. Here's an example: you spill some milk; instead of recriminating with yourself, you say to whoever is listening, "Gee, if the cat were here I wouldn't have to get the mop!" It is the best kind of humor, since it is nearly always appropriate. Jokes, on the other hand, require special care to make sure they're appropriate. Otherwise they seem forced and artificial. The common element in all humor is the bringing together of unrelated thoughts in a surprise ending: the punch line.

Remembering Jokes.

People say to me, "I don't see how you remember all those stories." I usually reply, "It's a disease." The key is much the same as in any other memory recall: association. We learn this as we learn anything else: by observing others and by practicing. The quickest way to improve your sense of humor is to associate with people who have one. You don't need to remember a whole story, only the punch line. The buildup is merely a description of the situation. That can be done in your own words.

Cautions.

Besides avoiding humor at the expense of other people, we should avoid humor that puts down races, nationalities, religious beliefs, or other ideas that people hold dear. Dirty stories are not humorous by my definition, though some very good humor may be "off-color." Like beauty, this judgment is in the eye of the beholder. Unless we know our audience well, we should observe the old motto: When in doubt, don't.

49. Wisdom

"When I was a boy of 14, my father was so ignorant I could hardly stand to have the old man around. But when I got to be 21, I was astonished at how much the old man had learned in seven years."
—Mark Twain

Wisdom is the distilled essence of what humankind has learned over the ages about truth and what's right and how to act. It resides in those who nurture their ability to learn continuously from experience, study and observation, unlike the man who had just been turned down for a raise. He protested, "Why boss, I've had 20 years of experience. The boss shook his head sadly: "No, Fred, you've had one year of experience 20 times."

While real wisdom is usually acquired through long experience, I believe there are ways to shorten the learning process:

- reading, as you are doing now;
- observing: listening and watching;
- analysis: sifting, sorting and organizing that which we read and observe.

I believe, by the way, that wisdom is not a substitute for religion. Rather, wisdom can supplement and combine with religion to help us enhance the quality of our lives.

When asked where the gold was, the old prospector said, "Gold is where you find it." Wisdom is the same way. Also, like gold, it's more apt to be found when you're looking for it.

We begin to acquire wisdom on the day we're born (some believe earlier than that), and continue until the day we die. The difference between the wise person and the fool is the rate at which wisdom is acquired. So it pays tremendously to accelerate the process as much as you can.

Hopefully, you will gain some wisdom from each chapter of this book. That is its main purpose. The rest of this chapter contains a few items that didn't seem to fit anywhere else.

Teaching by Example.

If a picture is worth is worth 1,000 words, I believe that a good example is worth ten times that much—especially in bringing up children. I tried never to preach to our children, but to show them by my actions what I really believe. I would also relate to them things that happened and how I viewed them.

Curiosity.

A wholesome curiosity about the world around us is a great asset. It enriches our life in a variety of ways. When we seek to satisfy our curiosity, we increase our wisdom and understanding, life becomes more enjoyable and interesting, and we become more interesting.

Asking questions is a wonderful way to get better acquainted with another person. Of course we must be diplomatic and considerate about delicate or sensitive subjects. We must also be attentive to the answers. If we make a habit of doing this, people find us more interesting.

Almost all of us are born with a natural curiosity. Too often it is dulled by parents, teachers or others who are too busy, too tired, or too preoccupied with their own thoughts to answer our questions. We do a great favor to our children, students and others when we take the time to answer their questions to the best of our ability. If we or they are not satisfied with the answer, say, "I don't really know, but let's see what we can find out."

Deal with the Other Person's Agenda.

If we wish to persuade someone to take a certain course of action we must "deal with their agenda." In other words, we must approach the subject from their point of view and with their objectives in mind. If we don't understand what these are, we need to ask questions until we do. All successful salesmen learn this skill, but it is important to all of us.

When we acquire this skill and practice it, marvelous things happen. We are far more successful in our endeavors. The other person doesn't feel pressured. Instead, they see us as being friendly, helpful and cooperative. And we truly are.

50. Wellness

> *"To become a thoroughly good person is
> the best prescription for keeping a
> sound mind and a sound body."*
> —Francis Bowen

> *"God gives you what you want, and then
> he makes you pay for it."*
> —Jacque Banarcewski

Physicians estimate that between 80 and 90 percent of the health problems they see are the result of the way people live, act and think. Think of this: Most of us have the power to become much healthier and happier than we are just by changing what we do and how we think.

Too often it is easier to blame circumstances, genes, upbringing, past experiences, parents, teachers, bosses and other people for our poor health, bad habits, bad thoughts and bad reactions than to take responsibility for them. Of course, all of the above factors, and more, have an effect on us. But we cannot escape the most important fact: We are what we think, eat and do. And we have the power to change all of these things.

Too many of us are like the old farmer who was being urged by the county agent to take some agricultural courses.

"Why should I?" asked the farmer, defensively.

"You'll learn how to farm better," answered the agent.

To which the farmer retorted, "Shucks, I don't farm half as well as I know how now!"

Weight Control.

Maintaining an ideal weight has many rewards. We look better, feel better, and have more energy. We are less apt to have high blood pressure or high cholesterol. In short, we are healthier, happier and likely to live longer and better lives.

Most Americans weigh more than their ideal weight. Many are grossly overweight. Most of us know that proper diet and exercise are necessary to control our weight. Many know also that crash diets are not the answer: We must have the right attitude about food.

With all of this knowledge at our disposal, why are so many people still overweight? I believe there are several reasons, all of which must be dealt with before one can hope to control one's weight.

The first is our upbringing. Most of us were brought up to believe it is a sin to waste food. But if we are served more than we need, particularly in a restaurant, the greater sin is to take on the excess calories. Here it is important to have some basic knowledge of nutrition. For example it is better to eat all the fresh fruits and vegetables and leave meat and, of course, the dessert. In restaurants look for the senior dinners: The portions are smaller.

Another is habit. Most of us have grown accustomed to serving and eating larger portions than we need. We must concentrate on eating smaller portions until it becomes second nature to do so. Closely related to habit is our attitude about different foods. We have become accustomed to eating more protein and fatty foods (butter, salad dressing, sour cream, etc.) than we need. Conversely, most of us should eat more fresh fruits and vegetables. Try this: when you are really hungry, take a small bite of raw carrot and chew it slowly. Discover the flavor that you may not have known before.

Similarly, take a small bite of a whole wheat roll without

butter or margarine. Chew it slowly and thoroughly. Look for the flavor you missed when it was slathered thick with greasy butter. Do these things for three months and your habits and attitudes will change. In the process, you will lose weight, feel better and enjoy life more.

Those People Who Can't Lose Weight.

Another unfortunate attitude is the belief that we are "one of those people who can't lose weight." It certainly does seem easier for some people than others. But, after close observation of people I know well, I am convinced that the differences are all explained by a combination of all the causes we have discussed.

Happily, recent clinical research supports these conclusions. I am reminded of the doctor who was renowned for his success in getting his patients to lose weight. When asked for his secret he replied, "Very simple: I merely put them on a strict diet of what they profess to have eaten the previous week!"

Among other things, notice the great difference in the amount of energy people use in their normal daily activities. We all recognize this difference between the manual laborer and the office worker. But it is also noticeable between different office workers. Some are more vigorous in their movements, move about more, use the stairs rather than elevator, and so on. All of these things affect the amount of calories we burn. The difference each day may be slight; but they add up over the months and years.

Motivation: the Real Key.

Finally, our motivation to maintain our ideal weight must be greater than our desire to eat. This is the real key to controlling our weight. Otherwise we are doomed to failure. Set a realistic goal. Let's say you are 20 pounds over your ideal weight. Your goal could be to lose those pounds in 20 weeks and maintain your new weight thereafter. Then tell your goal to a few people whose love and respect you cherish most. Then keep them posted on your progress.

There are other motivations. Rejoice frequently that you feel better and have more energy because you are controlling your weight. Congratulate yourself for having taken control of this important area of your life. Accept the compliments from your friends on how good you look. Revel in the fact that your favorite clothes fit better and look better. Most importantly, realize the great favor you have done yourself by making this major contribution to your wellness.

Bowen Said it All.

The quotation from Francis Bowen gives us the right perspective on wellness. It must be holistic. None of us will ever be perfect, but nothing is more gratifying and rewarding than moving in the right direction: that is, toward being a better person. That includes taking the best care possible of our mind, body and spirit.

Much of this book is focused on living a better, happier life, but you will want to do other reading as well. You will find the reading list in the back of this book to be helpful. That nice person at the reference desk of you public library will also be helpful.

Nine

Making A Difference

*"The only thing needed for the triumph of evil
is for good men to do nothing"*
— Edmund Burke

"Making a difference" is a phrase I hear repeatedly— to the point where I hesitated to use it. But it seems so appropriate to express a genuine test of service. Does what we do to serve others really make them or their situation better? If not, why are we doing it? Why aren't we spending our resources on something that does? That's what "making a difference" means to me. It is the standard against which I test all of my service activities.

I don't agree to serve on a board or a committee, unless there is strong evidence that my service will meet this test. Periodically, I assess my activities on these boards and committees. If one of them doesn't meet this test, I will resign (with a full explanation to the chair or executive director). Sometimes this means leaving an interesting and enjoyable situation and losing contact with good people, but it makes time for more worthwhile activities.

The same test applies to projects such as writing this book and other activities that I will define in the following chapters. The test may seem rigorous; but it fits my philosophy and helps me to fulfill my life's goals.

The sense of happiness and fulfillment that flows from engaging in activities that make a positive difference in other people's lives is difficult to describe to someone who hasn't experienced it. I believe these activities constitute one of the cornerstones of our salvation. There is no substitute or replacement for them. They help to produce that all-important sense of self-worth that nothing else can provide.

51. Volunteering

"Anything that really matters to us, anything that embodies our deepest commitment to the way human life should be lived . . . depends on some form of volunteerism."

—Margaret Mead

Almost every non-profit organization uses volunteers to some extent, and those that don't should! It's the American way—and a good one.

Many of my most rewarding experiences occur in volunteer settings. Sometimes I feel like the Lone Ranger riding off into the sunset as the executive director says "How can I ever thank you!" It does wonders to bolster my self-image.

One of the delights of volunteering is that you can be choosy about whom you work for and what you do. There is no job shortage. I have two criteria for picking volunteer jobs: First, I must believe wholeheartedly in the organization's mission. Second, I must be convinced that I can help accomplish the mission as well or better than anyone else they're apt to find.

Twin Cities magazine did an article on me a few years ago. It wasn't the best write-up (I didn't think the writer really knew me), but the title hit the spot: "He's doing

what he's good at." I think that's important in any job —
paid or volunteer.

52. Board Membership

> *"Instead of counting the years,*
> *make the years count."*
> — Author Unknown

Being a board member in a non-profit organization is a
special form of volunteering. The criteria (if you're going
to find the work fulfilling) are the same as those I described for choosing any other volunteer job.

What are the qualifications of a good board member? How
do you acquire the skills needed? Good questions. There
are good books on this subject. If you don't find the answers
in your local library, write the Association of Governing
Boards, One Dupont Circle, Washington, DC 20036. Their
focus is on colleges and seminaries, but the information is
largely applicable to any non-profit board.

Occasionally I am asked, "How does one get on a board?"
First, pick your organization as one in whose mission you
believe and as one who can use one or more of your areas
of expertise to good advantage. Remember that the normal
function of a board member is to help make policy, to
monitor operations and finances, and to evaluate the
effectiveness of the executive director. Then call the executive director, tell her(him) of your interest and suggest
a face-to-face meeting. This is the opportunity to verify your
information about the organization and learn more—also
to learn what is expected of a board member. Normally you
will be expected to serve on at least one committee. These
usually include executive, nominating, finance, marketing,
development (fund raising), planning, human resources. In

many organizations a major portion of the board's work is done in these committee meetings. Usually the more experienced board members are chosen to serve on the executive and nominating committees.

If you perform well on a board or two, you will not need to ask for further assignments. The nominating committees will seek you out.

What kinds of people usually make good board members? They may be those who have had decisionmaking experience in organizations, those whose advice is often sought by others, those with special skills in accounting, public relations, human resources—these are examples: There is no hard-and-fast rule.

What kinds of organizations are we talking about? Name a social need in your community and you will most likely find at least one organization trying to fill that need. These include mental health, family service, battered women, hospitals, United Way, scouting, historical societies, missions, counselling...the list goes on and on.

"But," you say, "I have no special skills in these areas." No matter. The executive director does. What (s)he is looking to the board for are complementary skills: business, finance, public relations, advertising, real estate—again the list goes on and on.

53. Service

> *"Ask not what your country can do for you,*
> *but what you can do for your country."*
> —John F. Kennedy

One of the real joys in this world is being of service to other people. We've already talked about volunteering and board membership. There are many less structured ways, and the opportunities are endless. Rabbi Kushner, in one of his marvelous talks,[10] suggests that we perform an act of loving service at least three times a week. My quota is usually more than met in the more structured ways; but some of my most fulfilling experiences have been in counselling (only, of course, when it is sought). People I've tried to help have included:

Three women with marital difficulties.

A teen-age girl whose parents were getting a divorce.

Our own children in a variety of matters.

A young man who thought he had learning disabilities having difficulty finding a career.

Numerous people who were considering starting their own businesses.

Still more numerous people trying to find a job or get established in a career.

A Caution to Women.

Women must be on guard against a compulsive need to over-serve their spouses, their children, and others to the detriment of their own mental well being. This compulsion derives from being over-socialized as a girl. It can be very difficult to overcome. Bepko and Krestan[5] have dealt with this problem, its sources and cures, very thoroughly.

54. Giving Material Possessions

"The more he cast away the more he had."
—John Bunyan

*"What I gave, I have; what I spent, I had;
what I kept, I lost."*
—Old Epitaph

*"If there be any truer measure of a man
than by what he does,
it must be by what he gives."*
—Robert South

The Joys of Tithing.

Doris and I have been tithers since the day we were married. Different people define tithing in different ways. The traditional biblical definition is a tenth of your gross income. Many people, including us, defined it as a tenth of their income after income taxes. Others define it differently. I don't think the exact definition is that important. What is important is that you have some definition and follow it. To follow it means setting aside that portion of every paycheck "off the top," and using it only for charitable purposes.

Like volunteer service, the joy of this process is indescribable to someone who hasn't done it. Without tithing, every charitable gift is a diversion of our hard earned money from some use that might have given us greater satisfaction (we think). You make the gift out of a sense of duty. Most of us don't derive much pleasure from doing our duty. At best, it's about as inspiring as brushing our teeth. Often we have negative feelings toward the persons who asked for the gift. They sense those feelings, and the process becomes unpleasant for everyone.

A Dramatic Change.

When you tithe, on the other hand, your whole attitude toward charitable giving changes. You become a steward of this precious fund. You are the lady bountiful, distributing this money where you think it will do the most good. Your only problem becomes an intellectual one: which organizations are most worthy? The people who approach you for gifts are now welcome. They bring you information about a worthy cause and help you with your deci sion. If you do send them away empty-handed, it is only because you feel there are more worthy uses for your tithe funds. You have no feelings of guilt, only regret that your funds will not stretch as far as you would like.

Perhaps you will feel a sense of concern for the asker. If so, you will be able to express it positively, perhaps by expressing a compliment about the excellent presentation. The asker may go away disappointed, but not with the negative feelings he might otherwise have.

Becoming a Philanthropist.

As a tither, the amounts you give to charity are three to five times what the average American family gives. You are able to do much more good and feel much better about yourself. People view you with respect and gratitude. They view you as a very generous person (which you are). You have become a philanthropist.

This doesn't mean you can't continue to enjoy life, of course. Many older Americans have more annual income than they need for life's necessities. We are fortunate to be in that group. What should we do with the excess? A few luxuries, including travel? Why not? Save some? Certainly, if we have not already accumulated enough to see us through our remaining years.

Making Your Charitable Dollars Stretch.

Doris and I work hard at making our charitable dollars

do as much good as possible. We gather as much information as we can about each of the myriad organizations that ask us for money. We belong to the Minnesota Council on Charities, which can provide valuable information on many of these organizations. Each year, after Thanksgiving, we review our information, rank the requests and do as much as our budget will allow.

A Rationale for Generous Giving.

How much should we give annually to charity? For many years the tithe seemed like an appropriate answer. As Doris and I approach our sunset years, we become more secure in the feeling that we won't outlive our assets. Accordingly we have increased substantially the part of our annual budget that we set aside for charities. Currently, we set this number at the level needed to keep us in the lowest tax bracket. We give as much in appreciated securities as we can get a tax deduction for. The rest we give in cash. There is a strong rationale for that: We believe that the 60 or so charities we support will use the money more cost-effectively than the government. That is part of our answer to the question: Who makes the best use of our money? Our children and grandchildren? charities? the government?

Happily, we have high respect for the judgment of all of our children. So the answer is simple: they and their children come first, then carefully selected charities, then the government. If our children come first, why do we give so much to charity? Good question. If we gave less to charity, the government would get much more.

Under the current tax laws, the most effective gift is not cash, but appreciated securities. When you give the latter, you receive a tax deduction for the current market value; but you pay no tax on your gain. You must be careful in handling these transactions with your broker. The security must not be liquidated in your account. It must be transferred to a brokerage account in the name of the charity.

There are other potential problems in giving appreciated securities. For example, the sale of odd lots (less than 100 shares) is not efficient. You may not wish to give 100 shares to one charity. Also, you want to give the security when its market value is high and when you need the tax deduction; but this may not be the time when the charity needs the money.

The Donor Advisory Account.

A donor advisory account overcomes all of these problems very neatly. Once you establish such an account with a public foundation, you can give securities to this account at any time and in any amount. You take your full tax deduction at the time of the gift. In return you give up all legal control of those assets. But you can "advise" the foundation to give a specified amount from this account to a specified charity at any later time.

There are a few simple restrictions. You have no legal or contractual right to direct what the foundation does with these funds. Under IRS rules, if you had retained such a right, you could not claim a tax deduction. You cannot use these funds to pay a pledge or similar commitment. The charity to whom the foundation gives the funds must be a tax-exempt organization, or a religious or educational organization, such as a church or public educational institution. These are organizations that the IRS has determined to be charitable organizations.

If your community does not have a public foundation with a donor advisory program, you can write to the St. Paul Foundation, Norwest Center, St. Paul, MN 55101 for information. If your community has such an organization and you don't know anything about it, you could ask for the names of some donors who have had a few years of experience with it. A little conversation with them should give you more confidence. Of course, any organization that purports to operate donor advisory accounts wouldn't last long if it didn't keep faith with its donors.

Estate Planning and Deferred Giving.

An important expression of our life's values—and how we wish to be remembered—is the thought we give to the disposition to be made of our material possessions when we die. The decisions we make in this regard make a very important statement of our interests and beliefs. In reaching these decisions, Doris and I use the same rationale we use for the annual disposition of our discretionary income, as described in the earlier part of this chapter. Our approach doesn't provide easy answers, but we are currently applying the most effective strategy we have been able to come up with. We have developed this strategy through conversation with many people: our children, trust officers, attorneys, estate planners, and development officers. (As chairman of the Deferred Giving Committee for United Hospital Foundation in St. Paul, I spent a significant amount of time with these people.)

Here are the key elements of our strategy:

1. Annually give our children all of our income we don't use, or the amount that is exempt from gift tax, whichever is less. The purpose of this is to minimize the estate tax when the second one of us dies by keeping the estate from growing.

2. Provide in our wills that, at the second death, after expenses are paid:

   - The first $600,000 that is exempt from estate tax will be distributed equally among our children (after a nice cash gift to each of our grandchildren);

   - The next $600,000 (or the amount remaining, if less) will be distributed among selected charities;

   - The remainder, if any, will be subjected to estate taxes and the remainder equally distributed equally among our children.

   - $600,000 is the amount exempt from estate tax under

current law. If this is changed, we will consider changing our wills.

Other Planned Giving Vehicles.

The will is still the most common vehicle for implementing your estate planning. There are a variety of other vehicles for this purpose. The development officer of any large charity will be glad to discuss these with you. Of course, you will want the help of your own attorney before you sign any documents.

One popular vehicle is the charitable remainder trust. There are several variations, but they all have some simple elements in common: The donor gives money to a charity; part of the money is used to provide income for him and/or his family, and the remainder goes to the charity when the commitment to pay the income has been fulfilled. It has several attractions. It provides a charitable deduction up front. It provides an excellent investment management vehicle. It is also quite tax favorable, particularly when you fund it with appreciated securities. Under current tax laws, the total gain on the appreciated securities is exempt from tax, even though a major portion of the "gift" provides an income for you and/or your loved ones.

The tax collector gets his due because the income from the trust is taxable. If the income beneficiary is age 14 or older, (s)he is taxed in his(her) his own income bracket. We found this to be a very attractive vehicle for funding educational subsidies for our grandchildren.

Seeding "Mini-endowment" Programs.

Suppose there is a cause of special interest to you that has not been endowed. You can find a community foundation that will work with you in setting up what I call a mini-endowment. They will start the program with as little as $10,000. The foundation invests the principle, and uses the income for the purpose you specify. The purpose must be such that it can be logically carried out by an organization that is, itself, a recognized, tax-exempt charity. You, the foundation, and the charity all work to promote additional contributions for the same purpose. These contributions can be in any amount. They all help to increase the income and enhance the program.

We have established three such programs. The first was to provide a scholarship each year to the Minnesota student who does best in the annual American High School Math Contest. The principle increased 50% in only the first three years and is still growing.

The second one provides a scholarship to the graduating senior of my high school who has the most outstanding record of community service and outreach. The third is identical except that it is for our children's high school.

Living Trusts.

We hear a lot these days about living trusts. They are urged on us as a way to save probate expenses. Whether the amount saved on probate expense exceeds the expense of the living trust depends on where you live. In Minnesota there is no great difference. In any event, consult an attorney in whose knowledge and integrity you have faith. Do not attend living trust seminars or go to the people who advertise the virtues of living wills. Some of them may have your best interests at heart, but many don't. And it is hard to tell one from the other.

Your Own Philosophy and Strategy.

Your own strategy for estate planning will vary according to your own circumstances and philosophy. The important things are: Discuss the issues openly with your spouse and children, decide your philosophy, seek expert counsel, develop your strategy, and execute the necessary documents. It is important to take the steps in that order. However modest your giving program may be, you can rest assured that it will give you more gratification and satisfaction than almost anything else you do with your material possessions. In the process you will have accomplished something else of great importance. You will have provided for an orderly disposition of your worldly goods in a manner consistent with your own philosophy. In doing so you will have left the soundest legacy possible. That is something that far too few people do.

Epilog

Well, my friends, we've come a long way together. I feel I can call those who read this friends, because I've shared openly as I would with a friend if we were face to face. The sharing has helped me to understand myself better: to "know the real me," as they say.

Writing this book has been hard work, but it has been most rewarding. And it has helped me answer the question I first asked: What caused my life to be so totally fulfilling, satisfying and triumphantly rewarding? I now believe it has been a combination of things:

- cherishing and building on the good parts of my heritage and ignoring, or consciously discarding the rest;

- viewing my environment and my circumstances realistically but with a strongly positive outlook;

- making a total commitment to the things I believe in;

- being fortunate enough to inherit a good mind in a sound body;

- having a set of sound, absolute values, started by parents and family, but refined and enhanced during the years.

A year-and-a-half ago my alma mater, White Bear High School, chose me as one of the graduates to appear on their newly created Wall of Honor. The Wall is a program designed to create role models for the present students. At the presentation ceremony they gave me five minutes to respond. I felt it was one of the greatest challenges I had faced in recent years. How do you convey your values to a gymnasium full of 11th- and 12th-grade students in five minutes?

I labored for hours over that speech. I didn't like the result because I didn't think the students would relate to it. Doris agreed. I got up at five o'clock the morning of the presentation, tore up my notes, and started over. The result was worth the effort. The students interrupted me at least twice with enthusiastic applause. Many of them gathered around afterward to talk more. The press and TV picked up on it.

Most important, it helped me bring my own values into sharper focus. Here is the complete text:

> *Good morning!*
>
> *Mr. Tesch, fellow honorees, students, teachers, friends, thank you for this honor and for the privilege of talking with you this morning. I had prepared a two-hour speech for this morning; but now I understand that I've only five minutes. So I won't need all of these notes. (Fling 'em). Let's just visit.*
>
> *How many of you would like to be happy and successful? (Hand up; pause) Yes! Aren't we fortunate to live in a country where we can have goals like that, and not have to spend every ounce of our energy in finding enough to eat and a way to keep warm?*
>
> *How do you define success? (Pause) well, let me tell you how I define success.*
>
> *You may read or hear that I was a poor farm boy from Canada who went on to become a senior vice president of one of Fortune magazine's 500 leading companies. That I became chairman of the executive committee of the largest printed circuit manufacturing company in the western world. That I've received community service awards and been written up in three of the Twin Cities' leading magazines. That I've*

been recognized by two of the major TV stations. That I've received service awards and recognition from over a dozen major community service organizations. That I was national vice president of one of the country's most prestigious professional associations.

Now these things are all very gratifying; but are they my measure of success? No way!! Here are my measures of success:

- *That my best friend is that beautiful lady sitting right there, to whom I've been happily married for over 54 years, to whom I owe a very significant part of my success.*

- *That I'm good close friends with five healthy, happy successful adults whom we call our children. And that they are showing us what good parents we were by being outstanding parents to their own children. And that we truly love and respect each other.*

- *That I've many other good friends with whom I can have intimate conversations. Whom I can love and respect and by whom I feel loved and respected in turn.*

- *That I've "made a real difference" in almost two dozen community service organizations on whose boards I've served. And many of whom I still serve.*

- *That I've made, and am still making, a difference in the lives of many people who seek advice.*

- *That I can still be an active giver of my time, talents and money. And that I've a strong desire to do so as long as I'm able.*

- *That I can and do still provide computer systems consulting services to half a dozen community service and major arts organizations, one as far away as Boston.*

- *That I've been able to learn from my failures and not be emotionally scarred by them.*

- *That I am totally free from anger; resentment; guilt; worry; depression; fear; envy; jealousy; and all of the other negative emotions.*

- *That, in my 79th year, I can still enjoy downhill skiing in the mountains, a couple of hours of vigorous tennis singles weekly or more often, cross-country skiing, sailing, biking 1600 miles a year, and other active sports.*

- *That I still can, and frequently do, put in 14 to 16 hours a day of vigorous mental effort.*

Well, my time is up. How did I achieve this enviable state? It's a long story. And you can read it in a book entitled Confessions of an 80 Year-Old Boy. *It will be in your library by August of 1994.*

In the meantime, seek out a few people whom you consider to be happy, fulfilled and successful. Don't be afraid to ask them what they think is important in their lives. They'll be happy to respond. And follow their advice.

Thank you very much for this honor and privilege.

Life continues to become even more rewarding. Two recent examples: First, the president of White Bear chapter of the National Honor Society heard the foregoing presentation at the Wall of Honor assembly. She asked me if I would give the principal address at their annual banquet. I told her I would be honored; I spoke to them on the importance of good communications and how to achieve them. I received many compliments from both parents and students afterwards, but one really stood out. It is my second example: A lovely senior class member came up to me; after complementing me she exclaimed, "I only wish you had spoken longer!" That was a mountain-top experience!

Speaking of mountain tops, just a few weeks ago I enjoyed five days in Vail with members of the United Hospital medical staff. I can honestly say I don't remember skiing as well, ever before. This was in addition to the mind-expanding continuing medical education sessions and the nightly bull sessions.

And so time goes on. My physical capacities will continue to diminish, but I rejoice in those that remain. And I will continue to rejoice in love and service as long as I draw breath and retain a few mental faculties. I wish the same for you . . .

Suggested Reading

4   Banks, Murray. Banks is an internationally known psychologist and speaker. He has also written a number of helpful pamphlets which can be obtained by writing E. Goshen, 8 E 63rd, New York, NY 10021.

5   Bepko, Claudia and Krestan, Jo-Ann. *Too Good for Her Own Good.* New York: Harper & Row, 1990. 256 pages. Emphasis on liberating women from a compulsive need to over-serve spouses, children, and others.

18 Berman, Phillip L. and Goldman, Connie, *The Ageless Spirit.* New York: Ballantine Books, a division of Random House, 1992. 282 pages.
    Another collection of inspiring essays by prominent people expressing their philosophies of growing old.

17 Berman, Phillip L. *The Courage to Grow Old.* New York: Ballantine Books, a division of Random House 1989. 314 pages. A collection of inspiring essays by famous people expressing their philosophies of growing old.

8   Brown, H. Jackson, Jr. *Live and Learn and Pass it On.* Nashville: Rutledge Hill Press, Inc., 1991. 160 pages. Easily read gems of wisdom for successful living submitted by people from ages 5 to 95.

11 Chapman, Charles F. *Piloting, Seamanship, and Small Boat Handling.* New York: Motor Boating, 1960-1961. 504 pages. The "bible" for owners and captains of boats and yachts. Covers all aspects of the vast array of knowledge required to take responsibility for operating a boat for other than short day cruises. Newer editions are probably available.

14 Jacobson, Stanley, Ed.D. "Attitude." *Modern Maturity* for December 1992-January 1993. AARP, P.O. Box 109, Long Beach, CA.

 7 Kushner, Harold S. *When All You've Ever Wanted Isn't Enough.* New York: Summit Books. Another inspiring book which will enrich your philosophy of life.

10 Kushner, Harold S. "The Challenge of Being Human." Address to the Westminister Town Hall. Tapes available. Minneapolis: Minnesota Public Radio.

Kushner, Harold S. *When Bad Things Happen to Good People.* New York: Schocken Books, 1981. 149 pages. This inspiring book will enrich your philosophy of life.

 6 Lair, Jess. *I Ain't Much Baby, But I'm All I've Got.* An easy-to-read book with many practical suggestions for improving your self image and increasing your peace of mind.

19 Lawson, Douglas M., Ph. D. *Give to Live.* How giving can change your life. La Jolla: ALTI Publishing, 1991. 195 pp. An inspiring and compelling book on the values and benefits of giving both your time and material resources.

 9 Maslow, A.H. *The Farther Reaches of Human Nature.* New York: Viking Press. 1972. 423 pages. Manuscripts published posthumously by the widow of this famous psychologist and philosopher. Somewhat difficult read-

ing, but contains excellent insights into what makes successful people tick. My quotes from this book are from this edition. Page numbering in other editions (such as Penguin Books) is different.

15   McLeod, Don. "Matilda Riley's Revolution." *Parade Magazine* for December 6, 1992.

3   Taylor, Glenn. *Wherever There's Water and Wind: A Complete Guide to the Sport of Windsurfing.* Palo Alto: The Bookmakers, Inc., 1979. 272 pages. A thorough study of this book and 100 hours of practice will enrich your life with an exhilarating sport.

16   Ubell, Earl "We Can Age Successfully," *Parade Magazine* for December 6, 1992.

* * * * * * * * * *

12   The quote is from the last line of a poem that reads:

> *"Dogs have fleas and fleas have fleas*
> *Upon their backs to bite 'em.*
> *And these fleas have littler fleas;*
> *So on, ad infinitum."*
> — Author Unknown

Index

NOTES

NOTES

NOTES

NOTES

NOTES

NOTES

NOTES

NOTES

ORDER FORM

Red Oak Press
P. O. Box 10614
White Bear Lake, MN 55110-0614

Please send _____ copies of *Confessions of an 80 Year-Old Boy* at $11.95 per copy
including sales tax, shipping and handling to:

_____

_____

_____

_____ Enclosed is my check for _____

_____ Please charge $ _____ to my:

_____ V I S A Account # _ _ _ _ - _ _ _ _ - _ _ _ _ - _ _ _ _ Expiring _____

_____ Master Card Account # _ _ _ _ - _ _ _ _ - _ _ _ _ - _ _ _ _ Expiring _____

(You may also order in any of the following ways):

TEL: **Minnesota 612-426-5704   National 1-800-426-5706**
FAX: **612-426-7039**   internet: **72317.1206@compuserve.com**